PLAYS FROM FOLKTALES
OF AFRICA AND ASIA

Plays from Folktales

of

Africa and Asia

*One-act, royalty-free dramatizations
for young people, from stories
and legends of Africa and Asia*

By

BARBARA WINTHER

Publishers   PLAYS, INC.   Boston

Library of Congress Cataloging in Publication Data

Winther, Barbara.
  Plays from folktales of Africa and Asia.
  SUMMARY: Nineteen plays including "Anansi, the African Spider," "Listen to The Hodja," and "The Great Samurai Sword."
  1. Folk-lore—Africa—Juvenile drama. 2. Folk-lore —Asia—Juvenile drama. [1. Folklore—Africa—Drama. 2. Folklore—Asia—Drama. 3. One-act plays. 4. Plays] I. Title.
PN6120.A5W5467   822   76-15558
ISBN 0-8238-0189-6

To my husband, Grant,
who has always listened
and helped

TABLE OF

CONTENTS

PLAYS FROM FOLKTALES
OF AFRICA AND ASIA

Introduction

In many parts of Africa and Asia, the art of storytelling still exists. It may take place in the marketplace, around a night fire, or in a sacred plaza, and the tales may be told by one person or a group of people. Pantomime, music, dancing, and singing are often woven through the tales. In some areas, a particular form of drama has evolved, handed down from generation to generation until it becomes a tradition, with specific techniques, such as the kabuki theater of Japan, the dance dramas of Southeast Asia, and certain tribal dances of Africa. For the most part, these tales are ancient, their origins often obscured by time. The stories have survived because they have special meaning and significance for the people in these cultures.

The plays in this volume are adaptations of African and Asian folktales. Some of the original stories have been altered, for the sake of simplicity, to enhance the flavor of the culture, or to fit the limitations of stage presentation. However, the basic plots, the theme and meaning of the stories, and the tone of each tale have been carefully preserved.

My sincere thanks for the help I received from my

American friends with roots in Africa and Asia, and for the generous assistance of those friends in the lands where I found these tales.

—BARBARA WINTHER

ANANSI, THE AFRICAN SPIDER

ANANSI, THE AFRICAN SPIDER

Anansi (sometimes Kweku Anansi or Kwaku Ananse) is the name given to the spiderman by the Ashanti tribe of Ghana, and he appears as one of the central characters in the folklore of that country. In the native tales of other West African countries, there are different names for him, but in every country where he is known, the spiderman is characteristically the same—sly, clever, and often full of mischief. (Anansi also appears in folktales of the Caribbean Islands.)

Although Anansi is small, this clever creature can usually outwit larger, stronger animals, and he often enlists the aid of his wife and children in his schemes. Sometimes, however, he gets into trouble and outsmarts himself, especially when he is greedy or pompous.

Anansi, the African Spider

Three folktales from West Africa

I.   How Anansi Brought the Stories Down

Characters

THREE STORYTELLERS
NYAME, *the Sky-god*
ANANSI, *the Spiderman*
CROCODILE
MONKEY

BEFORE RISE: THREE STORYTELLERS *enter before curtain.*
Each carries African rattle. They stand at one side of
stage.

1ST STORYTELLER: We are storytellers from an Ashanti
village in Africa.
2ND STORYTELLER: We are going to tell you three stories
about Anansi, the Spiderman.
3RD STORYTELLER: Anansi is a sly, clever spider. For this
is his way of living among larger, stronger animals. (2ND
and 3RD STORYTELLERS *sit.*)
1ST STORYTELLER: The story I will tell is called, "How
Anansi Brought the Stories Down." (*Shakes rattle and*
curtain opens; STORYTELLERS *remain onstage.*)

* * *

SETTING: *Forest of equatorial Africa. Kola nut tree and*
berry bush are near center. Hornets' nest hangs from

3

bush, and calabash gourd is on ground. Tall stool is up center.

AT RISE: NYAME *is sitting on stool, which represents his home in the sky.* ANANSI *enters as if climbing.*

1ST STORYTELLER: It all happened near the beginning of time, not long after animals were on the earth. Anansi thought it might be fun to tell stories in the evening. But Nyame, the Sky-god, was the owner of all the stories. (*Sits*)

NYAME: Here comes Anansi, climbing into my sky.

ANANSI: Good day to you, Sky-god.

NYAME: *All* my days are good, Anansi.

ANANSI: But of course. It is only we poor earth creatures who have bad days.

NYAME: I'm not going to change that. If that's why you've come, go home.

ANANSI: No, I'm here for another reason. I want to buy your stories.

NYAME (*Thundering*): What? Buy my stories? (ANANSI *cringes.*) You dare climb into my sky and ask me to sell you my stories? Great kings have tried to buy them. My stories are not for sale.

ANANSI: Don't be angry with me, Sky-god. I'm just a little spider trying to make my way in life. (*Pleading gently*) Isn't there any way I might talk you into giving up your stories?

NYAME (*Growling*): What a bother you are.

ANANSI: Why? Because I don't give up easily?

NYAME: Oh, all right, Spiderman. If you can show me a crocodile with no teeth, an empty hornets' nest, and a quiet monkey, I'll give you my stories.

ANANSI: Sky-god, those things don't exist.

NYAME: But if you're as clever as some say, then you can

make them exist. Now, go away. I must plan the weather for next week.

ANANSI (*Pantomiming climbing down*): A crocodile with no teeth, an empty hornets' nest, and a quiet monkey. That will take some doing. (*Sits as* CROCODILE *enters crawling*)

CROCODILE: Hungry! Hungry! (*Opens mouth wide*) I'm so hungry I could eat anything. I'm only happy when I'm eating more and more. (*Crosses stage, peering around for food.* ANANSI *watches thoughtfully, looks offstage, then claps some of his legs together.*)

ANANSI: I have an idea! (*Calling*) Say, Crocodile, I know where you can get a meal.

CROCODILE (*Hurrying to* ANANSI): Where, where, where?

ANANSI (*Pointing offstage*): Over there.

CROCODILE: I don't see anything but a big, green rock.

ANANSI: *I* see a plump juicy frog that looks like a rock.

CROCODILE: Yum, yum! A plump juicy frog. I see it now. That frog is trying to trick me into thinking it's a rock.

ANANSI: Why don't you sneak up quietly on that rock—I mean frog—open your mouth wide, and clamp your jaws shut as hard as you can.

CROCODILE: That's just what I'll do. Yum, yum! (*Sneaks offstage.* ANANSI *watches* CROCODILE'S *actions offstage. Sound of loud crunch is heard, followed by scattered pings.* CROCODILE *shouts from offstage.*) Ouch! That's the toughest frog I've ever eaten!

ANANSI: Aha! (*Calling to* NYAME) Did you see that, Sky-god?

NYAME (*With rumbling laugh*): Yes, Anansi. Greed broke the crocodile's teeth. Now, find an empty hornets' nest. (ANANSI *looks around.*)

ANANSI (*Spying nest in bush*): Ah, there's a hornets' nest. (*He crosses to nest. Sound of buzzing hornets is heard.*)

But it's full of hornets. (*Picks up calabash gourd, takes off top and looks inside*) This calabash gourd looks almost like a hornets' nest. That gives me an idea. (*Yelling*) Hornets, hornets, your home is too small. (*Sound of buzzing is repeated*) See this? I've brought you a bigger, more beautiful home. Just take a peek and see how much better off you'll be in here. (*Holds up gourd. Buzzing continues.* ANANSI *pantomimes watching hornets enter gourd, one by one. He suddenly bangs down lid and buzzing sound stops.*) Aha! (*Calling to* NYAME) Did you see that, Sky-god?

NYAME (*Laughing as before*): Yes, Anansi. Dissatisfaction emptied the hornets' nest. Find a quiet monkey and my stories are yours.

ANANSI: This is going to be the hardest job of all. (MONKEY *enters as if swinging from tree to tree.*)

MONKEY: Chitter, chitter, chatter. Look how pretty I am. Chitter, chitter, chatter. (*Stops to preen and pose*) What a perfectly gorgeous monkey I am!

ANANSI (*Aside*): I have an idea. (*Sighs loudly, in sorrow*)

MONKEY: Hello, Anansi. Is something wrong with you?

ANANSI (*Sighing again*): It's not possible. It simply can't be done.

MONKEY: What can't be done?

ANANSI: There's a great reward for the animal who can stuff its mouth with twenty kola nuts and still talk.

MONKEY: Twenty kola nuts? (*Indicates tree*) Like the ones on this tree?

ANANSI: Yes, and no one can do it.

MONKEY: What's the reward?

ANANSI: The animal who succeeds becomes king of the jungle for a week.

MONKEY (*Excitedly*): Oh, oh, oh! I must have that reward!

ANANSI: But you can't do it.

MONKEY: Yes, I can. Just watch me. (*Rushes over to tree and pantomimes stuffing nuts into mouth as* ANANSI *counts quickly from one to twenty*)

ANANSI: Excellent! Excellent! Now talk to me. (MONKEY *waves hands as if trying to speak, then points to cheeks, jumps up and down with distress, and finally exits.* ANANSI *calls to* NYAME) Did you see that, Sky-god?

NYAME (*Laughing as before*): Yes, Anansi. Vanity made the monkey speechless. I see you understand the ways of the world, Spiderman. From this day on, the Sky-god stories will be known as yours. (*Curtain closes behind* STORYTELLERS.)

* * * * *

II.   The First Talking Drum

Characters

THREE STORYTELLERS
FOREST KING
ANANSI, *the Spiderman*
ANTELOPE
LEOPARD
CROCODILE
MONKEY

BEFORE RISE: THREE STORYTELLERS *are sitting onstage.* 2ND STORYTELLER *rises.*

2ND STORYTELLER: I will tell you a story called, "The First Talking Drum." (*Shakes rattle. Curtain opens.*)

* * *

SETTING: *Same as Scene 1. Hornets' nest, stool, and calabash gourd are not onstage.*

AT RISE: KING *and* ANANSI *are talking in pantomime.*

2ND STORYTELLER: In the early days there was one Forest King. When he wanted to tell his subjects anything, it took weeks for messengers to reach the farthest villages. This made the King very unhappy.

KING: There must be a quicker way. What would I do if an enemy attacked? I would be defeated before help could come.

ANANSI: What you need, mighty Forest King, is something to make such a loud noise that everyone in the forest will hear it.

KING: But, Spiderman, I know of nothing that can make such a loud noise.

ANANSI: I can't think of anything either. But I'll have a meeting with some of the animals. We might come up with an idea. (KING *nods and exits one way;* ANANSI *bows and exits the other.*)

2ND STORYTELLER: That evening the animals met in a secret place in the forest. (ANANSI *enters, followed by* CROCODILE, ANTELOPE, LEOPARD, *and* MONKEY. MONKEY *immediately sits down and falls asleep.*)

ANANSI: And so, my friends, that's the situation. We must think of the loudest noisemaker there is.

CROCODILE: Nyame, the Sky-god, can make thunder. That's the biggest noise I know.

ANANSI: True, Crocodile. But Nyame wouldn't let anyone borrow his thunder.

ANTELOPE, LEOPARD *and* CROCODILE (*Ad lib*): That's right. Of course. Yes. (*Etc. Voices wake* MONKEY, *who nods, then falls asleep again.*)

LEOPARD: I have some loud cousins. You know—those lions.

ANTELOPE (*Leaping up; in terror*): Oh, those lions make such frightful roars! We antelope can hear them miles away.

ANANSI: I'll admit your cousins are loud, Leopard. But

I've never met a lion who was willing to carry a message for anyone. (*Animals ad lib agreement.*)

CROCODILE: Sh-h-h! Listen. (*Animals freeze. Sound of drum beating in distance is heard.* MONKEY *snores.*) Don't listen to Monkey snoring. Listen to the drum beating.

ANTELOPE: It's coming from the village. They must be dancing.

ANANSI: Hm-m-m. A drum makes a loud sound.

LEOPARD: It can be heard for miles.

CROCODILE: But a drum only beats out a rhythm for dancing.

ANANSI: Well, why couldn't a drum talk? Different beats could mean different things. And if a drummer were really skilled, he could beat out the sound of a voice.

CROCODILE *and* LEOPARD (*To each other*): A talking drum?

ANANSI (*Waving legs excitedly*): Yes! Yes! That's it! A giant drum to carry messages far away.

ANIMALS (*Ad lib, excitedly*): That's good! A talking drum! Great idea! (*Etc. Noise wakes* MONKEY *again.*)

MONKEY: I wish you animals would stop waking me up.

ANANSI: It's time you woke up, Monkey. We are all going to make a talking drum for the Forest King.

CROCODILE: We crocodiles will find the biggest log by the river.

LEOPARD: We leopards will use our sharp teeth to hollow out the log.

ANTELOPE: We antelope will give a fine skin to stretch over the drum and thongs to tie down the sides.

ANANSI: And I will decorate the drum. What will you do, Monkey?

MONKEY (*Yawning and scratching*): I'll pick some berries from this shrub. Then, I'll sit under this tree and eat them and watch the rest of you work. (*Others sigh in disgust and exit.* MONKEY *pantomimes picking berries, eating, and chattering.*)

2ND STORYTELLER: The animals worked very hard making the giant talking drum. All except Monkey. (*Sounds of chomping, chewing, pounding, creaking, and groaning are heard.*) At last the giant talking drum was finished. (ANANSI, CROCODILE, LEOPARD, *and* ANTELOPE *shove and pull drum onstage.* MONKEY *watches.*)

ANANSI: Now that the drum is made, it must be taken to the village and given to the Forest King.

ANTELOPE: That's a long way to travel.

CROCODILE: This is a heavy drum.

LEOPARD: Who will carry the drum?

CROCODILE: Antelope is the fastest. He should carry it.

ANTELOPE: No! Leopard is the strongest. He should carry it.

LEOPARD: No! Crocodile has the best jaws. He should carry it.

CROCODILE: No! I can't go so far from the river.

ANANSI: Wait! I know who should carry the drum to the King. It should be the job of the laziest animal. (*Animals ad lib agreement.*)

MONKEY (*Leaping up and rushing over*): Now, see here! I don't want to do anything. I don't feel like doing anything. I'm just going to sit here and eat and talk and (*Voice trails off as he sees other animals staring at him*) —and rest.

ANANSI: Well, well, Monkey. *We* didn't say you were the laziest. But you just admitted it.

MONKEY (*Sighing*): You win, Spiderman. All right. I'm the one who has to carry the giant talking drum all the way to the King. (*Starts pushing drum off while others laugh and pat* ANANSI *on back*)

2ND STORYTELLER: To this day the talking drum can be heard in the African forest. And when Monkey hears it, he stops his chattering. He sits still and remembers how lazy he was! (*Curtain*)

*   *   *   *   *

III. Tall-Tale Man

Characters

THREE STORYTELLERS
TALL-TALE MAN
LEOPARD
ANTELOPE
ANANSI, *the Spiderman*

BEFORE RISE: THREE STORYTELLERS *are sitting onstage.*
3RD STORYTELLER *rises.*

3RD STORYTELLER: Our last story is called, "Tall-Tale
Man." (*Shakes rattle. Curtain opens.*)

* * *

SETTING: *Same as Scene 2.*
AT RISE: TALL-TALE MAN *is sitting under tree, staring up.*

3RD STORYTELLER: There once was a man who told tales
that were so tall they could not possibly be true. Yet he
insisted they were the honest truth. (*Sits.* LEOPARD
enters.)
LEOPARD (*To* TALL-TALE MAN): Good day, sir. Why are
you staring up into the tree?
TALL-TALE MAN: I'm waiting for the magic kola nuts to
fall.
LEOPARD: Magic kola nuts?
TALL-TALE MAN: Oh, yes. Last week I caught two nuts
from this tree. They turned into two cows. I took the
two cows to the Frog King and he gave me two canoes.
But two old bull elephants stole the canoes while I was
asleep. And so I'm trying to catch some more magic
nuts.
LEOPARD (*In disbelief*): That's an unbelievable story!
TALL-TALE MAN: You must believe me, Leopard. I
swear it's true.

LEOPARD: You should be ashamed of yourself. I won't stay here and listen to any more of your false stories. (*Exits in a huff*)

TALL-TALE MAN (*Laughing*): Ho, ho, ho! I really fooled the Leopard. (*Looks off*) Aha! Here comes Antelope. I'll fool him, too. (*Stares up into tree;* ANTELOPE *comes bounding in*)

ANTELOPE (*To* TALL-TALE MAN): Good day, sir. Is there something important in that tree?

TALL-TALE MAN: I'm waiting for the magic kola nuts to fall.

ANTELOPE: Magic kola nuts?

TALL-TALE MAN: Oh, yes. Last week I caught two nuts from this tree. They turned into two cows. I took the two cows to the Frog King and he gave me two canoes. But two old bull elephants stole the canoes while I was asleep. And so I'm trying to catch some more magic nuts.

ANTELOPE: What a ridiculous story!

TALL-TALE MAN: You must believe me, Antelope. I swear it's true.

ANTELOPE: Sir, it is bad of you to tell such tall tales and call them true. Someone should teach you a lesson. (*Exits in a huff*)

TALL-TALE MAN (*Laughing*): Ho, ho, ho! I really fooled the Antelope. (*Looks off*) Aha! Here comes Anansi, the Spiderman. I'll fool him, too. (*Stares up into tree*)

ANANSI (*Entering*): Good day, sir. What's so important in the tree?

TALL-TALE MAN: I'm waiting for the magic kola nuts to fall.

ANANSI: Magic kola nuts?

TALL-TALE MAN: Oh, yes. Last week I caught two nuts from this tree. They turned into two cows. I took the two cows to the Frog King and he gave me two canoes. But two old bull elephants stole the canoes while I was asleep. And so I'm trying to catch some more magic nuts.

ANANSI: My, my! Next time hide your canoes so the two bull elephants won't find them.

TALL-TALE MAN (*Startled*): You mean you believe me?

ANANSI: Why, of course. And I'll tell you why. Last week I planted a field of okra. It grew so tall it touched the sky. I made seven hundred pots of soup and fed five villages. But two bull elephants came along and squashed the field with two enormous canoes. Then the Frog King stole the canoes and left two magic kola nuts in their place. I planted the magic kola nuts. And that's how *that* tree got here.

TALL-TALE MAN (*Stunned*): That's an impossible story!

ANANSI: You must believe me, sir. I swear it's true.

TALL-TALE MAN: I won't stay here and listen to any more of your silly tall tales. (*Exits in disgust*)

ANANSI (*To audience*): I have a moral to this tale. He who dishes it out should be able to eat it! Goodbye. (*Starts to exit as curtain closes.* STORYTELLERS *rise and start to exit, shaking their rattles, keeping step to beat.*)

STORYTELLERS (*Chanting*):
Anansi, the Spiderman,
Clever and sly.
Though nobody fools him,
Many still try.
(*Last two lines of chant are repeated until* THREE STORYTELLERS *are all offstage.*)

THE END

IJAPA, THE TORTOISE

IJAPA, THE TORTOISE

When the first European explorers landed on the West Coast of what is today called Nigeria, they were amazed to find highly civilized kingdoms, such as Benin and Ife, where beautiful bronze art objects were being made and life centered around sophisticated courts in large cities. Although these great kingdoms later fell into ruin, many of their art forms, folktales, myths, and tribal rituals have survived and continue to the present day.

The descendants of these ancient kingdoms comprise one of the major African tribes today, the Yoruba, numbering about ten million. Although there are modern cities in Nigeria, many Yoruba still live in small villages and try to preserve old tribal ways. They earn their living by farming or raising livestock. And their artwork, especially wood carving, is among the finest in Africa.

Ijapa, the tortoise, a shrewd trickster, is the parallel in Yoruba folklore for Anansi, the spiderman, in the folklore of the Ashanti tribe, and the Hare, who is the clever schemer in the folktales from other parts of Africa. The counterpart in American folklore is Brer Rabbit, Brer Fox, or Brer Terrapin. Except for differences in the settings, physical environment, and the individuality of the storytellers who draw on their unique cultural backgrounds, most of these animal trickster stories are basically the same, whether they have Ijapa, Anansi, the Hare, Brer Rabbit, Brer Fox, or Brer Terrapin as the main character.

Ijapa, *the* Tortoise

Two tales from Nigeria

I. The Dancing Palm

Characters

BUSSA, *a villager*
MUBI, *his wife*
BELLMAN, *also a villager*
VILLAGERS, *extras*
IJAPA, *the tortoise*
YANRINBO, *his wife*
OBA, *the chief*
ATTENDANT
SHANGO PRIEST

SETTING: *A Nigerian village. There is a dark backdrop curtain with cardboard cut-outs of huts, bushes, and trees. A large clump of bushes up left has vine-like rope hidden behind it. Down left is market area. Right is palm tree with a hollow trunk. Center is* OBA'S *throne-stool.*

AT RISE: VILLAGERS, *including* BELLMAN, BUSSA, *and* MUBI, *are buying, selling, and trading in market—nuts, utensils, and cloth.* BUSSA *and* MUBI *are selling yams.*

ALL (*Ad lib*): I'll give you five cowrie shells. No, not enough. My cloth is worth two of your bowls. No, one

17

bowl for your cloth. (*Etc.* IJAPA *enters right, crosses to market, and sees yams.* VILLAGERS *grow quiet as* IJAPA *speaks.*)

IJAPA: A fine morning (*Bowing to each*), Bussa and Mubi. Those are good yams you have there.

BUSSA: Of course. My wife and I grow only the largest and best.

MUBI: But not for you, Ijapa. We know you are a poor tortoise, always looking for free food.

IJAPA: True. (*Spreading arms*) I have nothing to trade for food and no money to buy any. Surely, though, there is no harm in admiring your yams and imagining how good they taste.

BUSSA: No harm. (*Holding yam under* IJAPA's *nose*) I will even let you smell this one. (IJAPA *sniffs deeply and then sighs.*)

IJAPA: Delightful! Ah-h-h, if only I were rich enough to buy them all.

MUBI: Move along, Ijapa. The market is no place for you. (IJAPA *shrugs, then crosses to palm.* VILLAGERS *freeze.* IJAPA *sits for nap. Soon he is snoring.* YANRINBO *enters right, sees* IJAPA, *and places hands on the rim of her turtle shell, disgusted.*)

YANRINBO (*Yelling*): Husband Ijapa! (IJAPA *jumps up guiltily.*) How dare you sleep under a palm tree while our children go hungry! Where is that breakfast you promised to bring home?

IJAPA: Ah-h-h, Yanrinbo, my beautiful, hard-shelled wife. Well, I—ah—I left the breakfast back there. (*Waves vaguely toward market*)

YANRINBO: Humph! Get your leathery feet moving and hurry up with the food. (*Exits right in a huff*)

IJAPA: I'd better find something to eat. If I don't, Yanrinbo will flip onto her back and wave her feet furiously. And my children will pull in their heads and refuse to speak at all. (*To himself*) Come now, clever tortoise, think. (*Taps head and walks around tree. Suddenly he stops, looks at tree, and jumps as he gets idea.*) I have it! I will use some tortoise magic and turn myself into this palm tree. Ho, ho! Wait until the villagers see this. (*Puts head into tree trunk and raises tree onto shoulders, steadying it with arms. In commanding tone*) Dance, palm, dance. (*African music is heard.* IJAPA *dances with swaying movements, first in place, then crossing to market. As he approaches,* VILLAGERS *resume ad-lib dialogue and pantomime as at start of play.* MUBI *is first to see the palm tree.*)

MUBI (*Pointing*): Look! That palm tree is dancing. (VIL- LAGERS *watch a moment, transfixed, until* IJAPA *lunges at them with a series of frightful grunts and growls.*)

BUSSA (*Shouting*): An evil spirit! (VILLAGERS *scream and scatter, exiting in different directions.* IJAPA *quickly removes tree, grabs yams, and carries palm to original position. Music ceases.* IJAPA, *laughing at his clever- ness, exits right.* VILLAGERS *peer onto stage, look about fearfully, then re-enter and cross to market area, back- ing up toward a central point at which they all bump into each other. All shriek and leap away in terror, then turn and laugh nervously as they recognize each other.*)

MUBI: The dancing palm has disappeared.

BUSSA (*Gesturing*): And so have our yams.

MUBI (*On knees, looking for yams*): Where did they go?

VILLAGERS (*Looking for yams; ad lib*): Where? Not here. There? No. Gone. (*Etc.*)

MUBI: The spirit of the dancing palm tree has eaten our yams.

BUSSA (*Rising*): Too bad, Mubi. We will have to dig more yams from our field to sell tomorrow. (*Blackout. Yams are returned to their original place. When lights go up a moment later,* VILLAGERS *ad lib and pantomime as at start of play.* IJAPA *re-enters, crossing to market.* VILLAGERS *grow quiet as* IJAPA *speaks.*)

IJAPA: Another fine morning (*Bowing to each*), Bussa and Mubi. (*Slyly*) I see you still have those good yams for sale.

BUSSA: These are not the same yams, Ijapa.

IJAPA (*Sniffing*): M-m-m! These smell just as wonderful as the others.

MUBI: Move along, Ijapa. The market is no place for you. (IJAPA *shrugs and crosses to palm tree.* VILLAGERS *freeze.* IJAPA *yawns and sits for nap. He snores.* YANRINBO *re-enters and sees* IJAPA *asleep.*)

YANRINBO (*Yelling; disgusted*): Husband Ijapa! (IJAPA *jumps up guiltily.*)

IJAPA: Ah-h-h-h, Yanrinbo, my beautiful wife with sparkling eyes like ripples in the river. I will bring the breakfast in a moment.

YANRIMBO: Humph! (*Exits right in a huff*)

IJAPA (*To himself*): What worked once will surely work twice. (*Puts on tree*) Dance, palm, dance. (*Music starts.* IJAPA *dances as before. As he approaches market,* VILLAGERS *ad lib and pantomime as before.* MUBI *sees palm tree.*)

MUBI (*Pointing*): Look! The dancing palm tree returns. (VILLAGERS *stare in amazement.* IJAPA *leaps and makes frightening noises as before.*)

BUSSA (*Yelling*): Evil spirit! Evil spirit! (VILLAGERS *scream and scatter, exiting as before.* IJAPA *quickly removes tree, grabs yams, and carries tree to original position. Music ceases.* IJAPA, *laughing at his cleverness, exits right.* VILLAGERS, *except* BELLMAN, *re-enter, and back into each other with shrieks, then nervous laughs, as before.*) Again the dancing palm has disappeared.

MUBI (*Gesturing*): And again our yams are gone.

VILLAGERS (*Ad lib*): Yes. Gone. Not here. The palm tree ate them. Yes, yes. The palm tree. (*Etc.* BELLMAN *enters left, carrying two bells, one large and one small. He strikes them alternately several times, ending by striking small bell three times. Then he stands at right of stool.*)

BELLMAN (*Announcing loudly*): The great Oba, ruling chief, will now sit on his royal stool to listen to the problems of the village. (OBA *enters left, regally, and sits on stool. He is accompanied by* ATTENDANT, *who stands left of stool, holds umbrella over* OBA's *head and waves away flies with palm frond.*)

BUSSA: We will tell the Oba about the dancing palm. (VILLAGERS *nod nervously and murmur to each other.*)

VILLAGERS (*Ad lib*): Yes, yes. Tell the Oba. Evil spirit. Eats yams. Dancing palm. (*Etc.*)

OBA: What is wrong? You all look upset.

BUSSA (*Rising*): Great Oba, for the last two mornings a palm tree has danced into the market. An evil spirit inside the tree has made horrible sounds and scared us away. Then the spirit has eaten our yams and disappeared.

OBA (*Rising in surprise*): Bussa, have you been dreaming?

MUBI (*Rising*): No, great Oba, my husband speaks the truth. We have all seen the tree in the market.

OBA: Hm-m-m. Very strange. (*Scratches chin thoughtfully, then calls*) Shango Priest, we need your help. (PRIEST *leaps onstage from right, carrying carved staff and rattle. He chants with dramatic gestures and dances with jumping and shaking movements.*)

PRIEST (*Chanting*):
> Shango, god of thunder.
> God of lightning, Shango.
> Ride into our village.
> Hear me, mighty Shango.

VILLAGERS (*Chanting*):
    Mighty Shango, mighty Shango, hear.
PRIEST (*Chanting*):
    Shango's magic power
    Will catch the darkest shadow,
    Will drive the bad away.
    Help me, mighty Shango.
VILLAGERS (*Chanting*):
    Mighty Shango, mighty Shango, help.
OBA: Shango Priest, for two mornings a palm tree has danced into the market and eaten yams.
PRIEST: Yams? A palm-tree spirit eating yams? That has never happened before. There is something peculiar about that. (*Suddenly jumps high, startling everyone*) Ha! We will capture this spirit, whatever it is. Bring more yams to market tomorrow. We will glue them to the ground with sticky tree sap and cover them with a thick layer of icky-sticky sap. Then we shall capture the spirit! (*Raises arms at audience and jumps, making an explosive "puff" sound. There is an immediate blackout. OBA and ATTENDANT exit. Yams are returned to original place. As lights go up a moment later, VILLAGERS, including BELLMAN, ad lib and pantomime in market as before. PRIEST stands near bushes, carefully watching all that happens. IJAPA re-enters and crosses to market. VILLAGERS grow quiet as IJAPA speaks.*)
IJAPA: And still another fine morning, Bussa and Mubi. (*Sniffing*) M-m-m. These yams have a slightly different smell today and their skins shine.
MUBI (*Brushing him away*): Move along, Ijapa. The market is no place for you. (*IJAPA shrugs, then crosses to palm tree. VILLAGERS freeze. IJAPA starts to sit under palm tree, changes mind, cocks ear to right, then chuckles and puts on palm tree as before. YANRINBO re-enters and looks for IJAPA. She peers at tree.*)

IJAPA: Dance, palm, dance. (*Music begins.* IJAPA *dances and makes weird noises at* YANRINBO, *who shrieks and exits right.* IJAPA *laughs and crosses to market.* VILLAGERS *ad lib and pantomime as he approaches.* MUBI *sees palm.*)

MUBI (*Pointing*): There it is! The dancing palm! (VILLAGERS *scream and scatter, exiting as before.* PRIEST *steps behind bushes, kneels, and peers out to see what happens.* IJAPA *quickly takes off tree and grabs yams. He pantomimes getting one hand stuck, then, in trying to get free, getting other hand stuck, then one foot, and then other foot.*)

IJAPA (*Bellowing*): Help! I'm stuck. (PRIEST *leaps out and dances around* IJAPA, *chanting and shaking rattle. During chant,* VILLAGERS *and* OBA *with* ATTENDANT *re-enter, sneaking up curiously to see* IJAPA.)

PRIEST (*Chanting*):
> Ijapa grabs once and twice,
> But doesn't know when to stop.
> Clever tortoise gets too greedy.
> That is why he's caught.

IJAPA (*With sigh*): All right, I'm caught. I promise I won't make the palm tree dance or steal yams anymore. Please, set me free. (*All look at* OBA *questioningly.* OBA *folds arms and glowers at* IJAPA *for a moment, then nods.*)

OBA: Ijapa, I hereby banish you from our village as punishment for stealing. (*To others*) Set the tortoise free. (PRIEST *pulls vine (rope) from behind bushes. He slips it around* IJAPA's *shell.* VILLAGERS *line up behind* PRIEST *and pantomime pulling as they grunt in unison, as in a tug of war. There is a loud popping sound.* IJAPA *comes free and all except* IJAPA *fall over backward.* YANRINBO *re-enters with hands on hips and sees* IJAPA.)

YANRINBO (*Yelling*): Husband Ijapa!

IJAPA: Yes, yes, Yanrinbo, my blooming flower of the rain forest. I am going to hunt for breakfast in the *river*. (VILLAGERS *laugh and point to* IJAPA *as he crosses left, shaking hands to get rid of stickiness. Curtain closes.*)

* * * *

II.   The Bush Spirits

Characters

IJAPA, *the tortoise*
YANRINBO, *his wife*
MUBI, *a village woman*
FOUR BUSH SPIRITS

SETTING: *The Nigerian bush. There is a dark backdrop curtain with cardboard cut-outs of bushes and trees. Large clump of bushes is up center.*

AT RISE: FOUR BUSH SPIRITS *are hiding behind center bushes.* IJAPA, *with a machete in his belt, and a pouch of corn kernels slung across shoulder, enters right, followed by* YANRINBO, *who is scolding him.*

YANRINBO: Ijapa, you lazy tortoise. You should plant cornfields of your own instead of stealing corn from other people's fields. What kind of example do you give our children?

IJAPA (*Waving her away*): All right, all right, Yanrinbo, my sweet, charming honeybee. Go back to our dear little children and tell them their father is planting corn in the bush.

YANRINBO: Humph! I'll believe you when I see the cornfield. (*Exits right in a huff.* IJAPA *looks about thoughtfully and stops center.*)

IJAPA: This is a good spot. I will clear this land and plant my cornfield.

MUBI (*Entering left, carrying jar*): Good morning, Ijapa. What are you doing here?

IJAPA: Hello, Mubi. I'm going to clear this land and plant a cornfield.

MUBI (*Horrified*): What? Here in the bush? Ijapa, nobody farms in the bush. It is too dangerous.

IJAPA: Fierce animals do not scare me. When I meet a leopard I merely hide in my shell until he goes away.

MUBI: I wasn't thinking of animals. Our ancestors say, "Travel through the bush quickly, or spirits will quickly make trouble."

IJAPA: Pooh! Bush spirits won't bother me. (MUBI *looks afraid.*)

MUBI (*Whispering*): Sh-h-h! There are frightful tales of what bush spirits do. (*Nervously*) I have stayed here too long myself. I must hurry to fill my jar in the river. (*Runs to edge of stage and pantomimes filling jar as if audience area is river.* IJAPA *waves as if brushing aside her words.*)

IJAPA: If bush spirits come, Mubi, I will be clever enough to put them to work for me. (*Suddenly, with wild yelps,* FOUR BUSH SPIRITS *leap out of bushes, up center, one from each side and two over middle. Their movements are abrupt, with jumps and hops, and they take funny poses when they talk. Seeing them,* MUBI *screams and exits left.* IJAPA *falls to hands and knees and draws himself under his shell.*)

1ST *and* 2ND SPIRITS (*Pointing at* IJAPA): Who is this?

3RD *and* 4TH SPIRITS (*Also pointing*): Who lingers too long on our land?

IJAPA (*Peering out from shell*): I am Ijapa, a poor, hard-working tortoise with a dependent wife and many little hungry children.

SPIRITS: Why are you here?

IJAPA (*Rising; uncertainly*): Er—ah—well, your land needs cleaning and clearing.

1ST *and* 2ND SPIRITS: Cleaning?

3RD *and* 4TH SPIRITS: Clearing?

IJAPA (*With growing courage*): A powerful ancestor told me what to do with your land.

1ST SPIRIT: Powerful ancestor?

2ND SPIRIT: Told you what to do?

3RD SPIRIT: With our land?

4TH SPIRIT: Could be a crocodile pretending. (*Gestures to other* SPIRITS. *They gather in huddle, speaking so* IJAPA *cannot hear.*) This foolish tortoise is either getting bad advice or making up a story.

1ST SPIRIT: Let us play along with him.

2ND SPIRIT: Yes. Play follow the leader. (*They giggle and nod in agreement.*)

1ST SPIRIT (*Chanting; to* IJAPA): Whatever you do, we will do too.

IJAPA (*Puffing with importance*): Excellent! A wise decision. First, let us clear the brush off this land. (IJAPA *pantomimes slashing away brush with machete.* SPIRITS *watch, then mimic* IJAPA's *movements, chanting, and doing all the work as* IJAPA *watches.*)

SPIRITS (*Chanting and pantomiming clearing brush*): Whatever you do, we will do too.

IJAPA: Now, this brush must be gathered into piles. (*Pantomimes piling brush into several piles*)

SPIRITS (*Chanting*): Whatever you do, we will do too. (*Mimic him*)

IJAPA: And the brush must be burned. (*Pantomimes rubbing flint; in breathy tones*) Tuh, tuh, tuh. (*Throwing up arms; making explosive sound*) Woosh! (*Wiggling fingers*) Crickle, crackle.

SPIRITS (*Chanting*): Whatever you do, we will do too. (*Mimic him*)

IJAPA: Last, the corn must be planted. (*Pantomimes taking kernels of corn from pouch, planting them, and tamping earth with foot*)

SPIRITS (*Chanting*): Whatever you do, we will do too. (*Mimic him*)

IJAPA (*Bowing*): Thank you, bush spirits. (SPIRITS *bow and leap back behind center bushes with yelps.* IJAPA *chuckles at his cleverness.*) Ho, ho! The bush spirits planted my cornfield. Now all I have to do is wait for the corn to grow. (*Claps hands gleefully. Blackout.* IJAPA *exists. As lights come up a moment later,* YANRINBO *re-enters. She stops in amazement, pantomiming seeing a field of corn.*)

YANRINBO: What is this? A field of full-grown corn. How can it be? Ijapa planted it only yesterday. (*Looking at "corn"*) M-m-m, the corn is ready to harvest. I'll pick a few ripe ears for breakfast. (*Pantomimes picking corn.*) Ah, here is a spoiled ear. (*Pantomimes throwing ear of corn into river. Suddenly* SPIRITS *leap out as before, terrifying* YANRINBO, *who drops corn and hides under her shell as* IJAPA *did.*)

SPIRITS (*Chanting over and over*): Whatever you do, we will do too. (*As they chant, they rush around and pantomime picking corn and throwing it into river, then laugh wildly, and leap back behind bushes.* IJAPA *re-enters, then stops, stunned.*)

IJAPA: What is this? My corn stalks grew high overnight.

YANRINBO (*Peering out*): Your corn ripened, too.

IJAPA (*Looking about*): My corn? My corn? Yanrinbo, where is my corn?

YANRINBO (*Nervously*): I picked a few ears, and four horrible bush spirits flew out of those bushes. They picked

all the corn and threw it into the river. (*Points*) They
kept chanting—

IJAPA (*Interrupting angrily*): I know what they chanted.
Yanrimbo, you have just lost my entire supply of corn.
You, you—(*He furiously chases* YANRINBO *around stage.*
SPIRITS *leap out as before.*)

SPIRITS (*Chanting*): Whatever you do, we will do too.
(*They chase* YANRINBO *around in a circle, until she escapes, exiting right.* IJAPA *strikes his head with his hands
in gesture of despair, staggering backwards.*)

IJAPA: Oh, no! What have I done? (SPIRITS *see this and
leap toward him.*)

SPIRITS (*Chanting*): Whatever you do, we will do too.
(*Pantomime hitting him on head.* IJAPA *breaks away,
yelling.*)

IJAPA: Help, help! The bush is no place for me. (*Exits
right, running.* SPIRITS *laugh and cross towards audience.*)

SPIRITS (*Chanting*): Whatever you do, we will do too. So
(*Pointing at audience in frightening way*)—when you
travel through the bush, go (*Jump at audience and
shout*)—quickly! (*Blackout. Curtain closes.*)

THE END

TWO DILEMMA TALES

TWO DILEMMA TALES

West Africans are especially interested in legal and ethical problems. Choosing sides on an issue and becoming involved in debating, judging, and solving problems make up an important part of their lives. Dilemma tales are a reflection of this concern.

In these stories, the storyteller presents the basic facts and premises with dramatic flair, using traditional introductions, mime, chants, songs, sound imitations, puns, and humor. The audience participates and responds.

The stories are open-ended, with the listeners invited to solve and comment on the problem. Unlike riddles, also popular in West Africa, the dilemma tales have no one answer. The same basic dilemma tales are told generation after generation, the answers and solutions of the audience changing, depending on the point of view, the times, and the social and political structure of the village. Magic or some special skill is usually an important part of these tales, and some of them are used as teaching devices, especially for young people, helping to establish values and relationships. Other dilemma stories pose ridiculous questions or impossible situations and are told mainly for fun.

Two Dilemma Tales

Stories from West Africa

I. The Snore or the Song

Characters

DRINN ⎫
MUKATA ⎬ *brothers*
⎭
CHIEF
GRANDMOTHER
VILLAGERS, *extras*
TWO SPIRITS

SETTING: *A village in West Africa. Backdrop shows a rain forest with huts under the trees. At left is a small hut with a circular, pointed roof made of palms. Hut has a working doorway and is set at an angle, so that rest of hut appears to be offstage. At center is a stool with a tall African drum beside it.*

AT RISE: GRANDMOTHER *sits on stool facing right.* VILLAGERS *sit on ground, right, grouped about her.*

GRANDMOTHER: Would you like to hear dilemma tales?

VILLAGERS (*Ad lib; excitedly*): Yes, yes. Dilemma tales. I like those. So do I. They're fun. (*Etc.* GRANDMOTHER *raises arms for silence.*)

GRANDMOTHER: As you know, in a dilemma tale there is never one answer to a problem. There may be two or

three or more. It is for you (*Gesturing to* VILLAGERS) to
seek out answers.

VILLAGERS (*Nodding; ad lib*): Yes, we know. That's right.
(*Etc.* GRANDMOTHER *begins to chant, gesturing dramatically. She alternates right arm and left arm movements,
keeping time to the rhythm of the following chant.*)

GRANDMOTHER (*Chanting*):
A story. (*Gestures with right arm, then with left arm*)
A story. (*Gestures as before*)

VILLAGERS (*Chanting*):
Let it go from you. (*Pointing to* GRANDMOTHER)
Let it come to us. (*Pointing to themselves*)

GRANDMOTHER (*Chanting*):
A story. (*Gestures as before*)
A story. (*Gestures*)

VILLAGERS (*Chanting*):
Let it go. (*Stamp twice and point to* GRANDMOTHER
    with each stamp)
Let it come. (*They stamp twice, pointing to themselves.*
    GRANDMOTHER *makes sweeping arm movement, as if
    stopping an orchestra.* VILLAGERS *grow quiet.*)

GRANDMOTHER: The first dilemma tale is about two
brothers, Drinn and Mukata. They had left their village to seek their fortunes. One evening (*Crossing up
right and gesturing off*) they arrive at a village such as
this. (*Gestures left.* MUKATA *and* DRINN *enter right,
wearily, each carrying a bundle of belongings.*)

DRINN: It is getting late, brother Mukata. I am tired.

MUKATA: So am I, Drinn. We will stop in this village for
the night. (*Goes to* GRANDMOTHER) Excuse me, Grandmother. May we speak to your chief?

GRANDMOTHER (*To* 1ST VILLAGER): Tell the Chief we have
two strangers in our village. (1ST VILLAGER *exits left,
running. Other* VILLAGERS *rise and cross to inspect newcomers, ad libbing as they giggle, point and chatter.*)

VILLAGERS (*Ad lib*): Who are they? Probably from a village to the north. This one is handsome. Sh-h-h! Don't say that. Where are they going? Maybe to work in the mines. (*Etc. Meanwhile* 2ND VILLAGER *pantomimes dipping a gourd into river at edge of stage, and crosses to offer it to* MUKATA.)

2ND VILLAGER: Here, travelers, a drink of water from our river.

MUKATA: Thank you. (*Pantomimes drinking from gourd, then handing it to* DRINN, *who also pantomimes drinking and returning gourd to* 2ND VILLAGER. CHIEF *enters left and crosses center, followed by* 1ST VILLAGER.)

CHIEF: Welcome to our village.

DRINN *and* MUKATA (*Bowing*): May we stay the night?

CHIEF: Of course. (*Gesturing to hut*) There is our guest house. However, I must warn you that there is a special law in our village.

DRINN: What is this law?

CHIEF: Our ancestor spirits (*Broad gesture, looking up*) desire silence at night. Therefore, anyone who snores will be immediately killed.

DRINN *and* MUKATA (*Gulping*): Immediately killed?

OTHERS (*Nodding*): Immediately!

MUKATA (*Clearing throat nervously*): Yes, ah—by all means we will obey your law.

CHIEF: Good. Then make yourselves at home.

DRINN *and* MUKATA (*Bowing*): Thank you, Chief. (CHIEF *exits left.* VILLAGERS, *murmuring to each other, exit right, followed by* GRANDMOTHER, *carrying stool.*)

MUKATA: Drinn, my brother, I seem to remember that you snore quite often.

DRINN: Me? Of course not.

MUKATA: Let us *hope* not—at least not tonight. (*They enter hut. Lights dim to show passage of time. From offstage, sounds of jungle animals are heard, then fade out.*

Offstage DRINN *begins to snore.* GRANDMOTHER *re-enters, stealthily, followed by* 1ST VILLAGER. *They cross to hut, listen, then grunt and move away.* MUKATA *peers out of hut, unseen by them, and listens.*)

GRANDMOTHER (*In stage whisper*): He is snoring. The village law is broken. Go tell the Chief. (1ST VILLAGER *exits left.*) The villagers must sharpen their spears (*Pantomimes sharpening spearhead, making hissing sound*), for he who snores must die. (*Pantomimes thrusting spear into ground; exits*)

MUKATA (*Looking into hut*): Sh-h-h, brother Drinn. Stop snoring. (*From offstage,* DRINN *makes strange snorts and grunts each time* MUKATA *speaks to him, but continues snoring.*) Brother, be still. Hush, hush! (*To himself*) Oh, dear, he sleeps too soundly. (*Pacing nervously*) I cannot awaken my brother, yet I cannot let the villagers kill him. I must think of a way to save him. (*Paces*) Perhaps if I do something to get everyone's attention, then Drinn's snoring will be forgotten. But what can I do? (*Stops, as he sees drum and idea comes to him*) This drum. I will play this drum and sing. But *what* will I sing? (*Looks at river, downstage, and gets idea*) About the river. I will make up a chant about animals in this river. (CHIEF, *wearing pouch at belt,* GRANDMOTHER *and* VILLAGERS *stealthily re-enter, pantomiming sharpening spears.*)

VILLAGERS *and* CHIEF (*In stage whisper*): Tss-ss, tss-ss, we sharpen our spears. Tss-ss, tss-ss, our spears grow sharp. (*Lights go up as* MUKATA *leaps to drum and begins beating out soft rhythm to astonishment of others, who look at each other in amazement.* MUKATA *softly chants to rhythm, swaying head and shoulders. For a moment, others stand and listen, then begin moving to rhythm, first their heads, then their shoulders. Next they pantomime dropping their spears, making a clattering noise.*

They wave arms, then bodies, and finally begin doing a dance, either rehearsed or ad lib.)

MUKATA (*Chanting*):

 Down in the river
 Lives tiny old fish,
 With a flippy-flop tail
 And millions of scales.
 He lies so low,
 So low he lies,
 Down in the river
 Over there. (*Points downstage to river*)

OTHERS (*Chanting*):

 Down in the river
 Over there. (*They point downstage.* DRINN's *snores grow louder.* MUKATA *chants loudly and beats drum hard, with others answering loudly.*)

MUKATA (*Chanting*):

 Down in the river
 Lives little old frog,
 With a grinchy-green head
 And fat, bumpy warts.
 He lies so low,
 So low he lies,
 Down in the river
 Over there. (*Points downstage*)

OTHERS (*Chanting*):

 Down in the river
 Over there.

(*Point downstage.* TWO SPIRITS *dance in, cross stage, and exit during next verse, thrilling* VILLAGERS. DRINN *snores even louder, and* MUKATA *shouts his chant and beats drum as hard as he can, with others answering in shouts.*)

MUKATA (*Shouting*):

 Down in the river

Lives old crocodile,
With a barky-big snout
And great sharp teeth.
He lies so low,
So low he lies,
Down in the river
Over there. (*Points downstage.*)

OTHERS (*Shouting*):

Down in the river
Over there. (*They point downstage. Last shout wakens* DRINN, *who peers from hut, rubbing eyes sleepily.*)

DRINN (*Re-entering*): What's happening out here? All this noise woke me up. (MUKATA *wipes forehead, relieved, and sinks to ground.* GRANDMOTHER *exits right.* VILLAGERS *rest on ground, laughing and slapping each other on backs with sighs and groans of happy weariness.* GRANDMOTHER *re-enters with stool.* CHIEF *crosses to* MUKATA, *who scrambles to feet.* CHIEF *claps him on shoulder.*)

CHIEF: Stranger, you have given us fine entertainment. We have enjoyed dancing and singing. Even the spirits of our ancestors (*Broad gesture, looking up*) came to dance with us. To show how grateful we are, here is a purse of money. (*Takes pouch from belt and hands it to* MUKATA, *who is astonished*) Villagers, since our ancestors seem to enjoy dancing and singing at night, we should do more of it. (VILLAGERS *clap hands and nod in agreement.*) And, since silence at night is no longer necessary, anyone who so desires may snore. (*All rise and cheer.* CHIEF *exits left.* VILLAGERS *and* GRANDMOTHER *cross right.* GRANDMOTHER *sits on stool, facing right.* VILLAGERS *sit on ground at her feet.*)

MUKATA (*Looking into purse*): I am rich! Brother Drinn, my fortune is made.

DRINN: You are very lucky, Mukata. What made you decide to sing and beat the drum for the villagers?

MUKATA: I did it to cover the sound of your snoring.

DRINN: Do you mean that if I had not snored, you would not have entertained the village?

MUKATA: True.

DRINN: Then, it appears half your money belongs to me.

MUKATA: What do you mean? You would have died by the villagers' spears if I had stayed silent.

DRINN: But if you had stayed silent, there would have been no purse. It is only because I snored that you received it at all. Therefore, we divide the money.

MUKATA *and* DRINN (*Ad lib*): I get the larger amount. No, you don't. Yes, I do. What are you talking about? Can't you see? See here! (*Etc.* MUKATA *and* DRINN *exit into hut, arguing.*)

GRANDMOTHER: And now, it is for *you* (*Pointing to* VILLAGERS) to decide between the snore and the song. Should the money be divided evenly? Or should it all go to Mukata? What is your answer? (VILLAGERS *call out answers and excitedly argue with each other, waving arms for emphasis, as curtain closes.*)

* * * * *

II. The Honey Hunter

Characters

TONVA, *the honey hunter*
HEAR-IT-ALL, *his wife*
FOLLOW-ANYTHING, *his son*
PUT-IT-TOGETHER, *his daughter*
GRANDMOTHER
VILLAGERS

SETTING: *A village in West Africa as before. Hut is moved to center, and there is no drum.*

AT RISE: GRANDMOTHER *sits up left on stool with* VIL-
LAGERS *on ground.*

GRANDMOTHER: This dilemma tale is about Tonva, who
lived in a village such as this (*Making wide gesture,
then crossing to hut*), in a hut such as this. (*She points
to hut.* TONVA *enters from hut and crosses right, holding stomach as if ill. He has a large honey pot hanging
from one shoulder.*) He made his living gathering honey
in the forest. Now, Tonva had a wife called Hear-It-All.
She could hear the slightest noise any place in the forest.
She could even hear this tiny spider (*Pointing to wall of
hut*) crawling up the wall. (HEAR-IT-ALL *enters from hut,
stops suddenly and puts hand to ear in listening pose.
Then she turns to hut, sees spider, and nods in under-
standing.*) Tonva had a son called Follow-Anything,
whose keen eyes could track the smallest animal—even
this spider. (*She gestures toward hut as* FOLLOW-ANY-
THING *enters from hut on hands and knees, with nose to
ground, tracking spider along ground and up wall. He
pantomimes gleefully grabbing spider, breaking off its
head, and throwing the two pieces on ground.*) And
Tonva had a daughter called Put-It-Together, who had
the power to mend anything that was broken. She could
even put together that spider. (GRANDMOTHER *points
to hut as* PUT-IT-TOGETHER *enters from hut and sees
spider. She pantomimes picking up the pieces, while
FOLLOW-ANYTHING snorts, disgusted, and turns his back.
She takes magic powder from pouch she wears at her
waist and chants, wiggling fingers over spider and
sprinkling powder on it.*)

PUT-IT-TOGETHER (*Chanting*): Ekululu jaboluka. Ko de
ba, ko de ba. Ekululu jaboluka. Ko de ba de ko. (*She
pantomimes putting spider on ground.* FOLLOW-ANY-
THING *tracks it as before, along ground and up wall, then*

snarls angrily at his sister, who smiles demurely and bats her eyes.)

GRANDMOTHER (*Crossing to* TONVA): Good day, Tonva. Are you ill?

TONVA: Yesterday I came down with a terrible stomach-ache. I think it was something I ate. My wife Hear-It-All is so busy listening to everything, she scarcely notices what she cooks. Oh-h-h, I feel weak and dizzy. (*Starts to exit right*)

GRANDMOTHER (*Calling after him*): Tonva, surely you are not going out to gather honey today. Not in your condition.

TONVA (*Stopping*): Of course I am. I gather honey every week on this day. Just because I feel ill does not mean I will give up my routine.

GRANDMOTHER: It will be difficult for you to climb a tree.

TONVA: I suppose so. (*Groans with pain, then shakes head to clear thoughts*) However, honey is valuable, and I wish to trade it at the marketplace. (*Whispers*) Besides, I must gather honey before the rest of my greedy family gets it. (*Exits*)

GRANDMOTHER (*Sitting on stool, to* VILLAGERS): And so, Tonva went off into the forest to hunt for honey. Several hours later, Hear-It-All suddenly heard strange sounds. (HEAR-IT-ALL *leaps forward, throwing up arms with shriek.* FOLLOW-ANYTHING *and* PUT-IT-TOGETHER *rush to her, one on each side.*)

FOLLOW-ANYTHING: What is it, Mother?

PUT-IT-TOGETHER: What do you hear?

HEAR-IT-ALL (*Listening intently*): Your father.

FOLLOW-ANYTHING *and* PUT-IT-TOGETHER: Father?

HEAR-IT-ALL: Somewhere in the forest, your father has fallen from a tree. I heard him fall. Now I hear him groaning.

FOLLOW-ANYTHING: I will track Father through the forest

and bring him back. (*Exits right, pantomiming tracking footprints*)

GRANDMOTHER: It was not long before Follow-Anything found his father. And just as his mother had said, Tonva lay on the ground groaning and holding his leg. (*FOLLOW-ANYTHING re-enters with TONVA, who has his arm around FOLLOW-ANYTHING's shoulder and is groaning and hopping on one foot. He still carries honey pot. They cross to hut doorway where, with grunts of pain, TONVA lies down, putting honey pot down beside him. HEAR-IT-ALL and PUT-IT-TOGETHER kneel upstage of him.*)

FOLLOW-ANYTHING: Father's leg is broken in three places.

PUT-IT-TOGETHER: Do not worry. With my powers I will mend his bones. (*She pantomimes sprinkling powder on leg and chanting as before.*) Ekululu jaboluka. Ko de ba, ko de ba. Ekululu jaboluka. Ko de ba de ko. (*TONVA sits up, feels leg, then jumps to feet.*)

TONVA (*Happily*): My leg is healed. Even my stomach feels better. Daughter, I am most grateful to you. Here. (*Handing her honey pot*) You may have all this fine honey for curing me.

FOLLOW-ANYTHING: But Father, I was the one who tracked you into the forest and brought you back to be healed. The honey should be mine. (*TONVA scratches head, then nods.*)

TONVA: You're right. Here. (*Taking honey from PUT-IT-TOGETHER and handing it to FOLLOW-ANYTHING*) This honey is yours for following me.

HEAR-IT-ALL: But, husband, I was the one who heard you fall. If I had not, no one would have gone to find you. The honey should be mine. (*TONVA scratches head, then nods.*)

TONVA: You're right. (*Taking honey from FOLLOW-ANYTHING and handing it to HEAR-IT-ALL*) You may have it all for hearing me. (*Others protest, waving arms and shaking fists. Family argues loudly.*)

ALL (*Ad lib*): The honey should be mine. Mine. Divide it three ways. No, four. No, two. No, no! (*Etc. Finally, TONVA grabs honey and exits into hut, followed by rest of family, still arguing.*)

GRANDMOTHER (*Pointing to* VILLAGERS): And now, it is time for you to decide. Who should get the honey? The hunter, the listener, the follower, or the healer? Should the honey be divided evenly? What is your answer? (*VILLAGERS excitedly call out answers as before. Meanwhile, curtain starts to close. Just before it closes completely* GRANDMOTHER *peeks out at audience, pointing at them and shouting*) What do you people think? (*Curtain closes.*)

THE END

AFRICAN TRIO

AFRICAN TRIO

In most parts of Africa, there are still storytellers who go from village to village telling tales, usually at night and around a fire. Animals are popular characters in their tales, especially clever little creatures who fool and outwit larger, stronger ones. Some stories are used to teach a moral; others are told for sheer entertainment.

In the first tale of "African Trio," the tiny Caterpillar fools Hare, Leopard, Rhinoceros, and Elephant. However, little Frog fools Caterpillar, not only because he is more clever, but also because Caterpillar has pushed his luck too far.

The second tale is an African myth about Hare, the hero-trickster of many tribal stories in which there is a struggle against nature for survival. The listeners identify with the small creature, who triumphs over the greater force.

The theme of the third tale is a familar one in world folklore: if you do not have inner beauty, your outward beauty will become ugly. This story also teaches that truth and knowledge should not be hidden.

African Trio

Tales from East, South and West Africa

I. The Fierce Creature

Characters

THREE STORYTELLERS
CATERPILLAR
HARE
LEOPARD
RHINOCEROS
ELEPHANT
FROG
STAGEHAND

BEFORE RISE: THREE STORYTELLERS *enter before curtain and sit on three stools at left.* 2ND STORYTELLER *beats African drum during opening lines.*

1ST STORYTELLER: Listen!
3RD STORYTELLER: Listen!
2ND STORYTELLER: Listen to a continent!
1ST STORYTELLER: Listen!
1ST *and* 3RD STORYTELLERS: Listen!
ALL: Listen to the rhythm. Boom, boom, boom, boom. Boomity boom, boom, boom.
2ND STORYTELLER: African beat! (1ST *and* 3RD STORYTELLERS *slap thighs.*) Up through your feet! (*All stamp feet*)
1ST *and* 3RD STORYTELLERS: Telling the folktales . . .

2ND STORYTELLER: Native, tribal folktales . . .

ALL: Of—(*They pause, then shout.*) Africa! (2ND STORY-TELLER *stops beating drum.*)

1ST STORYTELLER (*Rising*): The story I shall tell you is from East Africa. It is told by the tall Masai who live in the high country of Kenya. It is the story of "The Fierce Creature." (*Curtain opens.*)

* * *

SETTING: *The stage is bare. A slide of East Africa is projected on the screen which serves as a backdrop.*

AT RISE: STAGEHAND *carries on a large cut-out of a Masai house (see Production Notes) and exits.*

1ST STORYTELLER: A caterpillar came crawling along, looking for a place to rest. He entered the house of the hare. (*As he speaks,* CATERPILLAR *crawls onstage and behind house.*) When the hare came home, he noticed strange marks on the ground in front of his house. (HARE *enters and inspects ground in front of house.*)

HARE (*Shouting*): Who is in my house?

1ST STORYTELLER: The caterpillar did not want to be eaten by the hare, so he answered in a fierce voice.

CATERPILLAR (*From behind house*): I am the terrible warrior, deadlier than the leopard. I crush the rhinoceros to earth and trample the mighty elephant.

1ST STORYTELLER: The hare was most frightened. (HARE *hops about and trembles.*) He didn't know what to do, so when the leopard came padding by, searching for meat, the hare stopped her. (LEOPARD *roars off left, then enters stealthily, sniffing wind.*)

HARE: There is a fierce creature in my house, leopard. (LEOPARD *crosses to house, sniffing stage.*)

LEOPARD (*Loudly*): Who is in the hare's house?

CATERPILLAR (*From behind house; fiercely*): I am the terrible warrior, deadlier than the leopard. I crush the rhinoceros to earth and trample the mighty elephant. (LEOPARD *yelps in fear and hides behind* HARE.)

1ST STORYTELLER: Soon a rhinoceros came charging by on his way to the water hole. (RHINOCEROS *snorts off left and enters, charging, with his horn lowered.*)

HARE: Can you help me, rhinoceros? There is a fierce creature in my house. (RHINOCEROS *snorts, then charges to* HARE'S *house.*)

RHINOCEROS (*Loudly*): Who is in the hare's house?

CATERPILLAR (*From behind house; fiercely*): I am the terrible warrior, deadlier than the leopard. I crush the rhinoceros to earth and trample the mighty elephant. (RHINOCEROS *snorts in fear and hides behind* LEOPARD.)

1ST STORYTELLER: Soon an elephant came lumbering by, looking for bananas. (ELEPHANT *trumpets off left, then lumbers in, pantomiming looking in trees for bananas.*)

HARE: Can you help us, elephant? There is a fierce creature in my house. (ELEPHANT *lumbers to house.*)

ELEPHANT (*Loudly*): Who is in the hare's house?

CATERPILLAR (*From behind house; fiercely*): I am the terrible warrior, deadlier than the leopard. I crush the rhinoceros to earth, and trample the mighty elephant. (ELEPHANT *trumpets in fear and hides behind* RHINOCEROS.)

1ST STORYTELLER: Finally, a clever frog came hopping by on his way to catch bugs. (FROG *croaks offstage and enters, hopping.*)

HARE: Frog, can you help me? There is a fierce creature in my house. (FROG *hops to house.*)

FROG: Who is in the hare's house?

CATERPILLAR (*From behind house; fiercely*): I am the terrible warrior, deadlier than the leopard. I crush the rhinoceros to earth and trample the mighty elephant.

FROG (*Shouting*): I, the hideous leaper, have come. I am slimy, green and full of great big warts. (CATERPILLAR *squeaks in fear, crawls out from behind* HARE'S *house and off right.*)

CATERPILLAR (*Exiting*): Help! Help! (*Animals watch him go, then fall down, laughing.*)

FROG (*Bowing*): Kindly excuse me. I believe I just saw a fierce creature come crawling out of the hare's house. I, the terrible warrior, will pursue him, for my dinner is long overdue. (*Exits right, hopping;* 1ST STORYTELLER *sits. Curtain*)

* * * * *

II. When the Hare Brought the Sun

Characters

THREE STORYTELLERS
HEADMAN
CHIEF
SUN GIRL
MOON GIRL
HARE
PURSUERS, *animals from first play or extras*
STAGEHAND

BEFORE RISE: THREE STORYTELLERS *remain seated.* 2ND STORYTELLER *begins to beat drum.*

1ST STORYTELLER: Listen!

3RD STORYTELLER: Listen!

2ND STORYTELLER: Listen to a continent.

1ST STORYTELLER: Listen!

1ST *and* 3RD STORYTELLERS: Listen!

ALL: Listen to the rhythm. Boom, boom, boom, boom. Boomity boom, boom, boom.

2ND STORYTELLER: African beat! (1ST *and* 3RD STORYTELLERS *slap thighs.*) Up through your feet! (*All stamp feet.*)

1ST *and* 3RD STORYTELLERS: Telling the folktales . . .

2ND STORYTELLER: Native, tribal folktales . . .

ALL: Of—(*Pause, then shout*) Africa! (*Drum stops.*)

2ND STORYTELLER (*Rising*): I shall tell another story of the hare. It is told among the tribes who live on the flat grasslands of the veld in South Africa. It is called, "When the Hare Brought the Sun." (*Curtain opens.*)

* * *

SETTING: *Bare stage. A view of South Africa is projected on the screen.*

AT RISE: 2ND STORYTELLER *begins narration.*

2ND STORYTELLER: In the early days when the earth had no sun or moon, the hare took his musical instrument called the mbira and climbed up a giant spider web to visit the great country which was up above. (HARE *enters, playing mbira, or another simple stringed instrument.*) He came to the village, seeking shelter. (STAGEHAND *carries on cut-out of veld house, with working door, and exits.* NOTE: *See Production Notes for house description.*)

HARE (*Looking at house, then calling loudly*): Where is the chief?

HEADMAN (*Entering right*): I am the headman of this village. Why do you wish to see the chief?

HARE: I will play my instrument for him if he gives me shelter.

HEADMAN (*Calling off right*): Great chief, there is a hare who comes to our village playing the mbira. He seeks shelter.

CHIEF (*Entering right; to* HARE): Play for me. (HARE *plays instrument and dances.*) You play well. I shall give you lodging in this house. (*Points to house*)

HARE: Thank you. I have had a tiring journey. It will be good to rest. (CHIEF *and* HEADMAN *exit.* HARE *enters house.*)

2ND STORYTELLER: That evening the hare looked out of his door and saw a girl sitting in front of two large pots. (MOON GIRL *enters right with a large red pot and a large yellow pot. She sits and places pots before her.* HARE *peers out of door and watches. Suddenly,* SUN GIRL *enters, running, carrying a large red disc.*)

SUN GIRL: I bring the sun back from our sky. (*Puts disc into red pot*)

MOON GIRL: Then it is time for me to hang out the moon. (*Takes yellow disc from yellow pot and exits*)

SUN GIRL: It is time for me to go to bed. (*Yawns and exits*)

HARE (*Creeping out of house*): It would be a fine thing for my world below to have some of that sun. (*He takes red disc from red pot and tears off a piece of it.*) I'll climb back down the spider web to earth. (*Runs off right*)

2ND STORYTELLER: The next morning the two girls returned.

MOON GIRL (*Entering left with yellow disc*): It is time for me to rest. (*Puts yellow disc in yellow pot*)

SUN GIRL (*Entering*): It is time for me to hang out the sun. (*Reaches into red pot*) Something is wrong with the sun! (*Pulls out torn disc*) Look! Part of it is missing. (*Loudly*) Someone has stolen part of the sun! (HEADMAN *and* CHIEF *rush on from right.*)

CHIEF: How dare anybody do such a thing?

HEADMAN (*Looking at ground and pointing*): It must have been the hare. These are his footprints.

CHIEF: We shall follow him. (CHIEF *and* HEADMAN *exit left, running.* SUN GIRL *and* MOON GIRL *follow, carrying pots.* STAGEHAND *enters and removes house.*)

2ND STORYTELLER: The chief and his headman climbed down the great spider web to earth, and called together the animals to pursue the hare. (HARE *enters left and runs across stage in slow motion.* CHIEF, HEADMAN *and* PURSUERS—*animals from first play—enter left in single file and run after* HARE, *also in slow motion*) As the pursuers drew closer, the hare threw the three-spiked devil thorns across his trail. (HARE *pantomimes throwing thorns.* CHIEF, HEADMAN *and* PURSUERS *cry out in pain as they step on "thorns," rub feet or paws, and continue to track* HARE.) The hare pulled down huge vines to block his path. (HARE *pantomimes pulling down vines, and others pantomime fighting through them.*) The hare caused a great rain to wash away his footprints. (HARE *points to sky and others cover heads with hands, peering closer to ground.*) The hare came to a stream. He lay down and turned into a log. (HARE *lies down and remains motionless.*)

CHIEF (*Stopping and looking around*): I don't see the hare's footprints anymore.

HEADMAN: Neither do I.

1ST PURSUER (*Sniffing*): We don't smell him, either.

CHIEF: I guess we've lost him. Come on, let's go home. (*In single file,* CHIEF, HEADMAN *and* PURSUERS *pretend to walk across "log" and exit.* HARE *jumps up and leaps for joy.*)

2ND STORYTELLER: So the hare gave the sun to the earth, and we have had it ever since that day. (HARE *waves "sun" as curtain closes.*)

*   *   *   *   *

III. The Princess Who Was Hidden from the World

Characters

THREE STORYTELLERS
OLD CHIEF
PRINCESS
YOUNG CHIEF
SERVANT GIRL
EMISSARY
PROPERTY GIRL

BEFORE RISE: 2ND STORYTELLER *beats drum.*

1ST STORYTELLER: Listen!

3RD STORYTELLER: Listen!

2ND STORYTELLER: Listen to a continent.

1ST STORYTELLER: Listen!

1ST *and* 3RD STORYTELLERS: Listen!

ALL: Listen to the rhythm. Boom, boom, boom, boom. Boomity boom, boom, boom.

2ND STORYTELLER: African beat! (1ST *and* 3RD STORYTELLERS *slap thighs.*) Up through your feet! (*All stamp feet.*)

1ST *and* 3RD STORYTELLERS: Telling the folktales . . .

2ND STORYTELLER: Native, tribal folktales . . .

ALL: Of—(*Pause, then shout*) Africa! (*Drum stops.*)

3RD STORYTELLER (*Standing*): The story I shall tell you is from West Africa. It is told by the Vai tribe in the rain forests of Liberia. The name of the story is "The Princess Who Was Hidden from the World." (*Curtains open.*)

* * *

SETTING: *Slide of Liberia is projected on screen. Liberian house is at right (see Production Notes).*

AT RISE: OLD CHIEF *enters.*

3RD STORYTELLER: There was an old chief who was very good but not very wise. He had a beautiful daughter. (PRINCESS *enters and stands by* OLD CHIEF.) Although she was well trained at being a princess (PRINCESS *poses gracefully.*), she was kept hidden away from the world. (OLD CHIEF *puts his hand over his daughter's eyes and peers about suspiciously.*) The young chief of another tribe heard about this lovely girl. (YOUNG CHIEF *and* EMISSARY *enter at left.*) He sent an emissary with gifts and an offer of marriage. (YOUNG CHIEF *pantomimes handing gifts to* EMISSARY, *who staggers under their weight, then crosses to* OLD CHIEF.) The old chief agreed to the marriage. (OLD CHIEF *nods as he examines gifts.* EMISSARY *and* YOUNG CHIEF *exit.*) He called for a servant girl to take his daughter to marry the young tribal chief. (OLD CHIEF *beckons off right.* SERVANT GIRL *enters and takes* PRINCESS'S *hand.* OLD CHIEF *smiles happily and exits.*) The servant girl and the princess traveled through the rain forest. (PRINCESS *follows* SERVANT GIRL *offstage.* PROPERTY GIRL *enters and removes house, then re-enters carrying long blue streamers, and stands at center, representing waterfall.*)

PRINCESS (*Entering with* SERVANT *and seeing waterfall*): Look! The water is flowing down over the rocks. What is this?

SERVANT: It is a waterfall.

PRINCESS: Tell me about it.

SERVANT (*Sadly*): I can only tell you the story for a price. If I told you the story for nothing, you would become terribly ill.

PRINCESS: What is the price?

SERVANT: Your sandals.

PRINCESS (*Taking off sandals*): Take them. (*They exchange sandals.*)

3RD STORYTELLER: Then the servant girl told the story of how the waterfall flowed down to join a big river, and how the river flowed out to join the big ocean. The princess was amazed, and she walked on through the rain forest, thinking of all she had heard. (PRINCESS *and* SERVANT *exit, followed by* PROPERTY GIRL, *who re-enters with cut-out of a palm tree.*)

PRINCESS (*Re-entering with* SERVANT; *seeing tree*): What is this?

SERVANT: It is a palm tree.

PRINCESS: Tell me about it.

SERVANT: I can only tell you the story for a price.

PRINCESS: What is the price?

SERVANT: Your headdress.

PRINCESS: Here. (*Gives headdress to* SERVANT, *who puts it on.*)

3RD STORYTELLER: Then the servant girl told the story of palm trees and many other trees, and how some bore delicious fruit and others provided wood. The princess was amazed, and she walked on through the rain forest, thinking of all she had heard. (PRINCESS *and* SERVANT *exit, followed by* PROPERTY GIRL, *who re-enters with model of a peacock.*)

PRINCESS (*Re-entering with* SERVANT): What is this beautiful creature?

SERVANT: It is a peacock.

PRINCESS: Tell me about it.

SERVANT (*Sadly*): I can only tell you the story for a price.

PRINCESS: What is the price?

SERVANT: Your royal cloak and jewels.

PRINCESS: Take them. (*Hands cloak and jewels to* SERVANT, *who puts them on.*)

3RD STORYTELLER: The servant girl told the princess all about peacocks and other animals, those that flew, those that swam, those that crawled, and those that ran. The princess was amazed, and she walked on through the rain forest, thinking of all she had heard. (PRINCESS *exits, followed by* SERVANT *and* PROPERTY GIRL, *who re-enters with cut-out of a rainbow.*)

PRINCESS (*Re-entering, followed by* SERVANT): What is that beautiful sight in the sky?

SERVANT: It is a rainbow.

PRINCESS: Tell me about it.

SERVANT: This is the greatest secret of all, so the price is the highest.

PRINCESS: What is the price?

SERVANT: You must promise never to tell that you are a princess and I am a servant girl.

PRINCESS: I agree.

3RD STORYTELLER: Then the servant girl told the story of the sun shining through the water in the sky. She told about the clouds and the storms and the white, cold powder that fell on the high mountains far to the east. The princess was amazed, and she walked on to the village, thinking of all she had heard. (PRINCESS *and* SERVANT *exit, followed by* PROPERTY GIRL, *who re-enters with Liberian house and stands it at left.* YOUNG CHIEF *enters left and stands by house.*) When the princess and the servant girl came to the village, the young chief mistook the servant girl for the princess, and he married her. (PRINCESS *and* SERVANT *enter right and cross to* YOUNG CHIEF, *who beckons to* SERVANT *to follow. They exit into house.*) The real princess was treated as a servant and had to crush cassava roots and rice all day long, but she was so kind and good that everybody loved her. (PRINCESS *pantomimes pounding roots.*) But the servant girl acted as she thought a princess should. She was selfish and cruel, and everybody disliked her. (SERVANT *struts out of house, pretends to kick* PRINCESS, *and struts around with her nose in the air.* PRINCESS *exits.*) Several years later, the father of the real princess came to the village to visit his daughter. (OLD CHIEF *enters,* SERVANT *sees him and runs to hide in house.* YOUNG CHIEF *enters and shakes hands with* OLD CHIEF.)

OLD CHIEF: Where is my daughter?

YOUNG CHIEF (*Pointing to house*): In there, and I would be most happy if you would take her away.

OLD CHIEF (*Peering into house*): That is not my daughter!

YOUNG CHIEF: That is not your daughter? (PRINCESS *enters. Seeing* OLD CHIEF, *she kneels at his feet.*)

OLD CHIEF: This is my daughter!

YOUNG CHIEF: That is your daughter? I've been deceived.

(*He pulls* SERVANT *out of house and shoos her off left.*
To PRINCESS) You shall be my new wife. (*He enters*
house and PRINCESS *follows him.*)

OLD CHIEF: Now I realize that I should have taught my
daughter more about the world! I'm a wiser man than
I was when I left my village. (*Taps head and exits. Cur-*
tain closes. STORYTELLERS *exit, dancing and beating*
drum.)

THE END

THE MONKEY WITHOUT A TAIL

THE MONKEY WITHOUT A TAIL

The people of the Amhara tribe live in the mountains and on the high plateaus of Ethiopia. Most of the Amhara tales are about cleverness, which the people value highly. One of their favorite characters is the trickster monkey. The story of the following play is a variation of a tale told by the Amharas. In other versions, the monkey without a tail is not kind, but steals the King's honey and replaces it with mud. He then persuades other monkeys to cut off their tails so they will look like him and he won't be recognized as the thief.

The Monkey Without a Tail

An Ethiopian story

Characters

STORYTELLER
PALACE ATTENDANT
RAS WAKA, *a poor man*
MEJ, *his mule*
MONKEY WITHOUT A TAIL
KING OF SHOA
QUEEN OF SHOA
SUBJECTS, *extras*

SCENE 1

BEFORE RISE: STORYTELLER *enters before curtain and crosses center.*

STORYTELLER: Many, many years ago in the high African country of Ethiopia there lived a poor man by the name of Ras Waka who had a mule called Mej. (PALACE ATTENDANT *rushes in, talking nervously.*)

PALACE ATTENDANT (*To himself; ad lib*): The best. It must be the best. Yes, yes. (*Etc.*)

STORYTELLER: Excuse me. (*They bow.*) Who are you, and why are you so nervous?

ATTENDANT (*Breathlessly*): I am the palace attendant for the King of Shoa, and he always wants something for his Queen, and I must rush around to see that it's found,

59

and you can't imagine how nerve-wracking my life is. (*Wipes forehead*)

STORYTELLER: What does the King want this time?

ATTENDANT: The finest honey in the world. I hurry to tell his subjects.

STORYTELLER: They are to search for the honey, are they?

ATTENDANT: Yes, and, oh, the kingdom is falling apart because the King makes incessant demands. Farmers leave their fields, blacksmiths leave their metal, and merchants leave their shops to join the search. This time there is a two-week deadline and a fortune waiting for the winner. Everyone will give up everything to hunt for the best honey. And if nobody finds it—oh, oh, I tremble to think of the King's wrath. (*Exits, running*)

STORYTELLER: Poor Ras Waka will certainly join the honey hunt, for he has long dreamed of becoming rich and retiring to a peaceful, fertile valley. (*Exits; curtain opens*)

*　　*　　*

SETTING: *The forest near the Abbai River in Ethiopia. There is a backdrop curtain with several cut-outs of tropical trees. Left center there is a fire, with two stones for seats by it and a large jar.*

AT RISE: MONKEY WITHOUT A TAIL *is sitting by fire.* RAS WAKA *enters right, leading* MEJ, *who has a jar tied on back.* MEJ *is balky, wanting to rest.* MONKEY, *seeing them coming, hides behind trees to listen.*

RAS WAKA: Come along, Mej, please. You want to sit down every ten minutes. At this rate we'll never reach the palace by tomorrow's deadline. (MEJ *brays in protest.* RAS WAKA *shrugs and sighs.*) All right, we'll find a place to camp. It's almost evening, anyway. (MEJ *kicks up heels and brays happily.* MONKEY *sneaks closer to hear* MEJ *speak while* RAS WAKA *looks about for campsite.*)

MEJ (*To audience*): My back aches awfully; my hooves hurt horribly. For two weeks we've been tramping through the forest near the Abbai River, hunting from village to village. Poor Ras Waka wants to win the fortune from the King of Shoa, but I don't think he, or anyone, will find the best honey in the world. And I fear everyone who fails will be punished by that selfish ruler.

MONKEY (*To audience*): Hm-m-m. The King of Shoa wants the best honey. I have a jar of honey. (*Pointing to jar near fire*) This gives me an idea for a trick. You see, a monkey without a tail, like me (*Pointing*), has a great disadvantage in the forest. Ever since I lost my tail to a lion, I have had to grow clever in order to survive. Now tricks have become my trade.

RAS WAKA: Ah, a fire ahead. I shall ask to share the camp-site. (MONKEY *scurries to fire and sits as* RAS WAKA *and* MEJ *cross to fire.*)

MONKEY: Welcome to my humble fire, Ras Waka. (*Rises and bows.* RAS WAKA *returns bow.*)

RAS WAKA: Thank you, Monkey. But how is it you know my name?

MONKEY: The Monkey Without a Tail knows much about more.

RAS WAKA (*Observing* MONKEY): No tail. How interesting! (MEJ *brays, tapping* RAS WAKA *with hoof.*) Yes, Mej, I'll take that jar of honey off your back. (*Unloads jar to* MEJ's *great relief*)

MONKEY (*Feigning surprise*): You carry nothing but a jar of honey. Can that be true?

RAS WAKA (*Nodding*): Yes. I've been looking for fine honey for many days. At each village each chief told me he had the best. I kept trading one jar for another, giving up a few of my possessions with each trade. This is my seventh and last jar, since I have no more possessions and no more time to look.

MONKEY: Now you think you have the finest honey, do you?

RAS WAKA (*Shrugging*): May the water of Tisisat Falls cover my head if I know. (*They sit.* MEJ *grazes quietly.*) To tell the truth, Monkey, all honey tastes the same to me. That's my problem. I don't know how the best honey should taste.

MONKEY: Nobody does. However, I can help you.

RAS WAKA: In what way?

MONKEY: I own the finest honey in the world. (*Points to his jar.* MEJ *crosses to jar and sniffs it.*)

RAS WAKA (*Rising; excitedly*): Wonderful! Then I will give you my jar for yours, and also—(*Sighs and sits, dejectedly*) I forgot I have no possessions left, and so far no one has agreed to an even trade.

MONKEY: Never mind. You can have my jar of honey for nothing.

RAS WAKA: For nothing?

MONKEY: I will be rewarded in other ways. Even the King's fortune would do little good for a monkey in the forest.

RAS WAKA: You also know about the fortune. Is that right?

MONKEY: Yes.

RAS WAKA: Your knowledge impresses me. What makes you so sure you have the finest honey in the world?

MONKEY: I will only tell you that if I accompany you to the Palace with this jar of honey and speak to the King and Queen, they will definitely say my honey is the best. (MEJ *peers inside jar, scratching head with hoof.*)

RAS WAKA (*Rising, speaking to audience*): It seems strange to take the advice of a monkey. Yet this one seems very wise. (*To* MONKEY) All right, Monkey. In the morning we will take your honey jar to the palace. (MONKEY *and* RAS WAKA *perform a friendship ritual: they bow low to each other, then each leans over the other's right shoulder, then left shoulder and each touches ground with right hand, and finally brings hand to lips.*)

MEJ (*To audience*): My master is now friend to a monkey. That's enough to uncurl a python. (*Brays as curtain closes*)

* * * * *

SCENE 2

BEFORE RISE: STORYTELLER *enters before curtain and crosses center.*

STORYTELLER: When Ras Waka, his mule, and the Monkey Without a Tail arrived at the palace, other subjects had already gathered with their honey jars. (*Exits. Curtain opens.*)

* * *

SETTING: *The Palace of the King of Shoa. Up center are two thrones.*

AT RISE: SUBJECTS, *each with a honey jar, stand around speaking heatedly with each other.*

SUBJECTS (*Ad lib*): My honey is better than yours. No, mine is better. I have the best. I do. (*Etc.* ATTENDANT *enters, crosses center, and raises arms.*)

ATTENDANT: Sh-h-h! Hush, hush, everybody. (SUBJECTS *grow quiet.*) It's time for your honey jars to be judged by the King. May the Spirit Zar protect us all if the King doesn't think one is the best. (*Sound of drum is heard; announcing loudly*) The King and Queen of Shoa! (*Makes sweeping gesture to left.* SUBJECTS *bow and back across stage to right of thrones where they fall to knees.* ATTENDANT *stands, bowing, left of throne.* KING *enters left in a regal manner, followed by* QUEEN. *They sit on thrones.*)

KING (*Shouting*): The honey! I want the honey! (ATTEN-DANT *indicates each* SUBJECT *in turn, and each one presents jar to* KING, *bows, and then backs away left.* KING *tastes from each jar as presented, pauses to think and frown, then shakes head and passes jar to* QUEEN, *who repeats pantomime. The same pantomime is followed until all jars are presented.* KING *rises, bellowing.*) Is this all? Are there no more honey jars?

ATTENDANT (*Exclaiming*): Yeferas gooks!* It appears so, Your Highness.

KING (*Furiously*): It all tastes the same.

QUEEN (*Nodding*): All the same.

KING (*Pointing*): You people do nothing right.

QUEEN (*Nodding*): Nothing right.

KING (*Shaking fist*): If I don't get the best honey, everyone will have to crawl on hands and knees for two weeks. (*All move away fearfully.*)

QUEEN (*Nodding, then surprised*): Everyone?

KING (*Jumping with anger*): Yes! Where is my honey? (ATTENDANT *looks behind thrones, up in air, smiles weakly, and then shrugs.* RAS WAKA, MEJ, *carrying* MONKEY'S *jar on back, and* MONKEY *enter right.*)

SUBJECTS (*Surprised; ad lib*): What is this? It's Ras Waka and his mule. Look at the monkey without a tail. (*Etc.* RAS WAKA *quickly unpacks jar and presents it to* KING, *bowing, then backs right.*)

ATTENDANT (*Looking into jar*): More honey for your Highness to judge. (KING *starts to taste honey.* MONKEY *steps forward.*)

MONKEY: Wait! Before you taste, hear my words. (*All gasp with surprise.*)

KING (*Indignantly*): This monkey without a tail cannot speak to me.

---

* This exclamation is actually the name of Ethiopia's national sport, a game similar to jousting that is played on horseback.

QUEEN: How dare a lowly monkey talk to a king!

MONKEY: I am a monkey with great powers of perception. (*Moves about waving arms in dramatic, mystical manner.* SUBJECTS *draw together fearfully.*)

SUBJECTS (*Chanting*): A monkey witch. A monkey witch.

KING (*After a moment's consideration*): You may speak, monkey witch. (*Sits*)

MONKEY (*Bowing*): This jar which Ras Waka has brought to you contains the best honey in the world. However, when you taste it, you may find little difference from the honey in other jars. Yet I assure you this honey is the best.

KING: If there is little difference in taste, how can it be the best?

MONKEY: Because it is the clearest. It is so clear you can almost see through it. And therefore it makes everything and everyone else also become clear. You will see. Taste. (KING *tastes. All wait expectantly.*) Now look at your subjects there. Do they not appear to be frightened of you?

KING: They do indeed look frightened. I never noticed that before.

MONKEY: Look at your attendant. Is he [she] not nervous?

KING: Yes. Why, yes, very nervous.

MONKEY: Look at this mule. How does he look to you?

KING: Ah, let me see. The mule looks tired and extremely sore.

MONKEY: And this man, Ras Waka. What do you see when you look at him?

KING (*Considering thoughtfully*): He is kind but poor. His eyes contain dreams of a better life. (*Tastes again*) How extraordinary! This is the clearest honey I have ever seen. I see my kingdom more clearly than ever before. This honey must be the best in the world.

QUEEN (*Tasting*): M-m-m! How delicious. I believe this *is* the best honey in the world.

KING (*Rising*): Ras Waka, I hereby declare that for bringing this honey to the palace you win the fortune. (*All cheer.*) And you, my subjects (*Walks toward them*), do not be afraid of me any longer. I can clearly see that I have been a demanding ruler. Go back to your work in peace. (SUBJECTS *and* ATTENDANT *cheer and exit.* RAS WAKA *and* MEJ *rush forward to thank* MONKEY. KING *and* QUEEN *exit left as curtain closes.* STORYTELLER *enters before curtain.*)

STORYTELLER: So Ras Waka and his mule, Mej, were no longer poor. They found a fertile valley where they lived peacefully and happily for the rest of their lives. As for the Monkey Without a Tail—(MONKEY *enters.*) Excuse me, Monkey. (*They bow.*) Where did you find that excellent honey?

MONKEY: What honey?

STORYTELLER: The best honey in the world.

MONKEY: Oh, that. It was just plain, ordinary honey. You see, the best of anything is only what your mind considers so. My cleverness made it the best.

STORYTELLER (*Smiling and nodding*): I do see. You are indeed a clever monkey.

MONKEY: That's all that interests me.

STORYTELLER: Is that why you helped poor Ras Waka win the fortune, and why you helped the selfish King become a better ruler?

MONKEY: Of course. (*Glancing about to make sure no one is listening.*) Well, maybe I also like to bring happiness to others, but don't tell that to any forest creature or my reputation will be ruined. (*Exits, screeching and jumping in monkey fashion*)

STORYTELLER: So that, my friends, is the way of the Monkey Without a Tail. Peace be unto you. (*Bows and exits quickly through center curtain.*)

THE END

BATA'S LESSONS

BATA'S LESSONS

More than 3000 years ago in ancient Egypt, Ana the scribe wrote a story called, "The Tale of the Two Brothers," on which this play is based. It expresses in mythological terms the common concern about death in ancient Egypt, where the people spent much of their lives preparing for the next world.

Among the complicated beliefs held by the Egyptians in those days was the idea that each person had a Ka, a physical entity associated with the body, and a Ba or soul, an invisible entity which left the human body on death but could return in different forms after death.

In "Bata's Lessons," Ra, Ament, Isis, and Khnum represent the vast number of gods and goddesses in ancient Egyptian mythology. Almost every aspect of nature, every animal, every profession, and every milestone (such as birth, marriage, and death) had its special deities. Even the pharaohs who ruled ancient Egypt were considered to be sun-gods, and certain deities associated with them were popular during their reigns. These deities are not worshipped in modern Egypt. Since 640 A.D., when Egypt was invaded by Muslims, the religion has been that of Islam.

Bata's Lessons

A tale from ancient Egypt

Characters

NARRATOR
PALM TREE
BATA
ANPU, *his brother*
KHNUM, *god of the Nile*
ACACIA TREE
RA, *the sun-god*
AMENT, *goddess of the dead*
ISIS, *eternal mother goddess*
LOTUS, *Bata's wife*
PHARAOH
TWO SOLDIERS

SCENE 1

BEFORE RISE: *Lights go out as voice of* NARRATOR *is heard from offstage or over microphone, filtered to sound hollow and mysterious.*

NARRATOR (*Offstage*): In ancient Egypt, when gods and goddesses walked the earth, when magic deeds were done, when souls of the dead took many forms—in ancient Egypt, when Pharaohs ruled from golden thrones, then and there lived two brothers called Bata and Anpu. (*Soft Egyptian music is heard as stage lights go on and curtain opens.*)

* * *

69

SETTING: *Ancient Egypt. There is a yellow backdrop with a river painted on it extending from ceiling height at right down to stage level at left, gradually widening, then painted across and downstage as if continuing into audience. Against backdrop at right and center are small cardboard cut-outs of pyramids as if seen from a distance.*

AT RISE: PALM TREE *stands up center at right of river, holding arms curved at sides.* BATA *and* ANPU *stand on left side of river.* BATA *has sheathed sword at waist.* KHNUM *sits in river area of stage; he is always unseen and unheard by mortals.*

BATA: Anpu, my brother, it is time for us to part. I go to learn the lessons of life.

ANPU: Where will you go, Bata?

BATA (*Pointing right*): Across the River Nile, beyond that palm tree, and over the desert to some distant valley. There I shall rest my soul and build my new home.

ANPU: Guard your soul well, little brother. And do not forget to send for me if you need help.

BATA: I shall. And this will be the sign telling you I am in danger: The liquid of your drink will suddenly boil. Goodbye, brother. (*Claps* ANPU's *arm*)

NARRATOR (*Offstage*): That day Bata crossed the great river, while Khnum, the ever-changing god of the Nile, gave him safe passage. (BATA *pantomimes swimming across river.* KHNUM *rises, arms raised in protective gesture. After crossing,* BATA *brushes off water and waves to* ANPU, *who waves back, then exits.*) Bata journeyed far across the hot desert sand. (*Bell music plays as* BATA *walks in wide circle on right side of river. Bell music is repeated whenever desert is crossed, and same circle is followed.*) And it came to pass that one day Bata entered the Secret Valley of the Acacia Tree.

(ACACIA TREE *enters right, standing in classic Egyptian pose—body facing audience, feet, head, and arms facing left. Arms are bent, with right hand pointing up and held over head, and left hand pointing left at shoulder level. Music ceases as* BATA *stops beside* ACACIA.)

BATA (*Looking and gesturing*): This is a wonderfully green place. The hunting should be good, and the land appears fertile. Throughout the valley stand tall, fragrant acacia trees. In the top flower of this one, my soul shall rest. (*Pantomimes taking soul from body and placing it in right hand of* ACACIA, *who then closes hand.* BATA *yawns and stretches.*) Tonight I shall sleep well, for I have found my new home. (*Kneels, head down, eyes closed, as if asleep*)

NARRATOR (*Offstage*): Now it happened that Ra, the powerful god of the sun, also came into this valley, as did Ament, the goddess of the dead, and Isis, the eternal mother goddess. (*Music plays as* RA *enters left and walks across river to center, bowing to* KHNUM, *who bows back.* AMENT *and* ISIS *enter right, dancing around* ACACIA *and* BATA. *At end of dance, music ceases, and* AMENT *and* ISIS *pose on either side of* RA, *in manner described above for* ACACIA TREE.)

AMENT: Ra, why is this man (*Indicating* BATA) in our valley?

RA: He is here to learn about life, Ament.

ISIS: Then he should be protected.

RA: No, Isis. If we protect him, he will learn little.

ISIS: Then there should be a woman to share his life.

RA (*Thinking*): Hm-m-m. Yes. A wife could teach him much.

AMENT: Let us go to the Nile where the god, Khnum, molds images. (RA *nods, and the three gods cross to river. All bow.*)

RA: Khnum, create a woman to be Bata's wife.

AMENT: Make her lovely, but not perfect.

ISIS: For she must teach both the good and bad of life.

KHNUM (*Nodding solemnly*): Wait here. (*Exits left*)

NARRATOR: Then Khnum sat down before his giant potter's wheel. He took clay and fashioned it into a woman's form, the most beautiful in Egypt. (KHNUM *re-enters, leading* LOTUS, *who has head down, eyes closed, and arms hanging straight and stiff. She wears lotus flowers in hair.*)

RA (*Gesturing and blowing*): I breathe life into her. She shall be called Lotus, born of water and daughter to the sun. (LOTUS *raises head, coming alive.* AMENT, ISIS, KHNUM, *and* RA *gesture toward* BATA. LOTUS *crosses desert. When she reaches* BATA, *he rises and moves in a nine-step circle, followed by* LOTUS. *Then they reverse direction, making another nine-step circle. Meanwhile,* AMENT *and* ISIS *exit right, dancing, and* RA *exits left, exchanging bows with* KHNUM *as he crosses river.* KHNUM *sits as before.*)

NARRATOR (*Offstage*): For many years Bata and Lotus worked hard in the valley. (BATA *and* LOTUS *pantomime tilling soil.*) They prospered and were happy together. But one night (BATA *and* LOTUS *kneel in sleeping position as before*), at a time when the moon was dark and most of the gods and goddesses were walking in another land, Bata had a frightening dream. (BATA *wakes with a cry.*)

BATA (*Shouting*): No, no!

LOTUS: What is wrong, husband?

BATA (*Rising*): I dreamed my soul's tree (*Gestures toward* ACACIA) was cut down.

LOTUS: Your soul's tree?

BATA: Yes, it is a secret I have kept from you.

LOTUS (*Jumping up*): All the time, your soul was hiding here in this tree, and I never knew. (*Examines* ACACIA) Why would it be cut down?

BATA: I do not know. However, in my dream there were swords crossing the River Nile.

LOTUS: The River Nile? What is that?

BATA: A mighty blue stream of water giving life to Egypt. It flows far to the east.

LOTUS (*Staring left*): I would like to see this mighty stream.

BATA: No, Lotus. Stay here where we both are safe. I have a feeling it is dangerous to leave our valley. (*Glancing at sky left*) But now the day dawns, and I shall go hunting. We will forget my bad dream. (*Exits right. LOTUS moves up and down stage on tiptoe, trying to see into left distance. Meanwhile, NARRATOR speaks.*)

NARRATOR (*Offstage*): Lotus grew more curious about the River Nile. Somehow, at some time, she knew she had been there—so long ago, though, she could scarcely remember.

LOTUS: If only I could see the river—just once. Then I would hurry back home. (*Looks right to make sure BATA is not coming*) Surely there can be no harm in looking. (*Crosses desert. KHNUM, astonished, leaps up, gesturing her back.*)

KHNUM: Curious woman, you do not belong here. This is a bad sign.

LOTUS (*With excitement*): It is indeed a mighty stream as my husband said. Now I remember. It was here I was born.

KHNUM: I will frighten her. Then she will return to the valley. (*Pulls flower from her hair, throwing it in river.*)

LOTUS (*Gasping and holding hair*): A flower is gone—and a lock of my hair. (*Pointing*) There it is in the river. (*Turns in alarm and starts to cross desert but hears voices off left and again grows curious*) Voices. People. I wonder who they are. Surely there can be no harm in hiding to listen. (*Hides behind PALM. PHARAOH enters left, followed by TWO SOLDIERS.*)

PHARAOH (*Sniffing air*): There is a rare, sweet perfume in the air. From where does it come?

1ST SOLDIER (*Pointing*): Maybe from this flower in the river, great Pharaoh. (*Hands flower to* PHARAOH, *who smells it.*)

PHARAOH: Ah-h-h, yes. (*Examining it*) See here, a strand of fine, golden hair is attached. I am enchanted. Where is this woman whose hair shines like the sun?

2ND SOLDIER (*Pointing to* PALM): I believe a woman hides behind the palm tree. There, beyond the river. (LOTUS *peeks out.*)

PHARAOH: Yes, yes, a beautiful woman! Bring her here at once. (SOLDIERS *pantomime swimming across river.* LOTUS *backs away with fear.*)

KHNUM (*Disturbed*): I shall raise a wild storm so Lotus can escape. (*Waves arms and blows.* SOLDIERS *struggle, flounder, and fall to knees.* LOTUS *crosses desert, running, and collapses near* ACACIA.)

1ST SOLDIER (*Shouting*): Help, help!

2ND SOLDIER (*Shouting*): We will drown. Help! (KHNUM, *seeing* LOTUS *safe, stops, smiles, and nods with satisfaction.* SOLDIERS *crawl to right of river, then struggle to feet, gasping, brushing off water, leaning on each other in exhaustion.*)

PHARAOH (*Shouting*): Soldiers, I command you to follow that woman. Do not return to the palace unless you bring her back. (*Exits left.* SOLDIERS *pull themselves together, then cross desert, swords drawn.* KHNUM *sighs sadly, shakes head, and sits.*)

NARRATOR (*Offstage*): For many days Pharaoh's soldiers searched through the desert. At last they came to the Secret Valley of the Acacia. And there they found Lotus. (LOTUS, *seeing* SOLDIERS *approach, rises.*)

LOTUS (*Screaming*): Bata, Bata! (BATA *re-enters, sword drawn, and has fierce battle with* SOLDIERS, *while* LOTUS *watches in fear.* 1ST SOLDIER *collapses beside* ACACIA, *clutching shoulder.* BATA *continues driving* 2ND SOLDIER *left center.* 1ST SOLDIER *pulls himself to feet by holding onto left branch (arm) of* ACACIA, *bending it with his weight. Seeing this,* LOTUS *tries to push* 1ST SOLDIER *from tree.)* Get away! Do not touch this tree. My husband's soul is hidden here. Go, go! (1ST SOLDIER *shoves* LOTUS *away. She falls. He pantomimes chopping* ACACIA *down with sword.)*

1ST SOLDIER (*Loudly*): If your husband's soul is here, then when the tree is felled, he too will die. (ACACIA *groans, sways, and opening hand above head, falls. At same time,* BATA *groans, sways, and also falls.* LOTUS *rushes to* BATA, *kneeling beside him.*)

LOTUS: Oh, Bata, my husband. (*Weeps.* ANPU *re-enters left with goblet in hand and starts to drink.*)

ANPU (*Staring into goblet*): What is this? My drink boils. My brother Bata is in danger. I must go at once to help him. (*All freeze as curtain closes.*)

* * * * *

SCENE 2

BEFORE RISE: *Stage lights go out while* NARRATOR *speaks from offstage, as* LOTUS, *wearing crown, and* SOLDIERS *enter right, unseen by audience, before curtain.*

NARRATOR (*Offstage*): And the soldiers took with them Lotus, she who was born of water and daughter to the sun. When she stood before Pharaoh, he offered her precious jewels and gold, and exquisite robes of linen and silk. (*Lights come on before curtain area, revealing stylized Egyptian tableau of* LOTUS, *haughty and demanding, and* SOLDIERS, *cowering at her feet.*) Lotus became the chief of Pharaoh's wives, the most honored Princess of Egypt. With all her new riches and power, she soon forgot Bata. But Anpu did not. (*Blackout. All exit.* NARRATOR *continues speaking as, unseen by audience,* ANPU *enters right and kneels;* ISIS *and* AMENT *enter through center curtain, and* RA *enters left.*) He journeyed to the Secret Valley of the Acacia and there wept bitterly over his brother's death. That night he had a strange dream. (*Lights come up, revealing* ANPU *in sleeping position.* AMENT, ISIS, *and* RA *cross to him.*)

AMENT: Anpu, listen well to our words. Take a seed from the fallen acacia tree. Cover that seed with water. Then your brother will live again.

RA: Although living, he will not be in human form. Instead, Bata will become the sacred bull of Ptah.

ISIS: Therefore, Anpu, if your drink should boil again, it is to the sacred bull you must go. (*Blackout. All exit. Curtain opens, and stage lights go on.*)

* * *

SETTING: *Outside Pharaoh's palace. Two folding screens are at center, angled to represent corner of palace and placed so they encompass most of river area on stage floor. Left exit leads into palace. Right exit leads into city.*

AT RISE: PALM TREE *stands beside palace corner.* LOTUS *is center, scolding* 1ST SOLDIER, *who kneels right of her, bowing profusely.*

LOTUS (*Angrily*): I told you to have the best wine sent from the noble's vineyards. What arrived this morning was disgraceful. Poor wine will never be served at palace feasts.

1ST SOLDIER (*Shaking head*): Great Princess Lotus, the noble assured me this was his best.

LOTUS: Well, it is *not* the best. Go back and tell that stupid noble he had better produce superior wine or I shall have his head chopped off. (1ST SOLDIER *rises, backing right, bowing and nodding.*) And what is more,

I may have your head chopped off, too. (1ST SOLDIER *gulps, feeling neck nervously.* LOTUS *turns to exit left.*) Idiots, all of them. (*Exits proudly.* 1ST SOLDIER *wipes brow, crossing left to look after her.* BATA *enters right, as bull, wearing bull headdress and without sword. He is followed by* 2ND SOLDIER.)

1ST SOLDIER (*Surprised*): Why has this bull entered the courtyard of the palace?

2ND SOLDIER: Indeed it is a mystery. But what a magnificent animal!

1ST SOLDIER: I will inform Pharaoh. (*Exits left, running.* BATA *snorts, paws ground, and waves head like a bull.* 2ND SOLDIER *moves quickly away.* 1ST SOLDIER *re-enters, indicating* BATA *to* PHARAOH, *who also enters.*)

PHARAOH: Ah-h-h! (*Examining*) There is something magical about the sudden appearance of this creature. Perhaps he is sacred. (*Commanding*) Soldiers, guard this animal well. Revere and worship him. See that daily offerings are presented to appease his spirit. (SOLDIERS *fall to knees before* BATA. PHARAOH *muses as he starts to exit left.*) This bull has come here for a reason; yet I fear that only the gods and goddesses know why. I shall keep a close watch on what happens here. (*Exits.* SOLDIERS *rise, march right, and, drawing swords, stand guard.*)

LOTUS (*Re-entering, looking* BATA *over*): So this is what Pharaoh calls the sacred bull. I believe it is nothing more than a lost animal. Most certainly I shall not worship it. Far better if it worships me. (*Laughs, stopping short as* BATA *speaks*)

BATA: Lotus, Lotus, how mighty you have grown.

LOTUS (*Backing away*): What is this? The bull speaks my name. (*To* BATA) Who are you?

BATA: So soon have you forgotten. Do all the rich and powerful forget their humble beginnings?

LOTUS: You frighten me. (PHARAOH *re-enters, unseen by others, and hides behind* PALM TREE *to listen.*)

BATA: I am Bata, your husband in another time and place.

LOTUS (*Gasping*): Bata!

BATA: You have become far too proud and haughty, Lotus.

LOTUS: But I am a princess. I—I (*Sighs sadly*)—Bata, it is not easy to be humble when one is set above others.

BATA (*Nodding*): That is the third lesson I have learned through you.

LOTUS: What were the other two?

BATA: First: Knowledge cannot be withheld from the curious.

LOTUS: You mean when I crossed the desert to see the River Nile?

BATA: Yes, and second: A secret told to one will never again be secret.

LOTUS: You mean when you told me your soul was hidden in the acacia, and I told the soldier, and—oh, Bata, forgive me. (*Kneels*)

BATA (*Touching her head*): I forgive you, Lotus.

LOTUS: What would you have me do?

PHARAOH (*Rushing forward, yelling*): You will do nothing. (*Grabs her arm.* LOTUS *struggles.* BATA *lowers head and charges at* PHARAOH, *who releases* LOTUS *and dodges* BATA's *charges, shouting.*) Soldiers, soldiers, kill this mad bull. (SOLDIERS *pantomime killing* BATA *with swords.* BATA *dies.* LOTUS *sinks to knees, head in hands. Blackout. Curtain closes. Lights come on before curtain area.* ANPU *enters through center curtain, carrying goblet.*)

ANPU: My drink boils again. (ISIS *enters right;* AMENT *enters left.*)

ISIS: Go to the palace courtyard, Anpu. There you will find your slain brother.

AMENT: Take two drops of his blood and plant them

beside the River Nile. Then your brother will live again in still another form. (*All exit. Curtain opens on river setting of Scene 1.* KHNUM *sits in river and* PALM TREE *stands to right of river as before.* BATA, *holding papyrus plant, kneels down right of river.* LOTUS *kneels in river near* BATA. *They face each other. There is no movement.*)

NARRATOR (*Offstage*): Anpu obeyed the goddesses' command. From the two drops of blood, tall papyrus grew beside the River Nile. Then Lotus prayed to the god Ra, asking to be with Bata. And it came to pass that Ra sent Lotus to live in the water near the papyrus. Even today they dwell there, the lotus and papyrus, close to each other. (*Music plays as curtain closes slowly.*)

THE END

THE MAHARAJAH IS BORED

THE MAHARAJAH IS BORED

India is a land that is densely populated, and it has long been troubled by droughts and famines. As a result, millions of its people are poor and hungry.

For centuries, the caste system, which divided people into social classes and was woven into the ancient Hindu religion, has been practiced, but in 1955 part of it was abolished by law. In the villages where most Indians live, however, the caste system still prevails, for a deeply rooted, traditional social system cannot be quickly altered by the passage of laws.

This play, "The Maharajah Is Bored," dramatizes some of the problems arising from the continuing conflict between the rich and the poor in India. Maharajahs and cobras appear in many Indian folktales. The word maharajah means great king. Maharajahs were once the ruling chiefs of India's former princely states. The cobra usually plays the role of a guardian of treasure or the holder of secret knowledge.

The Maharajah Is Bored

A Hindu folktale

Characters

HERALD
GOPAL, *tailor*
PANDIT, *scholar*
SITARA, *poor girl*
RADHA, *rich girl*
MERCHANT
SNAKE CHARMER
COBRA
MAHARAJAH
SERVANT
VILLAGERS

BEFORE RISE: HERALD *enters before curtain to sound of drum roll. He is carrying scroll.* VILLAGERS *enter.*

HERALD (*Calling in loud voice*): *Dhian deejai! Dhian deejai!** I bring a message from The Magnificent Hindu Prince of Maharashtra to the villagers of Rajapur. (*Reading*) "I, the Maharajah, Prince of Maharashtra, am extremely *bored!* Therefore, I will conduct a contest tomorrow at noon under the banyan tree near the village well. If anyone knows how to make my life more interesting, let him appear before me. The person with the best suggestion will be awarded a thousand rupees,

---

* Approximate translation: "Hear ye! Hear ye!"

83

two white elephants, and my eternal gratitude."
(HERALD *exits, followed by* VILLAGERS, *ad libbing excitedly. Curtains open.*)

* * *

TIME: *The next morning.*

SETTING: *Street in Rajapur, India. Down left there is a canopy erected on poles representing tailor's shop. Money box and Radha's sari are on table under canopy. Patchwork sari is in basket on floor beside table, and stool stands next to it. Down right there is a banyan tree, and up center a stone well.*

AT RISE: GOPAL, *the tailor, seated cross-legged on stool, is sewing industriously on* MERCHANT's *jacket. Scraps of cloth are scattered about. Flute music is heard from off right.* PANDIT *enters left, reading book. He crosses right, sits on ground, lotus-style, under banyan tree, and continues to read.*

GOPAL: Good morning, Pandit.

PANDIT (*Not looking up from book*): Good morning, Tailor Gopal.

GOPAL: Why is it that each day you sit under the banyan tree and read?

PANDIT: Because I am a learned scholar. I shall not stop until I have read every book in the world.

GOPAL: Is that possible?

PANDIT: I will answer that question after I have read the last book.

GOPAL: But why must you read so much?

PANDIT: Everything important has been recorded. The answers to all problems are in books.

GOPAL: Indeed! And what problem are you solving today?

PANDIT: I am seeking ways to cure the Maharajah's boredom. In so doing, I have come upon other problems to which I must find other answers.

GOPAL: It is good to study, but I believe many problems can be solved through experience.

PANDIT: That, sir, is complete nonsense. (SITARA *enters right and crosses to well. She carries a water jar.*)

SITARA (*Calling happily*): Good morning, Gopal. Your shop is open early.

GOPAL: Yes. I must finish this jacket for a wealthy merchant.

SITARA (*Running over to him*): Let me see. Oh, lovely! Such soft silk!

GOPAL (*Gently pulling jacket away*): No, no, Sitara. You will get it dirty, and there is no time to clean it. The merchant will come soon.

SITARA (*Noticing material on table*): Ooh! What is this?

GOPAL: It is a sari for the rich girl named Radha.

SITARA (*Seeing more material*): And this? Gold threads all over!

GOPAL: Ah, ah, don't touch. These are fine clothes for people to wear before the Maharajah today at noon. A poor, ragged little girl like you must only look at them from a distance.

SITARA (*Backing away*): If I were rich, Gopal, I'd have you make me a sari so I, too, could appear before the Maharajah. I would win the contest, and my mother and father would ride the white elephants to the Arabian Sea and back again. And I would run beside them making up songs about the forest.

GOPAL (*Laughing*): You have such an imagination, little one. Do you really think you could win the contest?

SITARA: Of course!

GOPAL: And what would you tell the great Hindu prince so that he would no longer be bored? (*Bites off thread, having finished jacket*)

SITARA: I would say—(*Pauses*) I would say—(*Hangs head and sighs*) I don't know what I'd say.

GOPAL (*Smiling, as he folds jacket and puts it on table*): I am afraid you are full of childish dreams. (*Stuffs scraps into basket*) How is your mother today?

SITARA: She is no better. If only we had the money to take her to a doctor, she might get well. Someday, Gopal, someday I am going to find a hidden treasure chest on the banks of the Krishna River. Then, my mother will grow well, and we will never be hungry again. I will find enough to make everyone happy. Someday! (GOPAL *carries basket to right exit.*)

GOPAL (*Turning*): I hope you will have a good "some day," Sitara.

SITARA (*Calling after him*): What do you have in the basket?

GOPAL: Scraps of material from the clothes I make.

SITARA: What are you going to do with them?

GOPAL: Throw them away.

SITARA (*Running to him*): All those silks and satins and velvets? Those embroideries?

GOPAL: They are only small pieces. (SITARA *looks in basket.*)

SITARA: How pretty they are!

GOPAL: They are too little to make into anything.

SITARA: Gopal, wouldn't it be splendid if all the scraps were sewn together into a brilliant sari?

GOPAL (*Shaking his head*): Your head is full of coconuts. A patchwork sari?

SITARA: Why not?

GOPAL: It is not the style.

SITARA: I do not care about the style.

GOPAL: Aha! You wish to wear the patchwork sari *yourself!*

SITARA: Yes, for then I could appear before the Maharajah.

GOPAL (*Laughing*): Go home, child. You have too many ideas. (SITARA *crosses to well and fills water jar.*)

SITARA (*Sadly*): If I had no ideas, Gopal, there would be little in life for me. (*Exits.* GOPAL *again starts to exit, stops, looks at scraps in basket, then walks back into shop.*)

GOPAL: I will throw away these scraps later. (*He puts down basket, as* RADHA *enters and crosses to* GOPAL.)

RADHA (*Haughtily*): Tailor, have you finished my gown?

GOPAL (*Picking up folded sari and spreading it out for* RADHA *to see*): Here is your sari, Mistress Radha. (RADHA *walks back and forth, looking critically at sari.*)

RADHA (*Decisively*): I don't like it!

GOPAL (*Startled*): It is the material you chose. (*Bringing sari closer to her*) And, you see, I made it exactly as you commanded.

RADHA (*Pacing in front of shop in annoyance*): I don't care. (*Furious*) It isn't elegant enough. (GOPAL *sighs and folds sari up, replacing it on table.*) If I am going to win the Maharajah's contest, I must be better dressed than anyone. (*Stamping her foot with rage*) You are a stupid tailor! You sew no better than a monkey! (*She glares at* PANDIT *for a moment, gives an exclamation of disgust, and returns to shop.*) Oh, well, at least it's something new to wear. (*Rudely snatches sari, then takes coins from pocket and flings them at* GOPAL's *feet*) Here are your rupees, old man. (GOPAL *crouches and picks up coins. As she turns to leave,* RADHA *deliberately steps on his hand.* GOPAL *cries out with pain.* RADHA *laughs.*) It amuses me to see how the poor will grovel in the dust for a few rupees. (*Tosses her head arrogantly and exits.* GOPAL *rubs his hand, rises, and puts coins into money box.*)

GOPAL: Radha is a cruel woman. I hope she will not win the Maharajah's contest. (MERCHANT *enters and strides briskly to* GOPAL's *shop.*)

MERCHANT: Good morning, tailor. Is my new jacket finished?

GOPAL (*Bowing to* MERCHANT): It is finished, sir. (*Takes jacket from table and holds it up*) Do you wish to try it on?

MERCHANT (*Imperiously*): Of course. Help me with it. (GOPAL *helps him into jacket.*)

GOPAL: The jacket is a perfect fit. It makes you look so impressive that the Maharajah will surely listen to every word you say.

MERCHANT: He will listen anyway. I am the wealthiest merchant in the village. Here is your money. (*Takes coins from pocket and hands them to* GOPAL)

GOPAL (*Counting*): Excuse me, good sir, but you owe me ten more rupees.

MERCHANT (*Waving* GOPAL *aside*): I have paid you enough.

GOPAL: We agreed on the price before I made the jacket. It was understood that—

MERCHANT (*Interrupting*): If you do not feel I have paid enough, take back the jacket. (*Starts to remove it*) I shall pay no more.

GOPAL (*Protesting*): But, sir, the jacket was made to fit *you*. It would not look right on anyone else.

MERCHANT (*Sarcastically*): What a pity! Then you'd better keep the money I have given you and say nothing more. (*Strides right, snickering*) Hmph! It pleases me to make a good bargain, especially at another's expense. (*Exits, rubbing hands greedily*)

GOPAL (*Putting coins into box*): I think that merchant is a snapping crocodile, not fit to live with people. (*Sits on stool*) Sitara should win the contest. She is more deserving of the prize than any of these disagreeable people. (SNAKE CHARMER *enters right, playing flute. He sits down on ground cross-legged and continues to play.*

GOPAL *nods in time to music, smiles, and picks up scraps from his basket, sewing them together and chanting.*) A little bit of this, and a little bit of that. A sari for Sitara. *Yama tali tat. (He keeps repeating his chant. Neither* SNAKE CHARMER *nor* GOPAL *sees* COBRA *rising out of well, swaying to music, slithering over edge, still swaying, and crossing to center.* COBRA *always speaks with exaggerated hissing sounds.*)

COBRA (*Rising up behind* SNAKE CHARMER *and peering down at him*): Ss-s-top playing that flute! (SNAKE CHARMER *stops, his eyes wide with alarm. He looks up slowly, sees* COBRA *swaying over him, shrieks, and, terrified, stumbles over the well and hides behind it.* GOPAL, *seeing* COBRA, *drops sari, leaps to his feet and runs behind table in fright.*)

GOPAL: Great gurus! A giant cobra!

COBRA (*Moving toward him*): Sh-h-h. Be still! I am sick to my hood from waving around to music. What is your name?

GOPAL: G-g-gopal.

COBRA: The tailor?

GOPAL: Y-y-yes.

COBRA: I'm sorry.

GOPAL: Why?

COBRA: I'm looking for someone named Sitara.

GOPAL: The girl? She was here a moment ago.

COBRA: Find her. Be quick, before some villager comes along and throws stones at me.

GOPAL: You won't hurt her, will you?

COBRA: Of course not. I am here to help her. Run, run. (*Hisses at him.* GOPAL *runs off right.*)

GOPAL (*From offstage; yelling*): Sitara! Sitara!

COBRA (*Rummaging around in basket*): S-s-so. S-scraps! (*Looks around on ground and spies sari; stares at it, waving his head*) That must be the sari for Sitara. What *charming* colors! (SNAKE CHARMER *crawls over to get a closer look.* COBRA *sees him.*) I don't find *you* charming at all. (*Darts at him*) Shoo! (SNAKE CHARMER *shrieks and runs to* PANDIT, *shaking his arm.*)

PANDIT (*Not looking up*): My good man, will you please leave me alone so that I may read this important book. (SNAKE CHARMER *makes excited noises, pointing to* COBRA.) How am I going to find out about anything unless you let me *read?* (SNAKE CHARMER *shrugs and runs behind well.* GOPAL *re-enters, followed by* SITARA.)

GOPAL (*Shouting excitedly*): There it is—the giant cobra! (SITARA *crosses to center and falls to her knees.*)

SITARA (*Hands together, pleadingly*): Great Cobra, I am Sitara.

COBRA: Good. I have been sent here by the Goddess of the Krishna River.

SITARA: Why?

COBRA: She never tells me why. She merely said I must tell you to appear before the Maharajah at noon to tell him how his life can become interesting.

SITARA: Me? I have nothing to wear and nothing to say.

COBRA: The tailor is making a sari for you.

GOPAL (*Hurrying into shop*): Yes. It is almost finished. (*He sits on stool and starts to sew feverishly, casting furtive glances at* COBRA.)

COBRA: And you, Sitara, should know what to say.

SITARA: But I don't.

COBRA: Come closer, and I will hiss a hint.

SITARA (*Fearfully*): You will bite me.

COBRA: I bite only evil people. Don't be afraid.

SITARA (*Taking deep breath*): All right. I will trust you. (*Moves closer*)

COBRA: You must tell the Maharajah what makes you happy.

SITARA: He is a great man, Cobra. Do you think what makes me happy would ever interest him?

COBRA: Yes! Deep inside, you human beings are all alike, you know.

SITARA: No, I didn't know. (*She looks around thoughtfully; then, suddenly determined.*) I will tell him. (*To* COBRA) Oh, Cobra, may you have a long life and shed many skins! (*Impulsively hugs* COBRA)

COBRA: Shoo! You are wrinkling my hood. (*Flustered*) By all the muggy monsoons, I've never been hugged before. My snake friends will never believe this. (GOPAL *bites off last thread, rises, and holds up patchwork sari to full length.*)

GOPAL: Here, Sitara. The sari is done. (SITARA *takes sari.*)

SITARA: How beautiful! Gopal, you are the greatest tailor in all of India. (GOPAL *nods and smiles.*)

COBRA: Run, run, Sitara. Get ready, for it is almost noon.

SITARA (*Bowing, touching fingers to forehead*): Thank you, thank you, thank you. (*Turns and exits right, running.*)

COBRA (*Yelling*): Where is that silly Snake Charmer? (SNAKE CHARMER *peeks over edge of well, groaning.*) Play your flute, little man. It is time for me to return to the well. (SNAKE CHARMER *nods nervously and sits center as before, playing flute, while* COBRA, *swaying to music, slithers into well and disappears.* SNAKE CHARMER *stops playing, runs over to look into well, sighs in relief, and retreats to banyan tree. Sound of drum roll is heard from off left.* HERALD *enters.*)

HERALD (*In loud voice*): Dhian deejai! Dhian deejai! The Maharajah of Maharashtra is approaching on his elephant. All those entering the contest, come to the banyan tree by the village well. (SNAKE CHARMER *looks about nervously, then quickly retreats into shop.* RADHA,

MERCHANT, *in clothes made by* GOPAL, *and* VILLAGERS
enter, ad libbing excitedly.)

MERCHANT (*Pointing left*): Look! The Maharajah's elephant is covered with gold and silver. (*All turn, look off
left.*)

RADHA: The elephant kneels. The Maharajah steps down.

HERALD (*To* PANDIT): You with the book—go someplace
else. (*Shakes his arm*)

PANDIT: Sir, I am solving the world's difficulties.

HERALD: That is all very well (*Pulling* PANDIT *to his feet*),
but you cannot sit there and do it.

PANDIT (*Crossing to well*): I am finding more problems
and more answers than I ever dreamed existed. In fact,
each problem has so many solutions that I cannot decide
which solution is right for which problem. (*Sits in lotus
position at foot of well.* SERVANT *enters left, places chair
under tree, and quickly exits.* MAHARAJAH *enters left to
sound of slow drumbeat, followed by* SERVANT *waving
fan around him to keep away flies. All except* PANDIT
fall to knees, touching foreheads to ground. MAHARAJAH
sits in chair.)

MAHARAJAH (*Yawning with boredom*): Rise, villagers of
Rajapur. (VILLAGERS *rise and move right and left, some
sitting.* SITARA *hurries in, wearing patchwork sari.*) The
contest will begin. Who wishes to be first?

RADHA (*Crossing center*): I am called Radha, the daughter
of Sankar Lal. My father owns more water buffalo than
any man in Rajapur, and he is—

MAHARAJAH (*Interrupting*): I do not care what your
father owns. (*Yawns and stretches*) Just tell me, Radha,
how can my life be interesting?

RADHA: Great Prince, you are far too kind to your subjects. If you spend your time being a tyrant, going
about telling them all what they do wrong, punishing
them for their faults, making them work twice as hard

to please you, surely your life would become more interesting.

MAHARAJAH: Ho-hum. It is true that there are no perfect people in my state. I could spend a lifetime correcting everyone. I shall take your suggestion under consideration. (*Gesturing her away*) Next! (*She moves to one side.*)

MERCHANT (*Crossing to center*): Oh, mighty Hindu Prince, I am the wealthiest merchant in Rajapur, Karad, and Sangli. I sell teak and rosewood carvings, brass and ivory statues, jeweled necklaces—

MAHARAJAH (*Interrupting*): I do not care what you sell. (*Yawns*) Do you know how to make my life interesting?

MERCHANT: It is my suggestion that you spend your time buying the most expensive items in the world and building bigger and better and more beautiful palaces to house your treasures. Furthermore, I am experienced in obtaining the best prices and would be pleased to assist you, for a small fee, of course.

MAHARAJAH: Ho-hum. It is true that there are many fascinating objects in the world. I could spend a lifetime collecting them for my personal enjoyment. I shall take your suggestion under consideration. (*Gesturing him away.* MERCHANT *crosses back to crowd.*) Next! (*Silence.* MAHARAJAH *rises.*) If that is all, then I will return to the palace to decide. (GOPAL *pushes* SITARA *forward.*)

SITARA (*Shyly crossing to center*): Maharajah, I am a poor girl by the name of Sitara.

MAHARAJAH (*Surprised*): You? A poor child? What qualifies *you* to give advice?

SITARA: Only that I am a human being, and we are all that.

MAHARAJAH (*Smiling*): True. (*Kindly*) Tell me, child, how do you propose to make my life interesting?

SITARA: See the little things in life, meditate on them, then use them to create beauty.

MAHARAJAH: Such as?

SITARA: Look at my sari. It was sewn from pieces of left-over cloth.

MAHARAJAH: Hm-m-m! Who made this?

SITARA (*Pointing*): My friend, Gopal. (GOPAL *bows*.) He is an excellent tailor and a kind man.

MAHARAJAH: I must agree your sari is pleasing to the eye and most original. Tell me more.

SITARA (*Pointing to leaves on tree*): Have you noticed how delicate are the veins in the leaf of a banyan tree? And yet, the tree is so big, a hundred men could hide behind its roots. Is it not wonderful to see what nature forms? There is so much, Prince. (*Pointing off right*) See, there, how softly the butterfly rests on the jasmine flowers. (*Kneels, pointing*) And, here—how industriously the tiny ant marches about his business. (*Rising, she gestures widely.*) There is music in the sounds of the wind and the river. You could write poems and songs, whole books, about the little things around you.

MAHARAJAH (*Picking up leaf and inspecting it*): I have never really stopped to look before. It is indeed wonderful to observe how a leaf is formed. But how does one learn to know about such things?

SITARA: You listen to what your heart says, Prince. You are very still and you listen.

MAHARAJAH: Continue, little girl.

SITARA: A piece of discarded wood can make a crutch to help a lame old man. Clay from the banks of the Krishna River can form a water jar. Small stones joined together will build a strong wall for a neighbor's house. There are many little things that can help people and make them happy.

MAHARAJAH: How do you know what will make others happy?

SITARA: Again, I say, you listen to your heart.

MAHARAJAH: I am deeply moved by your words. There are those around who desire wealth and power. (*Gestures at* MERCHANT *and* RADHA, *who look away*) How can the greedy and cruel ever see beauty? (*Crosses to center*) There is no need to continue this contest. Sitara, you have shown me the way to true happiness. I award you a thousand rupees, two white elephants, and my eternal gratitude. I shall spend the rest of my life trying to create beauty out of little things, and I do not believe I shall ever be bored again. (*Returns to chair; sits.* GOPAL *and* VILLAGERS *rush forward to congratulate* SITARA. MERCHANT *and* RADHA *exit angrily.* SNAKE CHARMER *runs to side of well and plays flute.* VILLAGERS *break into small groups right and left.* SITARA *dances joyfully around well while* GOPAL *claps time.* PANDIT *sits reading.* COBRA *rises out of well in time to music. Curtains close.*)

THE END

LISTEN TO THE HODJA

LISTEN TO THE HODJA

In Turkey, the word *hodja* was once used as an honorary title for a scholar. A hodja wore a *kavuk,* a special white, turban-like hat with a felt cap underneath.

Nasr-ed-Din (Helper of the Faith) Hodja, a character in Turkish folktales, may have been a real person. According to some Turks, Nasr-ed-Din lived during the time of Ala-ed-Din, a sultan in the thirteenth century. Others claim he lived in the fourteenth or fifteenth century and knew Tamerlane, the Mongol invader. There is even a mausoleum in a Turkish city which has the date of his birth as being in the tenth century.

Some of the tales attributed to Nasr-ed-Din are also told by other folklore characters: The Mullah in Persian tales and Djuha and Abu Nuwas in Arabic tales. Furthermore, Nasr-ed-Din tales are found in Ethiopia, Greece, and the Balkans. So, as to whether or not Nasr-ed-Din Hodja ever lived, the best answer might be, "Of course he did. He has lived many times in many places." For this character, with his wry humor and his combination of cleverness and stupidity, humbleness and pomposity, appears very much a real person.

Listen to The Hodja

A Turkish folktale

Characters

TOURIST
STORYTELLER
THE HODJA
WIFE
JAMAL
TWO GUESTS
DONKEY
TAMERLANE
GUARD
TWO SERVANT GIRLS

SCENE 1

BEFORE RISE: *Spotlight shines on* STORYTELLER, *who sits on a pillow on the floor. Beside her, there are a cushion and two cups, and a coffeepot is heating on an open pan of coals (a "mongal"). From offstage, the musical chant of a muezzin is heard—the sunset call to prayer.* TOURIST *enters, center, wrapped in an enormous towel, gasps upon seeing* STORYTELLER *and starts to back away.*

TOURIST: Excuse me! I'm looking for the Turkish bath. Where am I?

STORYTELLER: Come in. This is the house of the old storyteller.

TOURIST (*Laughing nervously*): I'm really not dressed properly.

STORYTELLER: The Hodja would not agree.

TOURIST: The Hodja?

STORYTELLER (*Smiling*): You have not heard of him? (TOURIST *shakes head.*) Would you care for a cup of coffee? (*Pours coffee into cup*)

TOURIST (*Still nervous*): Well, perhaps a little. (*Sits down on pillow, and takes cup*) Thank you.

STORYTELLER: You appear tired.

TOURIST: I am! I flew to Switzerland this morning—the Alps, the yodelers, the cuckoo clocks—everything. Then, to Greece this afternoon to see the Parthenon and the Coliseum. Oh, no! That's wrong. The Coliseum was in Rome yesterday. (*Sighs*) Now I am in Turkey this evening. Whew! It's a lot to keep straight. (*Sips coffee*)

STORYTELLER: You are an American? (*Sipping from cup*)

TOURIST: Yes.

STORYTELLER: I thought so. Americans are always dashing about doing many things at once. Although you accomplish much, The Hodja might tell you that if you run too fast, you might lose part of yourself and stumble over it trying to find out where you are.

TOURIST: I am not certain that I understand. Who is The Hodja?

STORYTELLER: There are many hodjas in Turkey, for hodjas are teachers. Only one is called *The* Hodja. We think he may have lived hundreds of years ago. Nobody knows when or if he ever existed. However, we have many stories about him. Some people call The Hodja simpleminded. Others consider him wise.

TOURIST: Which is he?

STORYTELLER: Listen to The Hodja, and you be the judge. (*Puts cup down on floor*) One evening The Hodja came riding home on his little gray donkey. He had spent the day working in his vineyard, and his clothes were dirty and ragged. (*Spotlight goes out.*)

*   *   *

SETTING: *A Turkish village. There are two houses open to the street which runs across stage, so that action within houses is visible to audience. In Jamal's house, left, there is a low table set with four bowls and spoons and four pillows on floor around it. In The Hodja's house, right, there is a large pillow on the floor with a tall water jar beside it. The jar is empty.*

AT RISE: JAMAL *is sitting on pillow in his house.* THE HODJA *enters left, riding his gray* DONKEY *or walking beside it.* TWO GUESTS *are standing on street, in front of houses.* NOTE: *During the play, spotlights shine on each house as action shifts.*

1ST GUEST (*Calling to* THE HODJA): Are you going to Jamal's house for dinner?

THE HODJA: Yes! I am looking forward to it.

2ND GUEST: You had best hurry, or you will be late.

THE HODJA: I cannot insult my little gray donkey by calling him slow. (DONKEY *turns head and looks at* THE HODJA.) I realize that it is *I* who am moving slowly, and my little gray donkey cannot make *me* go any faster. (DONKEY *lifts head and brays.*) I do not have time to change my old clothes. I shall have to go to the dinner just as I am. (*Turns* DONKEY *around and rides up to* JAMAL'S *house, then climbs off, pats* DONKEY'S *head and ties him to a post*) Stay there and guard the house. (DONKEY *brays, lies down and goes to sleep.* TWO GUESTS *approach doorway of* JAMAL'S *house.* THE HODJA *gives one last look at* DONKEY, *shrugs, then goes to stand behind* GUESTS, *as* JAMAL *rises from pillow, and comes to doorway.*)

JAMAL (*To* GUESTS, *ignoring* THE HODJA): My dear friends, I am honored that you came to my house this evening.

1ST GUEST: Your dinners are always excellent, Jamal.

2ND GUEST: And your company is exceedingly entertaining.

THE HODJA: Good evening, everyone. (*The three men turn, look appraisingly at* THE HODJA, *then turn away and continue talking, ignoring him.*)

JAMAL: Although I do not like to brag, I do believe that the pilaf which my wife prepares is the finest in all of Turkey. Come in.

1ST GUEST: She is a fine cook, Jamal.

2ND GUEST: My mouth waters at the mention of good food. I have not eaten since morning. (JAMAL *walks to table, and* GUESTS *and* THE HODJA *follow.*)

THE HODJA (*Clearing throat*): Jamal, I have been out tending my grapes today. I noticed that your grapes were twice as large as mine.

JAMAL (*Ignoring him, to* GUESTS): Let us sit down at the table. (JAMAL *points to pillows for* GUESTS.) You sit here on this side of me, and you sit here on the other side. (JAMAL *and* GUESTS *sit.*)

THE HODJA (*Clearing throat louder*): Jamal. Where do you wish me to sit?

JAMAL (*Ignoring him, clapping hands and calling off*): Servants! Bring the food and place it before us. (*Veiled* SERVANT GIRLS *enter left, carrying platter of meat and bowls of pilaf and pistachio nuts, which they pass to* JAMAL *and* GUESTS. THE HODJA *stands back, coughs, then nervously strokes his beard.* SERVANTS *exit.* THE HODJA, *as if making decision, clears throat again very loudly, then steps over to table.*)

THE HODJA: Jamal, was I not invited to dinner at your house this evening?

JAMAL (*Ignoring him*): When our meal is over, honored guests, I have an excellent dancer from Constantinople to entertain us.

GUESTS: Ah! (THE HODJA *looks down at his clothes, shrugs, quietly turns away and goes into street. He unties* DONKEY.)

THE HODJA: Up, up, little gray donkey. We are going home. (DONKEY *rises with much effort, braying.* THE HODJA *climbs on.*) Forward! (DONKEY *walks slowly around stage to* THE HODJA'S *doorway.*) Whoa! (*He climbs off, pats* DONKEY'S *head, and ties him to a post in front of his house.*) Now you have *my* house to guard. (DONKEY *brays, lies down and goes to sleep.* THE HODJA *shrugs, scratches his beard, thinking. Suddenly he gets idea, leaps over* DONKEY, *and enters doorway of his house, shouting excitedly.*) Wife! My wife, where are you? (WIFE *enters right.*)

WIFE: Husband, it is late. Are you not going to the dinner at Jamal's house?

THE HODJA (*Shouting*): Soap and water, wife! At once!

WIFE (*Picking up jar*): Yes, husband. At once! (*Exits*)

THE HODJA (*Sitting on pillow*): All of the gentlemen were clean and finely dressed, and I was a disgrace to behold.

WIFE (*Re-entering with soap, towel, and water jar, which she gives to* THE HODJA): Do you wish your best turban?

THE HODJA (*Washing*): Yes! And bring my handsome new coat immediately.

WIFE: Immediately! (*Exits*)

THE HODJA (*Removing shoes and calling to* WIFE): I have no other shoes, and these are covered with dust.

WIFE (*Re-entering with turban and coat, and handing them to* THE HODJA): The dust will come right off. (*Bangs shoes together so that dust flies*) See? Now they are clean. (*Helps him slip on shoes and coat*) Oh, your beard is tangled, husband. (*Hands him brush*)

THE HODJA (*Brushing beard*): How do I look now, wife?

WIFE (*Standing back and admiring him*): Ah! I have not seen you look so fine in years. Surely you will impress your friends.

THE HODJA (*Swaggering out doorway and untying* DONKEY): Up, up, little gray donkey. Stand like the noble beast you are. (DONKEY *looks up at* THE HODJA *with surprise, brays, and jumps up.* THE HODJA *climbs on with great dignity.*) Forward! (WIFE *runs to window to wave as* THE HODJA, *nodding stiffly to her, rides down the street and crosses to* JAMAL's *doorway. Meanwhile* WIFE *gathers up everything but pillow and exits right.*) Whoa! (*Climbs off and ties* DONKEY *to post*) Guard my friend's house. Since you are the donkey of a gentleman, I suggest, indeed, I *insist* that you do not go to sleep. (DONKEY *brays loudly, sits down on rear haunches and peers down street.* THE HODJA *swaggers through the door.*) Good evening! (JAMAL *and* GUESTS *look up, smile, and rise.* JAMAL *rushes over to grasp* THE HODJA's *arm.*)

JAMAL: My friend, you are late. I was worried that some terrible disaster had happened to keep you away. Welcome! Welcome, my Hodja!

1ST GUEST: It is good to see you again, O great Hodja.

2ND GUEST: You will find the dinner a most delightful one, divine Hodja.

JAMAL: Sit beside me. (*To* 1ST GUEST) Would you mind moving over so that my dear friend can sit beside me?

1ST GUEST: Of course not, seeing that it is The Hodja who will sit next to *me*. (*All sit.*)

JAMAL (*Clapping hands, calling*): Servants! Bring food for The Hodja! (SERVANT GIRLS *enter left with food, bowing to* THE HODJA. *One offers pilaf.*)

THE HODJA: This is some of your wife's excellent pilaf. (*Takes a spoonful and drops it into a fold of his turban.*) Eat, turban, eat! (*Others gasp.*)

2ND GUEST (*Aside, to* JAMAL): Look! The Hodja is putting pilaf into his turban!

JAMAL (*To* THE HODJA): Effendi, are you feeling well?

THE HODJA: Quite well! Do I smell some wonderful roast mutton? (SERVANT *brings platter of meat.* THE HODJA *takes pieces of meat and stuffs them into pockets of his coat.*) Eat, coat, eat! (*Others gasp.*)

2ND GUEST (*Rising to knees and whispering to* JAMAL): Look! The Hodja is putting the meat into his coat pockets!

JAMAL: Yes, yes, I see, but I find it hard to believe.

THE HODJA (*Loudly, startling* 1ST GUEST): And now, the pistachio nuts! Jamal, you set a tremendous table for your friends. (SERVANT *offers him bowl of nuts.* THE HODJA *takes a handful of nuts and stuffs them into his shoes.*) Eat, shoes, eat! (GUESTS *gasp.*)

JAMAL (*Rising*): This is too much. Why are you taking my good food and wasting it that way?

THE HODJA: You do not wish my turban to eat?

JAMAL: No, of course not!

THE HODJA (*Rising to knees*): You do not wish my coat to eat?

JAMAL (*Striding away from table*): No, of course not!

THE HODJA (*Standing*): You do not wish my shoes to eat?

GUESTS: No, of course not!

THE HODJA (*Shrugging, looking around innocently*): When I came to this house a short time ago in my old, dirty clothes, I was ignored, and there was no place at the table for me. When I come to this house in my fine, new clothes, everyone notices me, and nothing is too good for me. Therefore, I thought it was my *clothes* you had invited to dinner. Certainly, it could not have been *me*. (*All look at each other in amazement. Quick blackout and curtain.*)

* * * * *

SCENE 2

BEFORE RISE: *Spotlight comes up on* TOURIST *and* STORY-TELLER *sitting in front of curtain.*

TOURIST (*Laughing*): The Hodja is quite a character!

STORYTELLER: He is a favorite with my people. Do you have time for another tale? (*Sips coffee.*)

TOURIST: Probably not, but I can't resist.

STORYTELLER: I am glad to see you more relaxed. So, once again we will listen to The Hodja. (*Sets cup down*) When Tamerlane the Great, the fearful Mongol conqueror, was ruling his vast empire, he took a liking to The Hodja because he found the little man amusing. One morning he sent word that he was coming to visit The Hodja in his home. (*Curtain opens.*)

* * *

SETTING: *Jamal's and The Hodja's houses, the same as in Scene 1. There is a bowl of figs on Jamal's table. Six large beets with tops are on the floor at center, as if growing in the ground.*

AT RISE: DONKEY *grazes near beets.* WIFE *is sweeping* THE HODJA's *house and beating the pillows.*

THE HODJA (*Entering right*): Wife, Tamerlane will not notice if the floor is swept or the pillows beaten. He is coming here to be amused.

WIFE: A clean house may not be amusing, but it is more pleasant. Have you considered what we shall give to him as a present?

THE HODJA: We'll give him nothing! We are not visiting him. He is visiting us.

WIFE: But, he is important—famous! It is a gift to us for him to enter our humble house. We must show our appreciation.

THE HODJA (*Scratching beard, thoughtfully*): Once again you are right. I shall pull some firm, red beets out of our garden and give them to Tamerlane.

WIFE: Good. (*Exits right*)

THE HODJA (*Humming happily, crossing to center*): Good morning, little gray donkey. (DONKEY *brays loudly.*) Will you kindly move so that I may pull up my beets? (DON-KEY *shakes head and sits down on haunches.*) You are still in the way. (*Pushes* DONKEY *from behind.*) There! (DONKEY *peers around as* THE HODJA *pulls on his beet tops. All six beets come out at once.* THE HODJA *falls over backwards.* DONKEY *brays in amusement, and* THE HODJA *rises with dignity.* JAMAL, *hearing the noise, enters and runs to his door.*)

JAMAL: What is the matter? Are you hurt?

THE HODJA (*Waving beets*): No effendi. I have six beautiful, firm red beets to give to Tamerlane when he visits my house.

JAMAL: Hm-m! They appear to be of good quality. Let me examine them. (THE HODJA *follows* JAMAL *into his house.* JAMAL *takes beets, thumps and sniffs them, and hands them back.*) Indeed, they will make a fine gift.

THE HODJA: Thank you, my friend. (*He turns to leave.* JAMAL *looks at bowl of figs on table, picks it up and sniffs it, and wrinkles his nose at the smell. Then he calls* THE HODJA.)

JAMAL: Wait, my friend. (THE HODJA *turns.* JAMAL *holds out bowl of figs, hiding his distaste.*) I think you should give this bowl of figs to Tamerlane instead of those beets.

THE HODJA (*Looking at figs*): But, your figs appear to be rotten.

JAMAL: Not so. They are at the peak of their ripeness. I have heard that Tamerlane has a fondness for very ripe figs.

THE HODJA: I did not know that.

JAMAL: I will show you what a good friend I am. We will make an even trade—the beets for the figs.

THE HODJA: It is done. (*Hands beets to* JAMAL *and takes figs, then crosses to his house, humming happily.* DON-

KEY *sniffs figs and brays loudly.* JAMAL *dances about gleefully with beets.*)

GUARD (*Entering*): Make way for Tamerlane the Great, lord of the land, military genius, expert horseman, fearless warrior, and winner of the local chess tournament. (*Drum roll is heard from offstage.* SERVANT GIRLS *enter, dancing and shaking bells, followed by* GUARD, *beating drum, and* TAMERLANE, *marching with arms folded and a fierce frown.* JAMAL *peers out window, suppresses mirth, and withdraws.* SERVANTS *stop at right, bowing, as* TAMERLANE *and* GUARD *pass; then they sit down to wait.* THE HODJA *rushes into his house, shouting excitedly.*)

THE HODJA: Wife! Wife! Tamerlane is here. (*He holds basket behind him and stands at left.* WIFE, *veiled, enters, and stands next to* THE HODJA. *Both bow low as* TAMERLANE *and* GUARD *stride into house.* GUARD *takes his place and stands at attention at right of door.*) Good morning, noble Tamerlane. Please sit down.

TAMERLANE: It is a *bad* morning! (TAMERLANE *sits on cushion on floor.*)

THE HODJA: I suppose it is. I have never seen such a bad morning. I do believe the world will end by this afternoon.

TAMERLANE (*With a sneer*): My soldiers are shooting poorly with their bows. Their arrows do not seem to know where the target is.

THE HODJA: What a shame! If you like, I shall speak to the arrows at once.

TAMERLANE (*Smiling a little*): That will not be necessary. What do you have hidden behind you?

THE HODJA: A gift for you.

TAMERLANE: I notice a funny smell. I trust it is not the gift that has such an odor.

THE HODJA: It might, but a gift which smells has more

meaning than one with no odor at all. (*Gives bowl of figs to* TAMERLANE) Figs for Tamerlane! Figs for you!

TAMERLANE (*Leaping up, holding nose*): What a smell! Guard, take these rotten figs away. (GUARD *takes bowl and rushes down street;* SERVANT GIRLS *squeal, hold noses, run off left.* GUARD *stops center, as if undecided what to do with figs.* TAMERLANE *rushes to window and shouts.*) Throw them at The Hodja. I have never been so insulted. He deserves to have the rotten figs on his head.

THE HODJA (*Dismayed*): Throw the figs at me? (*Bewildered, he runs through doorway into street, stops, peers around at* GUARD, *then rushes off right.* GUARD *follows, and, standing right, throws figs at departing* HODJA. TAMERLANE *laughs heartily, slaps his knees in amusement, then hurries out of house onto street.*)

GUARD (*Shouting excitedly*): I hit him. Right on target, noble Tamerlane. (*Continues to throw figs off*) Another hit. We should give figs to our soldiers. They might scare the enemy off. (*As he continues throwing figs after* THE HODJA) There's another. These are the squishiest figs I've ever seen—and the worst smelling! No one could stand up under these. There's the last one. (GUARD *turns, hands empty bowl to* WIFE, *who has been watching from doorway.*)

TAMERLANE (*Gesturing imperiously to* GUARD): Come, we must go back to our armies and make plans for using figs in our next battle. (*He laughs, then exits, followed by* GUARD. THE HODJA *re-enters, his turban askew, his clothes disheveled, his face dirty.*)

THE HODJA (*Shouting angrily*): Jamal, you villain, Jamal!

WIFE (*Going to him*): Oh, my poor husband! Are you all right?

THE HODJA: Quite well, wife! (*Shouts*) Jamal! (*Crosses left and enters* JAMAL'*s house*) Jamal, my friend!

JAMAL (*Entering his house, left; nervously*): I can explain everything. I know you must be upset. Before you do anything—

THE HODJA (*Falling to his knees*): I am extremely lucky to have a friend like you, Jamal.

JAMAL: What is this?

THE HODJA (*Rising*): I wish to thank you seven times above and seven times below the earth for the good you have done.

JAMAL: What good?

THE HODJA: You took my *hard* beets and gave me the *soft* figs.

JAMAL: I know!

THE HODJA: If it had been the hard beets which had been thrown at me, I might not be here at all. How wise it is to take the advice of a good friend. (*Quick blackout and curtain. Spotlight comes up on* TOURIST *and* STORYTELLER, *who sit on pillows in front of curtain.*)

STORYTELLER (*Laughing*): Come now, tell me whether The Hodja is simpleminded or wise.

TOURIST: It is hard to tell. I would say he is a little of both.

STORYTELLER: So it is with most of us, I believe. More coffee?

TOURIST (*Rising*): No, thank you. I still must find the Turkish bath.

STORYTELLER: It is next door.

TOURIST: You have been very kind. I wish I weren't leaving in the morning. I'd like to hear another story.

STORYTELLER: Next time you come to Turkey, stay a bit longer.

TOURIST: I shall. The Hodja could teach me many things. Goodbye.

STORYTELLER: Goodbye, my friend. (TOURIST *exits right.*)

THE HODJA (*Entering left, waving arms excitedly*): Wife! Come quickly!

STORYTELLER (*Rising*): What is it? What is wrong?

THE HODJA: I just looked into my well and saw the moon and seven stars in there. Surely they will drown if we do not pull them out.

STORYTELLER: What you see is only a reflection.

THE HODJA: Are you sure? How can we understand what is a reflection and what is real, if we do not have both? (*Exits right, calling*) Wife! My wife, where are you? (STORYTELLER *shrugs. Quick blackout.*)

THE END

THE FLYING HORSE MACHINE

THE FLYING HORSE MACHINE

This play is based on a tale called "The Ebony Horse," from *The Arabian Nights*. This book, more correctly known as *The Book of the Thousand Nights and One Night (Kitab Alf Laylah wa Laylah)*, is a collection of folk stories handed down by word of mouth for centuries. It is not certain if the stories originated in Arabia, Persia, or India, but sometime between the fourteenth and sixteenth centuries, a professional storyteller gathered the tales and put them into writing. A French translation in the early eighteenth century introduced *The Arabian Nights* to Europeans, and over a hundred years later, the first English translation was made.

In *The Arabian Nights,* there is a king who has the frightful custom of marrying and then putting his new wife to death the morning after the wedding. When Scheherazade marries the king, she cleverly tells him an interesting story each night, stopping at the most exciting place in the story and promising to finish the next evening. She escapes being put to death for a thousand and one nights, and the king decides to spare her life.

Scheherazade tells many magical tales—about the voyages of Sinbad, the Sailor, Aladdin and his wonderful lamp, Ali Baba and the forty thieves, Jinni rising from a jar, and carpets flying through the air—making *The Arabian Nights* one of the great treasures of fictional romance and adventure.

The Flying Horse Machine

A story from *The Arabian Nights*

Characters

PRINCE KAMAR
PRINCESS FAHAN, *his sister*
KING SABUR, *Sultan of Persia, their father*
MAROUDAH, *the old magician*
THE FLYING HORSE MACHINE
PRINCESS SHAMOUR, *of Ceylon*
GIANT ROC
TWO GUARDS
ATTENDANTS, *extras*
CLOUDS, *extras*

SCENE 1

SETTING: *King Sabur's palace courtyard, in ancient Persia. At an angle up right is his throne. Backdrop curtains, meeting at center, represent palace wall. Several tropical plants are grouped near backdrop.*

AT RISE: KING SABUR *is seated on throne.* 1ST GUARD, *with spear, stands beside him.* PRINCE KAMAR, *with a sword at his side, and* PRINCESS FAHAN, *veiled, stand left center, talking.*

KAMAR: The festival of Nau-Roz is almost over, sister Princess Fahan. I am impressed with the marvelous inventions entered in (*Gesturing to* KING SABUR) Father's annual contest. Which would you choose as the best?

115

FAHAN: M-m-m. Well, brother Prince Kamar, I believe I prefer the golden peacock that can tell the time of day.

KAMAR: It is beautiful, but what about the mechanical guard made of precious gems that holds a silver trumpet? Whenever an enemy approaches, the figure blows a fierce warning. Think of how beneficial it would be in ruling Persia. That is always Father's first concern.

FAHAN: Yes, perhaps you are right. However, Father has not yet declared the winner. Last year the prize was given by noon. Now it is almost evening, and his mind is still not made up. (*Commotion is heard from off left. 2ND GUARD enters left and falls on knees before KING.*)

2ND GUARD: King Sabur, sublime Sultan of Persia, an old man seeks admittance to demonstrate his invention.

KING (*Eagerly*): Send him in at once. (*2ND GUARD exits left.*) Strange. All afternoon I have felt it necessary to wait for one more contestant. (*MAROUDAH, the magician, wearing tousled white wig and beard, enters left, dramatically, with evil smile and sweeping bow. He is followed by 2ND GUARD.*)

MAROUDAH (*In sinister tones*): King Sabur, I am Maroudah, the magnificent magician. I have invented a miraculous magic horse machine. (*He makes a sweeping bow to left. FLYING HORSE MACHINE enters, snorting and neighing. HORSE consists of a wooden box on wheels as its middle or body section, covered by a fringed blanket, hanging to ground and hiding wheels, and large enough to be attached to papier-mâché horse's head which is worn by first actor. Blanket also covers second actor, in the rear, and a tail is sewn on end of blanket. A large key and removable knob are on horse's head. HORSE is followed by curious, veiled court ATTENDANTS, who murmur admiringly as HORSE, walking mechanically, circles stage and then stands, center.*)

KING (*Thoughtfully*): Your horse machine is interesting,

Maroudah, but there have been more remarkable inventions here today.

MAROUDAH: Ah, but you have not seen what my invention will do. This, great Sultan, is a flying horse machine.

ALL (*Amazed; ad lib*): A flying horse machine? (*Etc.*)

KING: Demonstrate that what you say is true.

MAROUDAH: With pleasure. (*Climbs onto* HORSE *and turns key.* HORSE *paws ground, neighs, and then, carrying* MAROUDAH, *quickly exits right. All look upward, point, gasp in amazement, as they pantomime watching* HORSE *flying overhead, crossing and circling stage.*)

ALL (*Ad lib*): Look! The horse is flying! See how it soars! (*Etc. They pantomime watching* HORSE *descend and finally land. In a moment* HORSE *with* MAROUDAH *riding it re-enters. All clap and murmur approval; ad lib*) Amazing! Wonderful! Fantastic! Surely this invention will win the prize. (*Etc.*)

KING (*Rising, holding up hands for quiet*): Never have I beheld such a marvel. (*Pacing excitedly, waving arms*) What possibilities this horse machine has for me! Every day I could fly above my kingdom. In a moment I could find anyone. I could visit the farthest city. I could spy on my enemies. I could cast fear into the hearts of entire armies. (*Crossing to* MAROUDAH) Maroudah, I declare you the winner of the Nau-Roz Festival Contest. Name your prize. Anything you desire shall be yours. Anything.

MAROUDAH (*Rubbing hands together and smiling sinisterly*): My prize, King Sabur, will be to marry your daughter, Princess Fahan. (*Whirls and gestures to her.* FAHAN *gasps and backs away.* KING *is astonished.* KAMAR *steps forward to protest. Others are alarmed.*)

FAHAN: No, no. (*Sinks before* KING) Please, please, Father, do not make me marry him.

KING: Hush, daughter. A king cannot go back on a promise. (FAHAN *weeps*.)

KAMAR: Although I have the highest respect for you, Father, I am shocked that you would force my sister, your obedient and gentle daughter, to marry this ugly and evil old wizard.

MAROUDAH (*Angrily*): Prince Kamar, though your words are sharp arrows, they fall only on parched desert sands. Princess Fahan is mine. I have won her fairly in exchange for this flying horse machine.

KAMAR: It may be a trick, Father. The horse may fly only when Maroudah rides it. The machine may have no value to anyone else.

KING: Hm-m-m. Maroudah, how can I be certain the horse will fly without you?

MAROUDAH: Try it, sire. (*Suddenly laughs wickedly as he gets idea. Turns to* KAMAR) But, no, since it is Prince Kamar who does not believe, he should be the one to test the horse.

KAMAR: I am eager to do so, for I feel this magician hides truth to gain his desire. (*Climbs onto* HORSE)

MAROUDAH (*Indicating key*): There is the key to make the machine go up. (*Laughs evilly, rubbing hands together, as* KAMAR *turns key.* HORSE *moves and* KAMAR *quickly exits right on* HORSE. *As before, all pantomime watching* HORSE *fly across stage, first left, then right. Then suddenly all shade eyes and murmur in growing horror, staring straight up.*)

ALL (*Ad lib*): Prince Kamar flies higher and higher. (*Etc.*)

FAHAN (*Rising, crying out*): Brother, brother, come back!

KING (*To* MAROUDAH): Why doesn't he come down?

MAROUDAH (*Laughing evilly*): Because he does not know how. I did not show him the secret knob for downward flight. Unless he finds it, he will continue to fly up and up. He will probably fly into the sun before he can find the knob. (*Laughs*)

KING (*Furiously*): You did this deliberately.

MAROUDAH: Yes. Prince Kamar tried to interfere with my plans. And now—(*Yanks* FAHAN *toward backdrop*) Now I have Princess Fahan. (FAHAN *struggles and cries out.*)

KING (*Yelling*): Guards, guards seize that evil magician! (GUARDS *rush toward* MAROUDAH, *who pulls* FAHAN *behind plants at rear. Concealed by plants and* GUARDS, *they "disappear" by crawling under backdrop curtains. At the same time the sound of an explosion is heard and* GUARDS *stagger back and fall as if stunned. Others shriek in fear.*)

ALL (*Yelling; ad lib*): Where are they? They have disappeared. It was evil magic. The princess has been kidnapped. (*Etc.*)

KING (*Shouting upward to* KAMAR): My son, search for the secret knob. (*Gesturing sadly to back wall*) My daughter, it is my fault you have been spirited away. (*Sinks onto throne, moaning unhappily*) May Allah forgive my lust for power. My greedy desire to own the flying horse machine has cost me my children. (*Others fall to knees, moaning, in imitation of* KING, *as curtain closes.*)

* * * * *

SCENE 2

BEFORE RISE: CLOUDS *enter left before curtain and crawl right along edge of stage to give effect of sky.* HORSE, *with* KAMAR, *who uses rocking motions to indicate riding, enters left and crosses right with* CLOUDS.

KAMAR: I am flying above the clouds. (*Points to* CLOUDS) The more I turn this key, the higher we go. (*Searching* HORSE) There should be another key, or button, or peg, or knob, or—(*Looking up, fearfully*) It is getting hotter. I am nearing the sun. Someplace on this horse machine there must be a device to make it fly downward. (*As*

Horse *reaches center stage he finds knob.*) Ah, here is a hidden knob. It turns. At last, we are flying downward. (*Wipes forehead with relief*) Another few minutes and I would have caught fire. (*Looking down*) Below me is a large, green island. And there is a shining, walled city. We shall land on the roof of that (*Pointing*) golden palace. (*Exits right on* Horse, *followed by* Clouds. *Curtain opens.*)

* * *

Setting: *Princess Shamour's room in the golden palace of Ceylon. Plants and throne used in Scene 1 have been removed. Center backdrop curtains are opened and draped to reveal cardboard cut-out of Oriental window frame. At right center is a couch made of large pillows.*

At Rise: Princess Shamour *is resting on couch, leaning on one elbow, and watching* Attendants *dance, left, to Indian music, heard from offstage.* Kamar *climbs through window, rear. Music stops.* Attendants, *seeing him, muffle screams and run fearfully downstage, huddling in a group.* Shamour *rises in alarm and starts to run right.*

Kamar (*Gesturing to stop her*): Wait, please. (*Bowing to* Shamour) Lovely lady, I mean you no harm. (*She stops and turns to look at him. They stare at each other, frozen for a moment, then speak as if enchanted.*)

Shamour: Who are you?

Kamar: Prince Kamar of Persia. And your name?

Shamour: Shamour, Princess of Ceylon.

Kamar: I am charmed by your grace and beauty.

Shamour: Thank you, handsome Prince. But how did you come to our island kingdom? I am certain our guards would have seen a ship arrive and spread the alarm.

Kamar: I flew here. (*All gasp.*)

Shamour: What powers you must possess! Are you part god, or do you cast spells in league with dark spirits?

KAMAR (*Smiling*): Neither, Princess Shamour. I flew here on a horse machine invented by the magician, Maroudah.

SHAMOUR (*Backing away*): Maroudah! I know that cruel man.

KAMAR: Indeed he is evil. He tried to kill me, but I learned his secret just in time, and escaped.

SHAMOUR: Few escape his clutches. I, too, was lucky enough to save myself from him. (*Crossing to window*) Look there, across the water to India. (KAMAR *crosses to window and looks out.*) It is said that Maroudah has a palace hidden in a valley between those two mountains. It is guarded by a fierce giant bird called a Roc. Each year the magician steals a new princess and carries her to that palace to be his slave. (*Crossing away*) Once he almost captured me, but I pretended to be insane (*Turning*), and he quickly disappeared, for Maroudah fears madness more than anything.

KAMAR: If only my sister had known that! I am afraid he may have captured her.

SHAMOUR: Since you have the horse machine, let us fly to the hidden palace to see if it be true.

KAMAR: Yes, I will fly there, but alone. (*Kneeling before her*) I have imposed too much on your kindness.

SHAMOUR: Let me go with you to help.

KAMAR: No, I would not have you risk any more danger. But I will return, lovely princess, to be your suitor, and if I find favor in your eyes, I will ask your father for your hand in marriage. For in all the world there is no other I would want for my wife.

SHAMOUR (*Smiling and touching his face*): May Buddha protect you and bring you safely back to me. (*He rises and exits through window.* ATTENDANTS *run excitedly to window to look after him.*)

ATTENDANTS (*Excitedly; ad lib*): How handsome he is!

Prince of Persia. Yes, yes, there he goes. The horse is flying over the water. (*Etc.*)

SHAMOUR (*Clapping hands*): Come, ladies, back to your dancing. (ATTENDANTS *cross downstage and take dancing poses.*) And I order that you tell no one what you have heard and seen here this day.

ATTENDANTS (*Bowing with palms of hands together*): Yes, Princess Shamour. (*Indian music is heard and* ATTENDANTS *dance as at beginning of scene, while* SHAMOUR *returns to rest on couch. Curtain slowly closes.*)

*　*　*　*

SCENE 3

BEFORE RISE: CLOUDS *enter right and crawl left.* HORSE, *with* KAMAR *riding on it, enters right and slowly crosses left as before.*

KAMAR: Now that we have flown over the water, I shall head for those two mountains. (*Points toward audience, peering at aisle.*) There it is! In that valley is the hidden palace. (*Turns knob*) Down we go, flying horse machine. We will land at the head of the valley. (CLOUDS *stop, center.* HORSE *crosses to left of* CLOUDS, *neighs, snorts, and paws ground.* KAMAR *climbs off* HORSE *and moves stealthily down steps of stage into aisle.* ROC *bursts through door at rear of auditorium and rushes down aisle toward* KAMAR, *flapping wings and screeching fiercely.* KAMAR *draws sword.*) The giant Roc! (*Draws sword and battles with* ROC, *who uses wings, beak, and talons to combat* KAMAR's *sword, all the while making frightening noises.* ROC *drives* KAMAR *back against stage; then* KAMAR *drives* ROC *up aisle, toward back of auditorium, but again is beaten toward stage steps. Half-way up the stairs,* KAMAR *manages to wound* ROC, *who staggers about dramatically, then, howling mournfully, flies away, exiting through rear auditorium door.* FAHAN *immediately enters through same door and runs toward stage.*)

FAHAN (*Calling*): Brother Prince Kamar! Praise be to Allah, you have rescued me. (KAMAR *helps her up steps and onto stage.*)

KAMAR (*Replacing sword*): Where is Maroudah, my sister?

FAHAN (*Upset*): He has returned to Persia.

KAMAR: Why so?

FAHAN (*Tearfully*): To capture Father.

KAMAR: Father?

FAHAN: Yes. Because I would have nothing to do with Maroudah and his orders, that miserable magician plans to torture Father before my eyes until I meet his demands.

KAMAR: The fiend! Quickly, onto the flying horse machine! (KAMAR *and* FAHAN *climb onto* HORSE. KAMAR *turns key, and* HORSE *turns and crosses to center, toward* CLOUDS. *Then* HORSE *and* CLOUDS *move right as before.*) First I will stop on the island of Ceylon. Then we will return to Persia to confront Maroudah and try to thwart his plans. (*All exit right. Curtain opens.*)

* * *

SETTING: *Same as Scene 1.*

AT RISE: KING *is seated on throne, head in hands.* 1ST GUARD, *with spear, stands beside him, also looking unhappy. Veiled* ATTENDANTS *stand left center, talking in hushed tones.*

1ST ATTENDANT: King Sabur has not eaten for days.

2ND ATTENDANT: The people of Persia are wondering if they still have a king.

3RD ATTENDANT: He has been this way ever since the loss of his son and daughter. I fear for our country. (*Commotion is heard off left.* ATTENDANTS *cross nervously to right of throne.* 2ND GUARD *enters left, running, and falls to knees before* KING.)

2ND GUARD (*Excitedly*): King Sabur, sublime Sultan of Persia, Maroudah the magician has come back. (*All gasp.* KING *leaps to feet.* 1ST GUARD *rushes forward with spear raised.* KING *waves him back.*)

KING: No, wait, guard. Only Maroudah knows where Princess Fahan is hidden. (*To* 2ND GUARD) Show the wizard into the courtyard, and, for now, be most courteous.

2ND GUARD (*Rising*): Yes, King Sabur. (*Exits left, immediately re-entering and making elaborate bow to present* MAROUDAH, *who enters in his usual evil manner.* 2ND GUARD *exits left.*)

MAROUDAH (*Bowing*): We meet again, King Sabur.

KING: Where is my daughter?

MAROUDAH: In India, sire. At my secret palace, living in magnificent splendor.

KING: Bring her here at once, or I will have your head cut off.

MAROUDAH (*Smiling evilly*): If you take my head, you will lose your daughter.

KING (*Sighing*): Why have you come here, Maroudah?

MAROUDAH (*Slyly*): Because your daughter is homesick. She misses her father and begs me to ask that you pay her a visit. Will you accompany me back to my palace so your daughter will be even happier than she is now?

KING (*After a pause*): Yes, I shall go with you. (*Whispers to* 1ST GUARD, *who nods*)

MAROUDAH: King Sabur, you must come *alone*.

KING: The King of Persia goes nowhere without guards.

MAROUDAH: If you wish to see your daughter, you will come by yourself. (KING *crosses right, pauses, then turns back with resignation.*)

KING: All right, Maroudah. You win. I shall go alone with you. Lead the way. (MAROUDAH *smiles and bows, then, rubbing hands, turns left to exit. Sound of commotion off left is heard.* 2ND GUARD *re-enters, waving his arms, excited.*) What is it, Guard?

2ND GUARD: King Sabur! King Sabur! Your son and daughter—they are here!

MAROUDAH: What? Impossible! (*Crosses left, peers offstage, sees them, then runs up center and stands behind plants to plot next move.* KING *gestures* 2ND GUARD *to step aside and happily crosses left as* PRINCE KAMAR, PRINCESS FAHAN, *and* PRINCESS SHAMOUR *enter left and bow.* KAMAR *has knob in pocket.* KING *claps* KAMAR *on shoulders and gently pats* FAHAN *on arm.*)

KING: This is the happiest moment of my life. (*Smiles*) Both of my children have returned safely to my kingdom. My prayers to Allah have been answered. And who is this lovely lady? (*Indicating* SHAMOUR. FAHAN *crosses center, not seeing* MAROUDAH, *who hides behind plants.*)

KAMAR: Father, I present Princess Shamour of Ceylon. Her father has agreed to our marriage. All we need is your blessing.

KING: You have it, my son. I could ask for no lovelier daughter-in-law. But before we speak of the wedding, tell me, what has happened? How did you find your sister?

KAMAR (*Gesturing left*): By riding the flying horse machine. (HORSE *enters left, neighing and moving in circle as at start of play.*)

ALL (*Ad lib*): The flying horse machine. The Prince must have found the secret knob. (*Etc. Suddenly* MAROUDAH *leaps forward.* FAHAN *screams and runs right to* ATTENDANTS, *who hover protectively over her.*)

MAROUDAH: Prince Kamar, you have outwitted me, but you shall pay for it. (*With a wild gesture*) You will all pay. I shall cast an evil spell on everyone in this palace. (*All gasp and back away in fear.*)

SHAMOUR (*Aside to* KAMAR): Remember, insanity is what the magician fears most. (KAMAR *nods and, to everyone's astonishment, drops to hands and knees and begins meowing like a cat.* SHAMOUR *also drops to hands and knees and begins barking like a dog, chasing* KAMAR *in a circle around* MAROUDAH. *They start leaping into the air with crazy laughs and weird motions, frightening* MAROUDAH.)

KING: What has happened? My poor son and daughter-to-be have lost their minds. (*Tears at hair*) What a terrible homecoming! (*Falls to knees, wailing, as do* ATTENDANTS, GUARDS, *and* FAHAN. MAROUDAH, *biting his nails nervously, tiptoes to* HORSE *and climbs onto it, turning key.*)

MAROUDAH (*Shouting*): I must leave quickly before I catch their madness. (*Laughing crazily, he exits right on* HORSE. SHAMOUR *and* KAMAR *rise and hold up arms for silence.*)

KAMAR: Do not worry. We are perfectly sane.

SHAMOUR: We acted that way to frighten away the magician.

FAHAN (*Pointing overhead*): Look, there he goes, flying into the sky. (*Others rise and pantomime watching him fly overhead.*)

KING: I fear he will come back to bring more trouble to my kingdom.

KAMAR: He will not return, Father. (*Takes knob out of pocket and holds it up*) I took off the secret knob which makes the horse fly down. It will fly up and up, into the sky, until it is consumed by the flames of the sun. It is fitting that Maroudah, the evil magician, will be destroyed by his own magic machine. (*All cheer as curtain closes.*)

THE END

PRINCE RAMA

PRINCE RAMA

The play "Prince Rama" is based on *The Ramayana,* a great epic of India composed in the fourth century B.C. by a sage named Valmiki, who probably collected the popular stories which celebrated the heroic deeds of Prince Rama, widely circulated by storytellers of the period. Many historians claim that the characters in *The Ramayana* were real people, that some of the events actually happened, and that the island home of the demon king is, in fact, the island of Ceylon, located off the southern tip of India.

Themes from *The Ramayana* appear again and again in South Asian art forms from India through Indonesia, in paintings, temple sculptures, songs, dance dramas, and shadow-puppet plays. But the greatest influence of *The Ramayana* is in the daily lives of South Asian people. Wherever the Hindu religion is practiced, the virtues of Prince Rama and Princess Sita are extolled as examples for children and adults to follow, with emphasis on the need to do battle against evil, as represented by demons.

"Prince Rama" may be presented entirely or in part in the ancient Southeast Asian theatrical form of dance drama, giving actors and dancers opportunities for imaginative, creative movement or stylized or informal improvisation. The battle between the monkeys and demons at the end of the play is a long dance-pantomime. Experiment with movements the demons and monkeys might use, and develop the movements into a battle pantomime, set to recorded or live music. Perform exaggerated movements, with full use of head, face, arms, fingers, and knees. Relate the movements of all performers to each other. In contrast, the dance movements of Rama, Sita and Lakshmana are more controlled, stylized and graceful.

Prince Rama

A story from the Asian folk epic, *The Ramayana*

Characters

STORYTELLER
PRINCE RAMA
PRINCE LAKSHMANA, *Rama's brother*
PRINCESS SITA, *Rama's wife*
RAVANA, *the demon king*
RAVANA'S SISTER
RAVANA'S FRIEND
MONKEY KING
HANUMAN, *the giant monkey*
MONKEYS
OTHER DEMONS

SCENE 1

BEFORE RISE: STORYTELLER *enters through curtain and stands center. Indian music is heard from offstage.*

STORYTELLER: In ancient India there was once a beautiful kingdom called Koshala. The king of Koshala had three queens. The first queen bore a son named Rama. Soon the second queen, too, had a son. And then the third queen gave birth to twin sons. Since Rama was the eldest, by right he was to become the next king. But the second queen was clever and ambitious. She wanted *her* son to be king, and she schemed until she succeeded in having Rama banished from the kingdom. And so the

129

good Prince Rama was sent off into the wilderness with his wife, Sita, and one of his brothers, Lakshmana. They lived in a forest that was full of fierce demons. One day the demons met in their stronghold, the city of Lanka, and discussed the newcomers. (*Music ends.* STORYTELLER *exits. Curtains open.*)

* * *

SETTING: *The city of Lanka, stronghold of the demon kingdom, on an island in the midst of a forest in India. There is a backdrop of tropical trees, brilliant flowers, birds, and butterflies. This backdrop is used for all scenes. A large rock which is decorated with a grotesque mask is right center.*

AT RISE: RAVANA, *the demon king, is squatting on rock as if ready to leap.* RAVANA'S FRIEND *and* RAVANA'S SISTER *stand before him.* OTHER DEMONS *watch them.*

RAVANA (*Enraged*): Why do you bother me?

FRIEND (*Pleading*): Listen to our sad story, O great demon king, Ravana.

RAVANA (*Impatiently*): I am too busy with evil deeds. (OTHER DEMONS *laugh evilly and jump in air.*)

SISTER (*Annoyed*): See here, Ravana. Surely you have time to listen to me, your sister, and to (*Points to* FRIEND) your friend!

OTHER DEMONS (*Chanting together*): Listen, listen, listen!

RAVANA: Well, be quick with it. Quick!

SISTER: Two men and a woman have come to live in our forest.

RAVANA: What of it? Just go about your evil business.

SISTER: But, Ravana, one of these men has such a good heart we find it difficult to live near him. His name is Rama. He helps the hermits and gives food to the animals. Every day he does good deeds.

FRIEND: It is rumored that Rama is an excellent warrior. I dare not try to do battle with him.

RAVANA (*Bellowing*): What? You dare not? This Rama is a mere human being.

FRIEND: I know, but—

RAVANA (*Interrupting; growling loudly*): Gr-r-r! Humans fear *us*! Gr-r-r! (*Leaps off rock, frightening others. All back away.* RAVANA *stops, grunts, and sits down. Inquisitively*) Who are the other humans with this Rama?

SISTER: There is Rama's wife (*Angrily*)—the beautiful Princess Sita. She is so loyal that she gave up everything and came with Rama to live in exile.

RAVANA (*Jumping up*): You say she is beautiful?

SISTER: Disgustingly beautiful!

RAVANA: Ha!

SISTER (*Furiously waving arms and shaking head*): Ee-ee! I despise her.

FRIEND (*Pushing* SISTER *aside*): The other human is Prince Lakshmana, one of Rama's brothers. He is honest and brave. He, too, gave up a royal life to live in the forest with Rama.

RAVANA (*Jumping up and down, chanting*): Good people are bad for the demon kingdom. (OTHER DEMONS *join in chant, also jumping up and down.*)

ALL: Good people are bad for the demon kingdom. Good people are bad—(RAVANA *suddenly motions wildly to stop chant, and shrieks.*)

RAVANA: We will get rid of them!

SISTER: Yes, yes!

FRIEND: But how?

OTHER DEMONS (*Ad lib*): Yes, yes! How? (*Etc.*)

RAVANA: We will play a trick on these people. I will kidnap Sita (*Rubs hands gleefully*) and bring her here to my island city of Lanka. (*Laughs evilly*)

FRIEND: That will make Rama so sad he will go away. (*Claps hands*)

SISTER (*Suspiciously*): I do not like the idea of having this Sita woman in our city.

RAVANA: Are you jealous of her beauty, Demon Sister?

SISTER (*Shrieking furiously*): Ee-ee!

FRIEND: I think this will be fun. (RAVANA, FRIEND, *and* OTHER DEMONS *leap about stage excitedly, howling, while* SISTER *folds arms and stares at them. Curtains close.*)

*   *   *   *

SCENE 2

BEFORE RISE: STORYTELLER *enters.*

STORYTELLER: So the demons made their plans. Meanwhile, unaware of this, Rama, Sita, and Lakshmana continued their peaceful life in the forest, not far from the demons' city. (*Exits. Curtains open.*)

*   *   *

SETTING: *A clearing in the forest, where Rama lives. There is a tree with a peg on the trunk at left, next to a stream.*

AT RISE: SITA *pantomimes picking flowers. She holds some flowers in her hands.* RAMA *pantomimes dipping wooden cup into stream. He drinks from it, then hangs it on peg on tree.* LAKSHMANA *is tying feathers on an arrow. He tries arrow in his bow, which is beside him.*

RAMA: It is a pity that the rest of the world cannot live in such beauty. I fear that ugliness presses in on many lives.

SITA (*Running to him*): You sound sad, Rama. Gaze on these flowers. Their perfection will gladden your heart. (*She puts flowers in her hair.* RAMA *smiles.*)

RAMA (*Affectionately*): Thank you, Sita. You, too, gladden my heart. (RAVANA'S FRIEND, *disguised as a deer, enters left, sees* SITA *and* RAMA, *and bounds across stage in front of them, then exits right.*)

SITA (*Delighted*): Oh, Rama. Did you see that golden deer? I have never seen such a charming animal! Will you catch it for a pet?

RAMA (*Going right*): It is indeed a bewitching creature.

LAKSHMANA (*Warningly*): Do not follow the deer, Rama. It may be a demon in disguise.

SITA (*Protesting*): But it is too beautiful to be bad.

LAKSHMANA: Outward beauty is often false.

RAMA: If Sita wants the deer, she shall have it. Lakshmana, you stay and guard her. (*Exits right*)

LAKSHMANA: I have a strange feeling about that deer.

SITA (*Playfully taunting him*): Lakshmana, do you see a demon behind every tree?

RAMA (*Shouting from offstage*): Help! Help! Save me!

SITA (*Horrified*): That is Rama's voice. (*She turns to* LAKSHMANA *beseechingly.*) Oh, Lakshmana, you must go to him at once! Your brother needs you!

LAKSHMANA (*Hesitating*): But Rama said I must guard you.

SITA (*Impatiently*): Go, go! Do not worry about me. Did you not hear your brother call? Do you not care for his safety?

LAKSHMANA: Of course I do, but I must—

RAMA (*Shouting from offstage*): Help! Help!

LAKSHMANA: All right. I will go. (*Pantomimes drawing circle around* SITA *with his bow.*) Sita, stay inside this circle and you will be safe. No demon will dare to enter it. (SITA *nods.* LAKSHMANA *exits right, running.* RAVANA *enters left, disguised as a hermit, wearing robe and hiding his demon mask behind him.* SITA *is staring offstage right and does not see him. He approaches her and grunts.* SITA *screams and jumps back.*)

RAVANA (*Softly*): Do not be frightened, lovely lady.

SITA (*Relieved*): Oh, you are only a hermit.

RAVANA: Yes. I am a weary hermit. (*Sits on rock*) How thirsty I am! Would you be kind enough to bring me a drink from that stream? (SITA *smiles and nods, runs to get cup, and pantomimes filling it from stream, while* RAVANA *throws off his robe and puts on his demon's mask.* SITA *returns, carrying cup and watching it, trying not to spill water. She does not look at* RAVANA.)

SITA (*Looking up*): Here you are. (*She sees his demon's mask, screams, drops cup, and tries to run back to circle.* RAVANA *grabs her arm and pulls her back.*)

RAVANA (*Evilly*): I have you now, Sita! Ha, ha! Away to my island city of Lanka!

SITA (*Terrified*): Help! Rama! Help me! (*She pulls flowers from her hair and drops them, as* RAVANA *pulls her off left after him.* RAMA *and* LAKSHMANA *re-enter right, running, and look around wildly.*)

RAMA: It *was* Sita calling to me. (*Despairingly*) As we feared, my brother, Sita is gone. (*Sinks to rock*) Never have I felt such unhappiness.

LAKSHMANA (*Pointing*): When I heard you calling, Rama, I left her here in this circle to be safe.

RAMA (*Sadly*): But it was not I who called, Lakshmana. It was the deer who imitated my voice.

LAKSHMANA (*Angrily*): That deer was a demon who tricked us both away from Sita!

RAMA: Yes. Another demon lured Sita out of this circle and carried her away. (*Rises, points to cup on ground*) Here is the cup she dropped. (*Picks it up*)

LAKSHMANA (*Seeing flowers*): Look, Rama. There are the flowers she was wearing in her hair. (*Picks up flowers, hands them to* RAMA)

RAMA: She must have dropped these flowers to let us know which way she went. Let us follow her, brother.

I will not rest until I find Sita and bring her back safely. (*They exit left. Curtains close.*)

* * * * *

SCENE 3

BEFORE RISE: STORYTELLER *enters.*

STORYTELLER: Rama and his brother searched through the forest for many days. At last they came to the land of the great monkeys. The Monkey King bid them welcome and offered them help. The strongest monkey, a giant who was called Hanuman, had seen the demon king Ravana flying overhead. (*Exits. Curtains open.*)

* * *

SETTING: *The land of the great monkeys. There is a throne at center stage.*

AT RISE: MONKEY KING *is seated on throne.* HANUMAN *is talking to* RAMA *and* LAKSHMANA. *Other* MONKEYS *stand or sit in groups around stage.*

HANUMAN: I was standing near this spot when Ravana flew past, blacker than ten thunderclouds. And as he flew over, he dropped this earring. Do you recognize it, Rama? (*Shows earring to* RAMA)

RAMA (*Examining it*): Yes, this is one of Sita's earrings! Hanuman, which way was the demon flying?

HANUMAN: South. I believe he was headed for the demons' stronghold, the city of Lanka, which is on an island.

MONKEY KING (*Rising*): Go, Hanuman. Find out if Sita is hidden in that city of Lanka.

LAKSHMANA: But Monkey King, how will Hanuman cross the water to reach the island?

MONKEY KING (*Confidently*): He will find a way. He can achieve impossible things.

HANUMAN: I shall return soon. (*Exits left*)

MONKEY KING: Rama, you see here the leaders of my great

monkey army. Each leader commands a thousand monkey soldiers. (*Faces* MONKEYS, *raises arms*) Monkeys, listen to your king. Will you join together to fight against the demons?

MONKEYS (*Together, shouting*): Yes!

MONKEY KING (*To* RAMA): We are all willing to help you fight these evil beings. It is time to make more room in the world for good creatures. (MONKEYS *cheer, waving arms and leaping about.* RAMA *and* MONKEY KING *salaam to each other. Curtains close.*)

* * * * *

SCENE 4

BEFORE RISE: STORYTELLER *enters.*

STORYTELLER: This is the way the giant monkey, Hanuman, crossed the water to reach the island city of Lanka: He crouched on a large rock on the mainland and gave a magnificent leap that carried him to the island. There he spied Sita, held prisoner in the city. With another wonderful leap, he returned to the mainland. Then the monkey army built a bridge to the island made of a forest of trees and a hundred mountaintops. When the bridge was finished, the army marched across it to the island. (*Exits. Curtains open.*)

* * *

SETTING: *City of Lanka, the same as Scene 1.*

AT RISE: RAVANA's SISTER *and* RAVANA's FRIEND *enter left and peer out into audience.* OTHER DEMONS *enter, rushing on from right and left, back and forth across stage, into audience, etc., pointing to back of auditorium. They ad lib shrieks, howls, and grunts.* RAVANA *enters.*

RAVANA (*Roaring*): Quiet! Quiet! (DEMONS *grow quiet.*) What is the matter with all of you?

FRIEND: Rama is coming with the monkey army. (*Points to rear of auditorium*)

SISTER (*Triumphantly*): I knew we shouldn't have kidnapped that Sita woman. Give her back to Rama.

RAVANA: No! I will not give her back. We will fight against that army. We will win.

FRIEND: But I fear that Rama has the gods on his side. I have heard that he has weapons against which we have no power.

RAVANA: Nonsense! (*Raises arms and shrieks*) Nothing in the world can defeat my evil forces. Follow me, demons! Forward to victory! (*Leaps off stage into audience and runs down aisle, waving sword and howling, followed by* DEMONS, *yowling. They exit at back of auditorium. Loud Indian music is heard.* RAMA, LAKSHMANA, MONKEY KING, *and* HANUMAN *enter, right, armed with swords and carrying banners, leading* MONKEYS. *They march around stage and take positions at right, as* RAVANA, FRIEND *and* SISTER *enter left, leading on* DEMONS, *also armed with swords and carrying banners.* MONKEYS *and* DEMONS *pantomime battle. At first,* DEMONS *seem to be winning, driving* MONKEYS *off right. Then* RAMA *pantomimes appeal to heavens, and, as if strengthened, leads* MONKEYS *forward to defeat* DEMONS *and drive them off left.* RAMA *exits after them, re-entering after a moment with* SITA. MONKEYS *cheer.* LAKSHMANA *goes forward to welcome* RAMA *and* SITA. RAMA *descends from stage, followed by* SITA, LAKSHMANA, MONKEY KING, HANUMAN, *and* MONKEYS, *in a triumphant march down audience aisle to rear of auditorium.* STORYTELLER *enters.*)

STORYTELLER: After Sita was reunited with Rama, they lived in the forest for fourteen years. Finally, Rama returned to claim his kingdom with Sita and Lakshmana. It is said that Rama ruled with great wisdom and kindness for many years, and his wife, Sita, was a most gracious and loving queen. (*Salaams to audience. Curtain*)

THE END

ABU NUWAS

ABU NUWAS

The ancient city of Baghdad is located on the Tigris River in what is today the country of Iraq. In the latter part of the eighth century A.D., this city became the religious capital of the Moslems and one of the leading trade and cultural centers of the world. It was the setting for the famous stories of *The Arabian Nights*. Among the many poets and storytellers of the city there lived a Persian poet by the name of Abu Nuwas. He died in the year 810 A.D. Because of his cleverness and wit, stories about Abu Nuwas are still told today in the Arabic lands of Northern Africa and Ethiopia and throughout the Middle East.

Abu Nuwas

Two tales from Baghdad

Characters

ZAKIA, *an old storyteller*
ABU NUWAS
DONKEY
HAJI, *a farmer*
INA, *his wife*
ALI, *a shoe merchant*
LEWA, *his wife*

I. The Stolen Shoes

BEFORE RISE: ZAKIA, *carrying mat, enters left before curtain, crosses to extreme right, spreads out mat, and then sits on it, facing audience. She remains there during play.*

ZAKIA (*Smiling and bowing head*): I am Zakia, a storyteller from Iraq. (*Dramatically, with gestures*) Some tales I tell are of magic carpets and genies who rise out of bottles. Others are about rich sultans from great domed palaces who ride horses through the clouds, and beautiful women wearing silken veils who hide in golden lamps. But to tell the truth, I am tired of those fairy tales. I would rather tell the funny stories of Abu Nuwas. He was a wise poet who really lived in ancient

141

Baghdad. Here is the Abu Nuwas tale of the stolen shoes. (*Curtain opens.*)

*   *   *

SETTING: *Backdrop painting of ancient Baghdad. Date palm trees are right and left. Under left palm is large, flat rock used as seat.*

AT RISE: ABU NUWAS *sits cross-legged on rock, composing a poem. He stares ahead, hands under bearded chin, thinking.* DONKEY *stands left, braying unhappily.*

ABU (*Waving to hush* DONKEY): Yes, yes, my hungry donkey, I shall feed you soon. At the moment I am creating food for the mind. (DONKEY *brays louder and with disgust.* ABU *raises arms, excitedly.*) Thank you, friend donkey. That is a splendid idea for a poem. (*Silently recites a poem, lips moving rapidly, hands waving dramatically.* HAJI *hurriedly enters right, barefoot, stops a moment in amusement to watch* ABU, *then hurries to him. Clears throat to gain attention.* ABU *bows head.*) Salaam, farmer Haji. I trust your millet fields are growing faster than locusts can eat.

HAJI (*Bowing*): Salaam, Abu Nuwas. My fields do well. And you? Are poems (*Pantomiming*) pouring from your head as sand slips through a man's fingers?

ABU (*With mock alarm*): I hope not. (*Pantomiming*) I would not wish my words to be as dry as sand nor as lost as what slips from a man's hand.

HAJI (*Smiling*): As always, you are clever. That, Abu Nuwas, is why I am here.

ABU: You have a problem?

HAJI: Yes.

ABU (*Looking at* HAJI's *feet*): It must be important, or you would not run here without first putting on shoes.

HAJI: My shoes *are* the problem. They have just been stolen.

ABU: Stolen, you say. Too bad, Haji. Tell me more.

HAJI: This afternoon I visited the house of Ali, the shoe merchant. My wife, Ina, came with me, claiming it was better than being left home alone.

ABU: Poor Ina. (*Shaking finger in reproach*) You are out visiting friends every afternoon and evening.

HAJI (*Spreading arms*): I like companionship. (*Smiling*) Besides, it saves money to drink another man's coffee.

ABU: I see. And so, this afternoon you went to the shoe merchant's home for coffee.

HAJI (*Nodding and pantomiming*): Today I worked in my dusty millet fields until my throat was dry. I stopped at home to wash my hands, and Ina decided to accompany me to Ali's house. As is the custom, we left our shoes outside the door. Then Lewa, Ali's wife, led us inside. An hour later, when we came outside, my wife's shoes were there, but mine were gone.

ABU: Do you suspect anyone?

HAJI: It could have been Ali. He left the room several times, and I owe him money for the shoes. It could have been his wife or my wife. They were talking in another part of the house. It could have been his wife—she thinks I drink too much of Ali's coffee. My wife could have done it to play a joke on me. But they all laughed and said they knew nothing about my shoes when I asked them. Perhaps a thief on the streets stole them.

ABU (*Stroking beard thoughtfully*): You can rule out a street thief, Haji. There are many clean shoes beside doorways. A street thief would not take shoes dusty from millet fields. (HAJI *shrugs and throws up arms.*)

HAJI: Alas! I was going to visit another friend tonight. How can I go without shoes? (ABU *suddenly gets idea and claps hands.*)

ABU: Ah, ho! Haji, tell Ali, Lewa, and your wife, Ina, to come to my rock in half an hour.

HAJI: Why?

ABU: Your shoes will then be found. (*Chuckles*) All will come, Haji, for they will be curious.

HAJI: So be it, Abu Nuwas. In half an hour. (*Exits right, running.* ABU *climbs down from rock.*)

ABU: Now, I have time to pick fragrant mint for my supper tonight. (*Crossing to scratch* DONKEY's *ears*) And then, my long-eared friend, I will feed you, and we will have a little talk together. (DONKEY *brays happily.* ABU *starts to exit left. Blackout of a few seconds. When lights come up,* ABU *is sitting on rock as before.* DONKEY *stands behind rock so tail is hidden from audience. As lights go on again,* HAJI, INA, ALI, *and* LEWA *enter right.* INA *has* HAJI's *shoes hidden in her sleeves, one on each side. They cross to rock. All bow.*) Salaam, my friends.

OTHERS: Salaam, Abu Nuwas.

HAJI: Have you found my shoes?

ABU: Not I.

HAJI (*Disappointed*): No?

ABU: No. But my donkey knows who took them. He knows everything.

OTHERS (*In surprise*): Everything?

ABU (*Nodding*): My donkey will name the thief.

HAJI: Wonderful! (*Peering left*) But where is your donkey?

ABU: Behind this rock. (*Jumps off rock and points*) Before he can name the thief, however, we must perform a test.

OTHERS (*To each other*): A test?

ABU: My donkey wishes to see us separately. He asks each (*Pantomiming*) to pull his tail once with the right hand. When the thief pulls his tail, my donkey will bray loudly. Then we will know who the thief is.

LEWA: You mean, only by pulling the donkey's tail will the thief be known?

ABU: Yes. I shall go first so you may be sure I did not steal Haji's shoes. (*Crosses behind rock. Others put hands to ears to listen. This is repeated each time person crosses behind rock.* ABU *quickly returns.*) There. I pulled the tail and nothing happened. You are next, Haji.

HAJI: Why me? *My* shoes were the ones stolen.

ALI: Ha! You probably hid them. You do not wish to pay me for them.

HAJI: What? Ridiculous! I will show you I am not the thief. (*Crosses behind rock, quickly returning*) There. I pulled the tail and nothing happened. You go, Ali. I think you stole my shoes. You want to sell them again.

ALI: What? Ridiculous! I will show you I am not the thief. (*Crosses behind rock, quickly returning*) There. I pulled the donkey's tail and nothing happened. I think it was your wife who stole the shoes. A barefoot husband cannot wander far from home.

INA: What? Ridiculous! I will show you I am not the thief. (*Crosses behind rock, quickly returning*) There. I pulled the donkey's tail and nothing happened. It must be you, Lewa. You have never approved of Haji's drinking your husband's coffee.

LEWA: What? Ridiculous! I will show you I am not the thief. (*Crosses behind rock, quickly returning*) There. I pulled the donkey's tail and nothing happened. (*All shrug and look at each other in bewilderment.* DONKEY *crosses down left, braying loudly and angrily, looking back at tail and then sitting on it. This startles everyone.*)

HAJI: Abu Nuwas, *now* your donkey brays. What is he saying? (ABU *crosses to* DONKEY, *whispers in each ear, listens at* DONKEY's *mouth, nods solemnly, and then returns to sit on rock.*)

ABU: My donkey tells me there is more to the test.

OTHERS (*To each other*): More to the test?

ABU: Each of us must touch the top of my nose with a finger of the right hand. It is a secret sign. (*Touches nose with index finger of right hand*) See, I will be first. Now, you, Haji. (*Each in turn passes by and touches* ABU's *nose with index finger of right hand.*) Now, Ali. Ina. And Lewa. Ah, ha! I know who the thief is. (*Leaps up*)

OTHERS: Who? (ABU *raises index finger in air, looking at each one, then suddenly points to* INA *and leaps off rock.*)

ABU: Ina is the one. Haji, your wife took your shoes. I am certain of it. (DONKEY *brays loudly, waving head up and down.*)

OTHERS (*Pointing at her*): Ina? (*A moment of silence as all stare at her.* INA *at first shakes head, then breaks down.*)

INA (*Tearfully*): Oh, all right. I was the one. I hid Haji's shoes. (*Lets shoes fall from sleeves. All gasp.* HAJI *glowers and puts on shoes.* INA *speaks in rush of words.*) Oh, Haji, I only wanted to teach you a lesson. Every day after work, you run to visit someone for coffee. Every night after dinner, you run off again. You never want to stay home and have coffee with me. I hid your shoes, hoping you would stay home this evening. (*Bursts into tears*)

HAJI (*Comforting her*): There, there. Stop crying, Ina. You sound like an overloaded camel.

INA (*Sniffing*): Forgive me, husband. I am so sorry.

HAJI (*Patting her shoulders*): My poor, dear Ina. It is all right. I understand. I have neglected you too long. Ali, would you and your wife care to join us for coffee this evening, in *my* home?

ALI: Certainly.

LEWA: Of course.

HAJI: Good. (*With a grin*) I might even pay for these

shoes, Ali. Excuse me, Abu Nuwas, would you like to come also?

ABU: No, thank you, Haji. I have a poem to finish.

HAJI: Then another time perhaps. I am most grateful for your help. May all your poems be as clever as your donkey. (ABU *strikes forehead in mock alarm as others bow and then exit right.*)

ABU (*Sighing*): People are strange. Everyone wants the answer to a problem. Few care how a problem is solved. (DONKEY *brays and crosses to get* ABU *to scratch his ears.* ABU *smiles.*) Ah, my donkey wants to know how I solved the problem. (*Climbs on rock, sitting as before, speaking to* DONKEY) You remember I rubbed mint on your tail this afternoon? You see, I knew the guilty person would *not* pull your tail for fear you would bray. So (*Points right finger in air*) the person whose right hand did not smell of mint (*Places finger on nose*) was obviously the thief. (DONKEY *brays with laughter.* ABU *joins in laughter.*) Yes, yes, my friend. It is another splendid idea for a poem. (*Curtain starts to close while* ABU *silently composes, arms waving, lips moving, as at start of play. Curtain*)

* * * * *

II. The Borrowed Cooking Pot

Characters

ZAKIA, *an old storyteller*
ABU NUWAS
DONKEY
HAJI, *a farmer*
INA, *his wife*

BEFORE RISE: ZAKIA *still sits on mat as before.*

ZAKIA: My favorite Abu Nuwas story is about the borrowed cooking pot. This tale is told in different ways

in different places—across Northern Africa, through
Arabia, Iran, and Iraq. Here is the way I tell the tale.
(*Curtain opens.*)

* * *

SETTING: *The same as Scene 1.*
AT RISE: ABU NUWAS *enters left.*

ABU (*Calling right*): Farmer Haji.

HAJI (*Entering right*): Yes, Abu Nuwas?

ABU *and* HAJI (*Bowing, to each other*): Salaam, my friend.

ABU: I have a favor to ask.

HAJI: What is it, great poet?

ABU: I wish to borrow a large cooking pot for making
pilaf.

HAJI: Hm-m-m, well, we are not in the habit of lending
our valuables, but for you . . . . (*Calling right*) Ina, my
wife, come here.

INA (*Entering*): Yes, husband? (HAJI *crosses to her.*)

HAJI: Abu Nuwas wishes to borrow a large cooking pot.

INA: Since he has always helped us, we should certainly
help him. (*Turns to exit right*)

HAJI: Wait, wait! (*With sidelong glances at* ABU, *he
speaks so* ABU *cannot hear.*) Do not bring our good
cooking pot, Ina. Bring the one with a hole in it.

INA: But, Haji—

HAJI (*Interrupting*): Sh-h-h, do as I say. I would not lend
our best cooking pot even to the Caliph of Baghdad.

INA: But how can he cook pilaf in a leaky pot?

HAJI (*Shrewdly*): He will have it repaired, of course.
Then we will have *two* fine pots. Now, hurry and bring
the old one here. (INA *shrugs, then exists right.* HAJI
crosses to ABU, *smiling.*) Ina will return in a moment
with the cooking pot.

ABU: I am most grateful. (INA *re-enters with large pot and gives it to* HAJI, *who inspects pot, with back to* ABU, *nods, and then dramatically presents it to* ABU.)

HAJI (*Bowing*): May your pilaf be as good as your poems.

ABU (*Bowing*): Thank you, Haji. May your day be as good as your cooking pot. (HAJI *looks startled, then quickly smiles and exits right. Meanwhile,* ABU *holds pot up to light and notes hole in bottom.*) Well, well, my good friend, farmer Haji, gives me a pot with a hole in the bottom. (*Chuckles*) He probably thinks I will repair it. (*Exits left, still chuckling. Blackout. As lights go up a few seconds later,* ABU *re-enters, carrying the large pot with small pot inside. Calling*) Haji, Haji. (HAJI *re-enters.*) A wonderful thing has happened.

HAJI: A wonderful thing?

ABU: Yes, about this leaky pot of yours.

HAJI (*Faking surprise*): Leaky? Do you mean there was a hole in it? Oh, I am so sorry. Thank you for repairing it.

ABU: I did not repair it. But look at what is inside.

HAJI (*Looking*): A small cooking pot.

ABU: Yes. A miracle has happened. Just as I was about to use your cooking pot, it suddenly gave birth to a little cooking pot.

HAJI: That is difficult to believe. (*Holds up small pot thoughtfully.*)

ABU: Lately miracles keep happening in my house. Why, only yesterday, another friend lent me a large and beautiful teapot, and it gave birth to a small and beautiful teapot.

HAJI: Hm-m-m. Amazing. (*Suddenly yells*) Ina, Ina, come quickly. (INA *re-enters.* HAJI *crosses quickly to her.*) Look, we have a new little pot in our home. (INA *holds small pot up to light.*)

INA: It is not new. It has a hole in it. (HAJI *speaks so* ABU *won't hear.*)

HAJI: Sh-h-h. Ina, I think Abu Nuwas has gone a bit crazy.

INA (*Loudly*): What?

HAJI: Sh-h-h, sh-h-h! He believes miracles are happening at his house. (*Taps head indicating* ABU *is unbalanced*) He obviously put this little pot inside. But he claims our big leaky pot gave birth to this little leaky pot. Now, if we lend him our big new pot (*Chuckles*), it will probably give birth to a little new pot, and we will have another good pot in our home. (*Rubs hands greedily*) Ina, bring our finest cooking pot for Abu Nuwas.

INA (*Shrugging*): As you wish. It sounds silly to me. (*Exits right with pots*)

HAJI (*To* ABU): Since you still need to make your pilaf, we will lend you a better cooking pot, Abu Nuwas. (INA *re-enters with second, new-looking large pot.* HAJI *takes pot and gives it to* ABU *with bow. Dramatically*) I pray for more miracles in your home.

ABU (*Bowing*): Thank you, Haji. (*Exits left.* HAJI *exits right, rubbing hands together in expectation. Blackout. When lights go up a few seconds later,* ABU *is sitting cross-legged on rock.* DONKEY *is left.* HAJI *re-enters right.*)

HAJI *and* ABU (*Bowing, to each other*): Salaam, my friend.

HAJI: How was your pilaf?

ABU: Delicious.

HAJI: Good, good. (*Rubbing hands together*) And my fine cooking pot, did it give birth to a little one?

ABU (*With mock sadness*): I have bad news for you, Haji.

HAJI: The pot did not give birth?

ABU (*Shaking head*): No.

HAJI (*Annoyed*): Then bring back my cooking pot at once.

ABU: I wish I could, but your cooking pot died.

HAJI: Died!

ABU (*Gazing upward*): May it rest in a world of peace.

HAJI (*Crossing angrily to rock*): Now, Abu Nuwas, you know very well a cooking pot cannot die.

ABU: It cannot? But Haji, you were quick to believe your leaky old pot could give birth. You prayed your fine, new pot would also give birth. (*Rising with outstretched arms*) And any fool knows where there is life there is death. (*Folding arms*) So, you must believe your cooking pot died. It was very sudden, you know. I buried it just this morning. (HAJI *strikes head in alarm.*)

HAJI: Buried it! Where?

ABU: In the bottom of the river, where all good pots go at the end of their days on earth. Please give my sympathy to your wife. (HAJI *staggers backward.*)

HAJI: In the river! Oh, no! My best cooking pot! (*Moves right, mumbling, tearing at robe, acting a bit crazy.*) I am a fool. I have killed my cooking pot. (*Exits right as* DONKEY *brays with laughter.* ABU *holds up arm to stop laughter.*)

ABU: We must not laugh at this serious time. (DONKEY *gives a loud snort of disgust.*) Ah, thank you, friend donkey. That is another fine idea for a poem. (*Curtain slowly closes while* ABU *silently ad libs poem, as at start of play.* ZAKIA *rises, bows to audience, then rolls up mat and exits.*)

THE END

PACCA, THE LITTLE BOWMAN

PACCA, THE LITTLE BOWMAN

Tales called Jatakas (birth stories) are among the most important collections of folktales still in existence and have been told in India for well over two thousand years. These 547 birth stories, narratives of former incarnations of Buddha, tell of his adventures in his former lives as he advanced toward perfection by being kind and helpful to others. They include fables, moral tales, maxims, and legends, and are a part of the Buddhist sacred writings. Sculptures on ancient Indian temples show scenes from these tales.

In the Jatakas, Buddha appears as a man, as a god (deva), or as an animal. He is always the best character in the story, teaching a moral or presenting a truth. In this play, adapted from a Jataka tale, Pacca, the little bowman, represents Buddha.

Pacca, the Little Bowman

A Jataka tale of India

Characters

PRINCE
OLD SAKKAR
PACCA, *the little bowman*
KATTI, *the big firewood merchant*
QUEEN
VILLAGE GIRL
CITY MERCHANT
THIEF
TWO ROYAL GUARDS
OTHER GUARDS
ELEPHANTS
MONKEYS

BEFORE RISE: *Large pillows are placed in front of curtain, at right of stage. One pillow, used as a backrest, is propped against wall. PRINCE enters center through curtains, striding angrily to right. He is followed by OLD SAKKAR, who is trying to speak with him. They remain there during the play.*

PRINCE: No, Old Sakkar, I am far too busy to listen to you. Today I shall ride about the city, showing off the tremendously expensive new jewel in my turban. Tomorrow my lazy but charming friends are coming over

155

for a huge party. And the day after that I will be equally busy.

SAKKAR: But Prince, your father has sent me to discuss your education. Soon you will rule the kingdom, you know.

PRINCE (*Interrupting*): I know, I know! What more must I learn? I can read and write, I have memorized the laws of the realm, and I look splendid upon a horse. What's more, I walk, talk, dress, and act in an exceedingly royal manner. Furthermore, my friends consider me a magnificent prince.

SAKKAR: It is about your choice of friends the king is most concerned.

PRINCE: Oh, bother! Father is forever trying to interfere with my good times.

SAKKAR: Perhaps he thinks your good times are too many, while your good deeds are too few.

PRINCE: Others can do my good deeds for me. Now see here, Old Sakkar, although my father considers you the wisest person in the realm, I am certain there is nothing you can teach me. So run along and spread your wisdom elsewhere. (SAKKAR *sighs, shakes head sadly, and starts to exit, then pauses thoughtfully, turning back.*)

SAKKAR: Prince, allow me to tell you just one tale. After that I will annoy you no longer.

PRINCE: One tale? Is it amusing?

SAKKAR: Perhaps. It is a story I told your father when he was about your age. (*As* PRINCE *considers,* SAKKAR *adds quickly.*) And if there is nothing left for you to learn, as you claim, you can prove it when the tale is done.

PRINCE: How so?

SAKKAR: By explaining how the tale's moral does not apply to you.

PRINCE (*Sitting, laughing*): You are persistent, Old Sakkar. Very well, be quick, and for goodness' sake keep it interesting. I am eager to show off my new jewel.

SAKKAR (*Bowing*): I believe your time will not be wasted. (*Sits*) This is the story of a little archer by the name of Pacca and a big firewood merchant by the name of Katti. (*Bells jingle as curtains open.*)

* * *

SETTING: *A clearing near a river in India. Painted on backdrop is a jungle with many animals among the trees. Brilliant colors are used and the style is that of traditional Indian painting.*

AT RISE: *Stage is empty. Then* PACCA *enters, carrying bow and wearing quiver.* SAKKAR *and* PRINCE *remain seated on pillows, down right, watching. Whenever* SAKKAR *speaks, actors freeze.*

PACCA: I'd like to join the Queen's Royal Guard. But I'm too small. Only tall men are allowed to join. (*Sighing*) That's too bad, for I'm a hard worker and an excellent shot. If only there were some way I could be in the Queen's service! (*Looking off*) Here comes a tall man poling a boat. If he were a bowman, the Royal Guard would take him in a minute. (KATTI *enters, pantomiming lazily poling boat through water in time to slow drumbeat heard from offstage.*)

KATTI: Every day the current seems stronger. This boring job of mine tires me out.

PACCA (*Calling out to* KATTI): Hello, where are you going?

KATTI: To gather firewood in the grove up there. (*Yawns*) Every day I cut and bundle wood. Every afternoon I carry huge bundles to my boat and float downstream to market. (*Yawns*) People say, "Katti, you're stronger than a bull elephant." That's true, but it's small help for a poor man who doesn't like to work. (*Continues to pole.* PACCA *watches thoughtfully, then suddenly waves his bow.*)

PACCA: Wait, Katti, Let me, Pacca, be your friend and advisor.

KATTI: What sort of advice could you give me?

PACCA: Well, in the first place, I'd advise you to join the Queen's Royal Guard.

KATTI (*Making a face*): Oh, no, that's too much work. Besides, I can't send an arrow straight.

PACCA: Ah, but *I* can. If you join the Royal Guard, I will be your page and do all your archery for you. Then we will divide the pay—five hundred pieces for you and five hundred pieces for me.

KATTI: That's good money, friend. (*Thinks*) You'll do all the archery, hey? (PACCA *nods.* KATTI *pantomimes throwing away pole and jumping out of boat, pulling it ashore and tying it to a tree.*) There, you heavy old boat. You can stay here by the river while I, big Katti, will go to the palace. Lead the way, Pacca. (PACCA *and* KATTI *march around stage, chanting, joined by* GUARDS, *who enter left and right.* GUARDS *have bows and quivers.* 1ST GUARD *is beating drum and* 2ND GUARD *is shaking bells.* PACCA *waves bow.*)

PACCA *and* KATTI (*Chanting*): Guard the kingdom; guard the Queen.

GUARDS (*Chanting*): Guard and guard and guard and guard.

PACCA *and* KATTI (*Chanting*): Help the people, rich and poor.

GUARDS (*Chanting*): Help and help and help and help. (*All freeze as* SAKKAR *speaks.*)

SAKKAR: So Katti joined the Queen's Royal Guard, and little Pacca became his faithful page. Katti was very careful to hide the fact that Pacca did all his archery for him. (KATTI *holds edge of his cape in front of* PACCA.) And because Pacca was such a skilled bowman, Katti soon gained a fine reputation as an archer. It wasn't long before the Queen herself knew about his excellent service. (QUEEN *enters regally with bag of gold hidden in her sari and wearing large jeweled necklace.* VILLAGE GIRL *enters, running, from opposite side.*)

VILLAGE GIRL (*Screaming*): Help, help! Wild elephants are trampling our village. (*Falls to knees*) Merciful Queen, please save our homes.

QUEEN (*Calling*): Katti?

KATTI (*Crossing to her, bowing*): Yes, Your Highness.

QUEEN: Take care of that herd of elephants.

KATTI: At once, Your Highness. (*Bows and, to drumbeat, marches to edge of stage, followed by* PACCA, *as* GUARDS *chant*)

GUARDS: Katti, Katti, the Queen sends Katti. (KATTI *and* PACCA *peer into audience.*)

PACCA: The village is straight ahead of us. I hear the elephants. (*Sound of* ELEPHANTS *outside back of auditorium door is heard.*)

KATTI: What is your advice, Pacca?

PACCA: First a volley of arrows, followed by a ferocious charge. (KATTI *nods as* ELEPHANTS *burst into auditorium, stomp down aisle, and trumpet angrily at audience.* PACCA *pantomimes shooting arrows from bow, taking arrows from quiver in quick succession.* ELEPHANTS *hold trunks or knees, squealing in pain, as if injured.* PACCA *leaps off stage and yells and stamps at them.* ELEPHANTS *exit through rear door, squealing and pushing each other, trumpeting in distress. Meanwhile* KATTI *watches from stage, arms folded, aloof and unconcerned.* PACCA *returns to stage and bows to* KATTI, *who snaps fingers nonchalantly, does an about-face and, followed by* PACCA, *marches back to rejoin* GUARDS, *accompanied by drumbeat.* VILLAGE GIRL *kisses hem of* KATTI's *cape.*)

GIRL: Thank you, great warrior, thank you. (*Exits, moving backwards, bowing prayerfully.* QUEEN *crosses to* KATTI, *who puts cape over* PACCA *to hide him.*)

QUEEN: Katti, as a reward for your excellent service, I give you this bag of gold. (KATTI *bows and takes bag of gold she hands him, stuffing it into belt.* GUARDS *cheer.* QUEEN *crosses to stand at side.* KATTI *struts about pompously.* PACCA *is still under cape. He tries to keep pace with* KATTI, *but accidentally steps on* KATTI's *toes, making* KATTI *cry out and jump. No one notices.*)

GUARDS: Hurrah, hurrah, hurrah for Katti! (CITY MERCHANT *enters, waving arms and groaning loudly.*)

MERCHANT: Oh-h-h! I have been robbed. (*Staggers across stage, lamenting*) Every day for a whole week, a thief has broken into my shop and stolen the best silks and spices. (*Kneeling*) Most magnificent Queen, please help me.

QUEEN (*Calling*): Katti?

KATTI (*Bowing*): Yes, Your Highness.

QUEEN: Take care of that thief.

KATTI: At once, Your Highness. (*Bows and, to drumbeat, marches to edge of stage, followed by* PACCA, *as* GUARDS *chant.*)

GUARDS (*Chanting*): Katti, Katti, the Queen sends Katti. (KATTI *and* PACCA *peer out at audience as if searching for thief. Then* PACCA *points to a spot just below stage.*)

PACCA: There's the merchant's shop, Katti. Let us hide and wait for the thief to come. (*They crouch.* THIEF *enters from back of auditorium, sneaks down aisle to "shop," and pantomimes filling bag with merchandise.*)

KATTI (*Whispering*): What is your advice, Pacca?

PACCA (*Whispering*): An arrow in the seat of the pants will teach a lasting lesson. (KATTI *nods.* PACCA *pantomimes shooting arrow.* THIEF *yelps and holds seat of*

pants, looking up at PACCA *with growing terror as* PACCA
rises, ready to shoot again. KATTI *rises in aloof manner
as before.* THIEF *backs away.*)

THIEF (*Yelling*): No, no, let me go. I promise never to
steal again. (PACCA *makes a frightening face and gives
a loud cry.* THIEF *retreats down aisle, shrieking.*) Help,
help! A demon is after me! Help, help! (*Exits at back
of auditorium.* PACCA *bows to* KATTI, *who snaps fingers
in flippant manner, and, as before, marches back to*
GUARDS, *in time to drumbeat, followed by* PACCA.
MERCHANT *kisses hem of* KATTI'S *cape.*)

MERCHANT: Thank you, great warrior, thank you. (*Exits,
moving backwards, bowing gratefully, as* QUEEN *crosses
to* KATTI. *He hides* PACCA *with cape, as before.*)

QUEEN: Katti, as a reward for your bravery, I give you
this necklace of emeralds and rubies. (*Removes necklace
and places it around* KATTI'S *neck.* KATTI *bows and
struts around even more pompously, as* GUARDS *cheer.*
PACCA, *under cape, tries to keep up, but steps on*
KATTI'S *foot, accidentally, and* KATTI *jumps and cries out
as before. No one notices.* QUEEN *crosses to stand at one
side.*)

GUARDS: Hurrah, hurrah, hurrah for Katti!

KATTI (*Arrogantly*): The Queen gives me gold for my
excellent service and jewels for my bravery. People
praise my name and kiss the hem of my cape. Indeed
I must be a great warrior, for everyone thinks I am. Ah,
Katti, what a fine, handsome, extraordinary man you
are!

PACCA: Katti, listen to me. I am your true friend. Have
you forgotten me?

KATTI (*Interrupting disdainfully*): Listen to *you*? Listen to
a lowly, insignificant page who couldn't even get into the
Queen's Royal Guard? Go away!

PACCA: But, Katti—

KATTI (*Gesturing him away*): Go away! I am too big a man
to be bothered with a little person like you. (*Struts about
as* PACCA *sadly crosses up left, standing with back to
audience. All freeze.*)

SAKKAR: Then one day a fierce horde of monkeys charged
out of the jungle, snatching food from people's homes
and scaring children. (VILLAGE GIRL, CITY MERCHANT,
and THIEF *run in, screaming ad libs.*)

ALL (*Ad lib*): The monkeys! Help, help! They're taking
everything. I'm frightened. (*Etc.* GUARDS *rush about
jangling bells.*)

GUARDS (*Chanting*): The monkeys are coming. The monkeys are coming. What shall we do? The monkeys are
coming.

QUEEN (*Shouting with hands to her mouth*): Katti, Katti!
(*All freeze as* KATTI *bows extravagantly.*)

KATTI: Yes, Your Highness.

QUEEN: Take care of those monkeys.

KATTI: At once, Your Highness. (*Bows and raises hand
in signal for* GUARDS *to follow. He leads them around
stage, to beat of drum and bells, in chanting march.
After a moment of hesitation,* PACCA *follows them.
Meanwhile,* MONKEYS *enter from back of auditorium
and leap along aisle, pantomiming snatching food from
people in audience and scaring them.*)

GUARDS (*Chanting*):
Guard the kingdom; guard the Queen.
Guard and guard and guard and guard.
Help the people, rich and poor.
Help and help and help and help.
(*Finally,* KATTI *stops at edge of stage.* GUARDS *peer into
audience, see* MONKEYS, *and point.*)

GUARDS (*Together*): The monkeys are there.

1ST GUARD: They're getting ready to attack us.

2ND GUARD: What is your advice, Katti?

KATTI (*Surprised*): *My* advice? Er, ah, hm-m-m.

1ST GUARD: Our leader must shoot the first arrow, as is the custom. (KATTI *glances about nervously.*)

KATTI (*Muttering*): Leader? Leader? Me, shoot an arrow?

GUARDS (*Chanting*): Yes, yes, Katti first. Yes, yes, Katti first. (*Their words die out as they realize* KATTI *has no bow and looks frightened.*)

2ND GUARD: Katti, where is your bow?

KATTI: My bow? What bow? Er, ah, hm-m-m. . . . I have none.

1ST GUARD: No bow?

KATTI (*Backing up*): No, no bow! I—ah—think I'll run back to the palace and look for it. Er—ah—you men hold back that advancing horde of fierce monkeys, and I'll look for my bow someplace or other. (*Turns and bolts up left, where he stands shaking, back to audience.* GUARDS *are shocked.*)

1ST GUARD: Katti ran away.

2ND GUARD: Who will lead us now?

GUARDS (*Ad libbing excitedly*): No one. We'll all be killed. What shall we do? Retreat. No, there's no time. Here come the monkeys. (*Etc. They sink to knees, groaning and hiding heads fearfully. At this sign,* MONKEYS *jump onto stage, pantomiming grabbing food, and making noises to scare* GUARDS. PACCA *leaps forward to* KATTI'*s former place.*)

PACCA (*Shouting*): Stand, guards. (MONKEYS *freeze in surprise.*) I, Pacca, the best bowman in the land, will lead you. (*He pantomimes shooting an arrow. A* MONKEY *yelps, and grabs tail, pantomimes pulling arrow out of tip of tail, then holding up tail with dismay.* GUARDS *rise, give wild battle cries, make fierce faces, and stamp. They pantomime shooting arrows at* MONKEYS. MONKEYS *shriek in alarm, leap from stage, and, chattering loudly and dodging arrows, run up aisle and exit at back of auditorium.*)

SAKKAR: When the Queen heard how Pacca had led the

Royal Guards against the monkeys, she was extremely grateful. (GUARDS *move up center as* QUEEN *enters and crosses to* PACCA. KATTI *stands motionless to one side.*)

QUEEN: Little Pacca, you deserve many gifts for your excellent service and bravery. From this day forth you shall be the leader of my Royal Guards. (*Crosses to* KATTI, *takes bag of gold and necklace from him, crosses back to* PACCA *and presents them to him*)

PACCA (*Smiling shyly*): To have been helpful is reward enough, my Queen. I need no other reward. (*Bows.* QUEEN *smiles, and then, with great respect, bows to* PACCA. *She exits, followed by* PACCA *and* GUARDS, *marching and chanting to sound of drum and bell.*)

GUARDS:
Little Pacca's brave in heart.
Brave and brave and brave and brave.
Little Pacca's big in deeds.
Big and big and big and big.

(*They exit.*)

SAKKAR: Katti left the palace in disgrace. He returned to his boat and began to collect firewood. (KATTI *pantomimes untying boat, shoving it into water, and jumping in, poling boat through water with great energy.*) Katti was so ashamed of himself that he worked much harder than before, seldom stopping and never complaining. (KATTI *pantomimes poling boat in opposite direction.*) One day Pacca came to the riverbank to see his old friend. (PACCA *re-enters.*)

PACCA (*Calling*): Katti, my friend, may I help you?

KATTI: No, Pacca. You helped me too much, only I didn't realize it until too late. I would rather help *you.*

PACCA: Help me?

KATTI: Yes. Do you think it is possible for me to be your page, as you were once mine? Of course, I would have to leave the archery to you, but I could do all the other work.

PACCA (*Nodding happily*): Agreed, agreed! Come along, Katti. We will share the pay just as we did before. (KATTI *pantomimes dropping pole, jumping from boat, and pulling boat ashore, tying it as before.*)

KATTI: I am indeed lucky to have you for a friend.

PACCA: Friends are not luck, Katti. They are born out of time and trouble. (KATTI *and* PACCA *march toward exit, their arms about each other's shoulders, to beat of drum and bell, heard from offstage.*)

KATTI *and* PACCA (*Chanting*):

Guard the kingdom; guard the Queen.

Guard and guard and guard and guard.

Help the people, rich and poor.

Help and help and help and help.

(*Curtains close as they exit.*)

* * *

SAKKAR (*Rising*): Thank you for listening, Prince. I trust I did not bore you.

PRINCE (*Rising*): Old Sakkar, your tale has been most instructive. I now see how important friends can be. And I now realize how my lack of humility has kept me from making any true friends. (*Crosses thoughtfully to center curtain, followed by* SAKKAR, *then removes jewel from turban*) Take this jewel to my father. (SAKKAR *bows as he accepts jewel.*) Tell him—tell him his son begs forgiveness. (*Exits, followed by* SAKKAR)

THE END

THE GREAT SAMURAI SWORD

THE GREAT SAMURAI SWORD

For many centuries, public storytelling in Japan was a profession. The teller of tales, or hanashika, wore special clothes, used formal language, and narrated his tales in a large room. One familiar folktale concerned Naoto and Osada, who were said to have lived during the third shogunate of the Tokugawa regime (1603-1651). Naoto was a young samurai, a soldier bound to defend and protect his lord, with his life, if necessary. In this feudal system, for a samurai—like Naoto in "The Great Samurai Sword"—to shirk his duty or fail to uphold the family honor was a disgrace.

"The Great Samurai Sword" is presented here in kabuki style, a form of drama native to Japan, which has specific conventions. The word "kabuki" was originally borrowed from the Chinese word *kabu* (*ka,* song; *bu,* dance) by the Japanese, and in the late sixteenth century, they gave the name kabuki to a kind of dance. This later developed into a musical drama, originally performed by female actress-dancers, but now, in the style of the classic No drama, performed entirely by males, with female parts taken by specially trained male actors.

Japanese actors spend years learning the true kabuki style of acting, in which symbolism is the keynote, gestures are exaggerated, and movement and speeches are synchronized— poses are held by the actors after the more important speeches, for example. The costumes and makeup are elaborate, and the actors' faces are painted in expressive, decorative patterns.

Plays are usually chosen from a standard list. "The Great Samurai Sword," though not one of these, is based on a Japanese folktale of the kind that often serve as the source of kabuki plays.

The Great Samurai Sword

A Japanese folktale in kabuki style

Characters

NAOTO, *a young samurai warrior*
SUDO, *his father*
SAGAMI, *his mother*
GRANDMOTHER
COUSIN
OSADA, *a lovely lady*
KASAI, *her father*
KANAMI, *her mother*
FOUR SINGERS
MUSICIANS

SETTING: *A large Japanese screen stands up center, covered with a painting of a lake, Mt. Fuji, and houses to right and left of lake. In front of the screen is a long, narrow platform. Down left are four large pillows arranged in a row.*

AT RISE: FOUR SINGERS *enter right, moving stiffly, and cross to pillows. They sit cross-legged, staring straight ahead.* MUSICIANS *enter left in a similar manner, carrying their instruments, and sit cross-legged on the platform. Music begins.*

SINGERS (*Chanting together*): In the days of the third shogun* lived Naoto, a young samurai.

* 1603-1651 (shoguns were military rulers of Japan).

1ST SINGER: For ten generations,

2ND SINGER: His people taught the sword.

SINGERS (*Together*): Most honorable family of Sendai City. (SUDO, SAGAMI, GRANDMOTHER *and* COUSIN *enter and kneel in a half circle.*)

SUDO: Our son, Naoto, has proven himself an excellent warrior. (*Folds arms proudly*)

GRANDMOTHER (*Nodding sleepily*): True.

COUSIN: He now teaches the art of fencing with the sword. (*Pulls out sword*)

GRANDMOTHER (*Nodding*): True.

SUDO: His annual income is three thousand bushels of rice. (*Pantomimes eating with chopsticks*)

GRANDMOTHER: True.

SAGAMI (*Wiggling fingers, moving hands back and forth*): But, have you not noticed restlessness in our son?

GRANDMOTHER: True.

SUDO: Naoto needs a wife. (*Slaps one hand on floor*) That would settle him down. (*Slaps other hand on floor*)

GRANDMOTHER: True.

SUDO: Honorable Grandmother has only one word. (*Holds one finger up*) Either she needs dictionary or long nap.

GRANDMOTHER (*Still nodding*): True. (*Falls asleep, snoring*)

SUDO (*Looking upward*): Ah, so! Grandmother sleeps like owl. (*Spreads arms*) Rest of family must think like fox.

SAGAMI (*Rising*): There is a lovely daughter of the Tokugawa house. (*Dances*)

COUSIN (*Jumping up to join her*): Ah, she is charming. Osada is her name.

SAGAMI: Her mind (*Points to head*) works well. She is quick (*Raises one hand*) and clever (*Raises other hand*) in everything she does.

COUSIN (*Leaping around*): Her brothers have taught her

the use of the sword and spear. (*Fences with imaginary enemy, grunting and leaping wildly*)

GRANDMOTHER (*Waking suddenly*): The enemy attacks! (*Looks at* COUSIN) What is the matter, Cousin? Do you have fleas?

SUDO: Hm-m-m. (*Scratches chin*) I did not call meeting for purpose of Cousin leaping about or Grandmother snoring like owl and making bad jokes.

COUSIN (*Quickly returning to kneeling position*): Oh, so sorry!

SUDO (*Rising*): I shall go to House of Tokugawa and look at this young lady called Osada. If she is all you say, then perhaps a marriage can be arranged. (*Exits left, followed by* SAGAMI, COUSIN, *and* GRANDMOTHER)

SINGERS (*Together*): The next afternoon in the hour of the Ram. . . . (MUSICIAN *strikes gong twice.*)

OSADA (*Entering right with dainty, shuffling steps, smiling*): I am Osada. My elders have told me that I will soon marry the handsome Naoto. (*Raises hands to cheeks*) It makes my face feel as warm as the burning incense. (*Puts hands on heart*) It makes my heart beat as the dragonfly's wings. I shall go to our garden and dance about the plum trees, for I am filled with joy. (*Exits right, dancing*)

NAOTO (*Entering left with large strides, frowning*): I am Naoto. My elders have told me that I will soon marry the lovely Osada. (*Points to feet*) It makes my feet feel cold as icicles. (*Points to hair*) It makes my hair stand up as the porcupine quills. I shall go to the teahouses to play and throw my money about, for I do not wish to settle down.

SINGERS (*Together*): Away went Naoto, tossing his money, forgetting his sword. (NAOTO *leaps around, tossing arms in air, then exits left.*)

1ST SINGER: Alas, how his relatives worried! (SUDO, SAGAMI, COUSIN *and* GRANDMOTHER *enter left, run around in a circle making worried gestures, and exit left.*)

3RD SINGER: How his friends groaned! (*Loud groans from offstage*)

2ND SINGER: What a great insult to Osada's family! (KASAI *and* KANAMI, OSADA's *parents, enter right, run around in a circle making angry gestures, and exit right.*)

4TH SINGER: Then, as the young silver moon hid behind the silent pines—(KASAI *and* KANAMI *enter right as* SUDO, SAGAMI, COUSIN *and* GRANDMOTHER *enter left. They bow to each other, then face audience.*)

KASAI: We come to tell you we do not like the life your Naoto lives.

KANAMI: He shows no interest in our daughter, Osada.

KASAI: She sits sadly under our plum trees, her tears flowing like waterfalls.

KANAMI: Your son must have butterflies in his head. (*Taps head*)

KASAI: Therefore, we say, unless Naoto changes his ways by the time the next moon touches the sides of Mount Fuji (*Points to mountain on screen*), we cancel agreement of marriage. (*Makes chopping motion*)

SUDO (*Rubbing hands nervously*): Please accept humble apologies.

SAGAMI: Naoto is not very old in his manners.

COUSIN: It is a bad time. Even the spiders are restless these days.

SUDO: We shall speak to our son and correct his fluttering ways.

GRANDMOTHER (*Aside to* SUDO): What has Naoto done?

SUDO *and* SAGAMI (*Putting fingers to lips*): Sh-h-h!

GRANDMOTHER (*Aside*): Sh-h-h, yourselves. Where is respect for ancient grandmother? (*Points to self*) I might as well sleep.

SUDO (*Touching forehead, bowing to* GRANDMOTHER): Honorable Grandmother, we are trying to get son married, but son would rather be butterfly.

GRANDMOTHER (*Shrugging*): Butterfly? Ah, so! (*All bow to each other, then* KASAI *and* KANAMI *exit right.*)

SUDO (*Loudly*): Cousin, bring Naoto here.

COUSIN (*Speaking quickly and dancing around*): This is greatly disturbing. I have not been able to eat my noodles. My soybean soup tastes like straw, and my shark fins have lost their flavor. Naoto must be punished for his idleness. He does not practice his sword anymore. He thinks because of his money and good name that he is a great man. Oh, the sadness of—

SUDO (*Interrupting*): I did not ask for speech from Honorable Cousin. Where is my son?

COUSIN (*Bowing*): Oh, please excuse. (*Exits left, re-entering with* NAOTO, *who bows to* SUDO.)

SUDO (*Loudly*): Naoto, open your eyes and see what you do. (*Points to* NAOTO's *feet*) You set your sandals in the mud. (*Waving arms*) You play all day and all night without a serious thought. You bring ruin upon our good name. (*Shakes his fist*) You disgrace your forefathers.

GRANDMOTHER (*Shaking her finger at* NAOTO): Shame on you, butterfly!

SUDO: Naoto, we beg you, give up your childish actions, marry the lovely Osada, and become a fine husband (*Gestures widely*), bringing honor to your family.

GRANDMOTHER (*Shaking her finger*): Butterflies do not live long lives.

NAOTO (*Humbly*): Forgive me for the unhappiness I have caused you. O Father, you fill me with shame.

GRANDMOTHER (*Shaking her finger*): Butterflies may be pretty, but they come from *worms!*

SUDO: Honorable Grandmother, now is not time for butterfly lessons. Naoto, we forgive you.

NAOTO: I swear by my great ancestors that I shall follow wiser paths. (*Points left, then exits with great strides.* SUDO, SAGAMI, COUSIN *and* GRANDMOTHER *clasp their hands, sigh with relief, and exit left.*)

SINGERS (*Together*): Naoto did change his life . . . (*Pause*) for awhile.

1ST SINGER: Blow, blow the winter winds.

2ND SINGER: The nightingale has gone away.

3RD SINGER: The temple wears a cap of snow.

4TH SINGER: Beside the fire, Osada waits for spring. (OSADA *enters right and dances as if moving around fire, warming hands.* KASAI *and* KANAMI *enter right.*)

KANAMI: The marriage gifts have been exchanged. (*Spreads arms*)

KASAI: In the time of the cherry blossoms (*Makes tree shape*), our daughter, Osada (*Points to her*), marries the young samurai (*Draws imaginary sword*), Naoto.

SINGERS (*Together*): From the tall bamboo the cuckoo calls,

1ST SINGER: To tell us spring is here.

2ND SINGER: And by the lake the cherry trees

SINGERS (*Together*): Are bursting clouds of pink.

KASAI: Go to your husband's house, Osada. (*Points off left*)

OSADA (*Bowing*): My heart is full of gladness. My feet will fly on the wings of the hummingbird. (*Exits left, running lightly.* KASAI *and* KANAMI *exit right.*)

1ST SINGER: The summer locusts came to sing their song.

2ND SINGER: Poppies lit the fields with glowing light.

3RD SINGER: Then autumn winds gave color to the leaves,

4TH SINGER: Waving their arms through fields of yellow rice.

OSADA (*Entering left, shuffling sadly*): Oya-oya! My husband has returned to his unhealthy ways. (*Stands at center*)

NAOTO (*Entering left, cheerfully leaping about*): I have forgotten what my family told me. It is fun to lose my money here and there. I waste my time, singing in the streets. Ho, what a jolly time I have. (*Continues leaping*)

OSADA (*With her arms outstretched*): Dear husband, will you not come home and stop your running?

NAOTO: All of my money is gone. I shall mortgage my rice income for a half-year in advance. (*Continues leaping*)

OSADA (*With arms outstretched*): Dear husband, will you not come home?

NAOTO: I need more money. I shall sell our furniture. (*Continues leaping*)

OSADA: Dear husband! (*Puts her hands over her face.*)

NAOTO: Osada, give me your wedding robes and your jewels. I must sell them to pay these debts. (*Continues leaping*)

OSADA: Oya-oya! (*Sinks to her knees*)

NAOTO: Osada, go to your father and ask him for the loan of two hundred yen. Do not tell him why you need this money. My luck will soon change. I shall pay him back before the year is gone.

OSADA: I go, but it does not make me happy to do so. (*Exits right, shuffling sadly.* NAOTO *exits left, leaping gaily.*)

SINGERS (*Together*): The House of Tokugawa heard many rumors. (KASAI *and* KANAMI *enter right, with hands to ears, shake heads sadly, and exit right.*)

1ST SINGER: Yet, Osada's father trusted his daughter's wisdom.

2ND SINGER: He asked no questions.

3RD SINGER: But he wondered much.

KASAI (*Entering right, stroking beard*): My daughter has come to visit. (*Gestures for her to enter*)

OSADA (*Entering right and falling to her knees before him*): O Honorable Parent, I come to ask a great favor.

KASAI: Speak, little flower.

OSADA: I know of a samurai sword (*Draws imaginary sword*) which you have locked up (*Twists fingers as if locking*) in a special room. It was worn by your grand-father.

KASAI: Indeed, it is my dearest treasure. (*Puts hands on chest*)

OSADA (*Holding out arms to him*): Give me that great sword, Father. (KASAI *strokes his beard, walks away, returns, and strokes his beard again.*)

KASAI: I shall give it to you, daughter. (*Exits right, followed by* OSADA)

SINGERS (*Together*): How beautiful was the sword!

3RD SINGER: A long, curved blade with sharpest edge.

4TH SINGER: A handle carved and set with precious stones.

SINGERS (*Together*): The Great Samurai Sword! The Great Samurai Sword! (NAOTO *enters left and* OSADA *enters right, carrying sword.*)

NAOTO: Where is the money, Osada?

OSADA: I was too full of shame to ask for it without a reason, so instead I asked my father for this valuable sword. I told him that I wanted it to practice fencing with you, as I once did with my brothers.

NAOTO (*Looking at sword*): I can see that this sword is worth much. It should bring a good price.

OSADA: You shall have it, dear husband. However, there is a condition. I may only give the sword to one who defeats me fairly with it.

NAOTO (*Smiling*): Ho, ho! Let us put on fencing gear, and I will show you my fine skill as a swordsman.

OSADA: My skill is only that of a woman, but my brothers taught me well. For the sake of honor, I must fence my best.

NAOTO (*Laughing*): Of course! Quickly now, for I wish to sell the sword tonight. (*He exits left and* OSADA *exits right. Music plays. They re-enter wearing masks and chest armor, and carrying swords. They fence in a stylized, dancing manner, to musical accompaniment. Finally, with a blow,* OSADA *knocks the sword from* NAOTO's *hand.* NAOTO *is shocked and shamed. In a rage he picks up his sword and exits left, slashing the air, groaning, and making faces.* OSADA *removes her mask, smiles, and exits right in a dainty, shuffling manner.)*

SINGERS (*Together*): For five days Naoto lived in the tea-houses,

1ST SINGER: Trying to forget his shameful defeat.

2ND SINGER: At last he gathered himself up.

SINGERS (*Together*): To take a serious look at his life.

NAOTO (*Entering left sadly, then facing audience*): Oh, what a fool I am. Before you is a bold, brave samurai, who receives three thousand bushels of rice each year. My father, my father's father, and my many, many fathers' fathers were excellent swordsmen. I, too, was once good. But, look at me. I have wasted away my money and lost my skill at fencing. My own wife defeated me. (*Groans and makes a face*) I shall go away to the greatest fencing master in the city of Edo, and there I shall labor hard and learn much. (*Points right and exits with great energy.*)

OSADA (*Entering right, looking back and pointing*): There goes my husband. While he is gone, I shall live simply and help pay back his debts. (*Exits left*)

SINGERS (*Together*): Naoto studied hard for five years.

1ST SINGER: He no longer played in teahouses.

2ND SINGER: He no longer threw away his money.

3RD SINGER: He listened to the wisdom of great men.

4TH SINGER: He practiced with his sword every day.

NAOTO (*Entering right*): Ho, Osada, my little wife, I have returned.

OSADA (*Entering left, carrying sword in both hands, and bowing to* NAOTO): Welcome home, Naoto. I have missed you. Time has crawled on the snail's back.

NAOTO: Forgive me, Osada. I have not treated you well. I believe that now you will find me a different man. Shall we have another fencing match for your father's sword?

OSADA (*Kneeling, holding sword out*): Never again, my husband, for now I *know* you would win. The sword is yours. Sell it if you wish.

NAOTO (*Taking sword*): Rise, my wise little wife. Return this great sword to your father and tell him that it has served its purpose and is no longer needed.

OSADA (*Rising and smiling, taking sword*): Most excellent husband, I shall always obey your commands. (*Exits right.* NAOTO *exits left.*)

1ST SINGER: Come to the celebration.

2ND SINGER: A thousand lanterns light the gardens.

3RD SINGER: All night long the temple bells ring. (MUSICIAN *rings bells.*)

SINGERS (*Together*): Naoto, Naoto. Naoto returns with honor. (KASAI *and* KANAMI *enter right and* SUDO, SAGAMI, COUSIN *and* GRANDMOTHER *enter left. All bow to each other and face audience.* NAOTO *enters left and* OSADA *enters right. They meet in center between the others, bow to each other, and face audience.*)

ALL (*Together*): May the fireflies light your way to good fortune. (SINGERS *sing a Japanese or suitable song while others dance. All bow.* SUDO, SAGAMI, COUSIN *and* GRANDMOTHER *exit left as* KASAI *and* KANAMI *exit right.* NAOTO *and* OSADA *circle the stage and exit left.* SINGERS *and* MUSICIANS *exit left. Curtain.*)

THE END

WHITE ELEPHANT

WHITE ELEPHANT

Customs of Burma and Thailand (formerly Siam) differ, and the two bordering countries have not always been on friendly terms. The Burmese and Thais, however, do share religious beliefs, folktales and legends, and a style of theater called dance drama, performed in many Southeast Asian countries. In dance drama, the play is acted out with dance movements.

The classical drama of Burma is called *zat;* in it, acting and dancing are important. It is the tradition in this form of drama for a problem to be brought to the attention of the King for solution, as in this play, "White Elephant." In performances of this play, dances may be added, possibly in the opening scene or at the end. Or, characters may make their entrances in *zat* style, in which they imitate marionettes: 1) elbows pointed out and held up with forearms dangling down and away from body; 2) knees bent and jutting forward.

In the folktales of Burma and Thailand, goodness is not always rewarded. Sometimes the fool turns out to be wise, and the rascal becomes the hero. Good luck, humor, and often a wry twist at the end are features of these tales. Elephants are considered lucky and valuable, especially the rare white elephant. According to legend, the white elephant originally came from the world of the sky, bringing needed rain to the rice fields.

White Elephant

A folktale from Burma and Thailand

Characters

PON KHIN, *washerman*
SAI, *his wife*
NU AUNG, *potter*
PA SONG, *his wife*
KING BINNYA DALA
MESSENGER
SERVANT
GRAY ELEPHANT
WHITE ELEPHANT

SCENE 1

TIME: *Long ago.*

SETTING: *City of Ava, in Burma. This scene is played before curtain.*

AT RISE: NU AUNG *enters right before curtain, yawns, stretches, looks about to make sure he is not seen, and then sits against right proscenium arch, falling asleep. PON KHIN, carrying cut-out of small washtub, and SAI, carrying two white shirts, enter at center through curtain. They kneel and, as they talk, pantomime scrubbing shirts in the tub. NU AUNG, annoyed at being disturbed, opens one eye, sighs, crosses arms, and listens.*

SAI: Are these the last shirts to wash, husband?

PON KHIN: Yes, Sai. It was a large load today. Each week more and more people bring their clothes to us.

181

SAI: That is because we are the finest washers in the city of Ava. (*Rising to hold up shirt*) We can turn the *dirtiest, darkest things into gleaming white.*

NU AUNG (*Snorting in disgust*): Stop bragging, Sai.

SAI (*Seeing* NU AUNG): Look, there is the potter, Nu Aung, sleeping again.

NU (*Rising angrily*): I am not sleeping. I am thinking—designing pottery in my mind. You do nothing but scrub; I am an artistic potter.

SAI: Ha! You only think you are. You spend one day a week making pottery. The other six days you are lazier than a lizard in the sun. And so is your wife, Pa Song. I have seen her dozing in the marketplace. Maybe if she had more pottery to sell, she could stay awake longer. Nu Aung, once you were a fine potter, but now you are only a lazy lizard.

NU (*Furiously*): Pon Khin, your wife babbles like a monkey in the trees. She has no respect for talent.

PON: My wife gives respect when and where it is due. Neither of us thinks highly of anyone who does a job poorly. (NU *rushes to center and shakes fist in* PON's *face.*)

NU: You, too, are a monkey. One of my beautiful pots is better than a hundred of your clean shirts. *For me, no pottery job is too difficult.*

PON: Come on, Sai. Let us spread out the shirts to dry. (*Picks up tub*) Those who work little often claim to do much. (*Exits center, followed by* SAI, *who carries shirts and shakes her head in disgust.* NU *stalks about, puffing angrily.* PA SONG *enters left, yawning and stretching.*)

PA: Husband, there is one pottery cup left, but it is slightly cracked. I doubt if anyone will buy it. Until you get around to making more pottery, I think I will (*Yawns*) work at home.

NU: All right, all right. It does not matter to me. Pon Khin and Sai were just here bragging about their good fortune.

PA: They do appear to eat and dress far better than we.

NU: They are mere scrubbers. Our fortune will grow, in time.

MESSENGER (*Shouting from off left*): Royal announcement! Royal announcement! (*Enters, reading from scroll*) Binnya Dala, King of Burma, magnificent lord of a thousand elephants, has no white elephants in his herd. The King of Siam has two white elephants in his herd, and therefore, it is extremely important for the King of Burma to have two white elephants in *his* herd. Anyone with information about the whereabouts of white elephants, come to the palace immediately. (*Exits*)

NU (*Thoughtfully*): White elephants are rare and difficult to find. (*Suddenly slaps thighs and laughs*) Pa Song, we will get even with those bragging washers. We shall go to the King.

PA: To the King?

NU: Yes. You will see how clever your husband can be. (*Exits left, followed by* PA. *Curtain opens.*)

* * * * *

SCENE 2

SETTING: *Courtyard of King's palace. Upstage is backdrop painting of palace wall with temple tops and trees showing above. Scene may be played against simple backdrop curtain, if desired. At right center, at an angle, is King's throne.*

AT RISE: KING *sits cross-legged on throne.* SERVANT *holds large golden umbrella over his head.* MESSENGER *enters left and bows to* KING, *hands together in prayerful manner, touching forehead. All bow in this way.*

MESSENGER: Magnificent lord of a thousand elephants, a

man and woman have come to the palace gate with information about white elephants.

KING: Ah-h-h! Bring them into the courtyard. (MESSENGER *bows and exits left.*) My royal announcement brought quick results. (MESSENGER *re-enters, followed by* NU *and* PA, *who bow.*)

NU: King Binnya Dala, I am Nu Aung, and this is my wife, Pa Song. We make fine pottery to sell in the marketplace.

KING: I do not care who you are or what you do. I am only interested in white elephants.

NU (*Quickly*): Yes, of course. (*Clears throat*) Within the city of Ava there lives a washerman by the name of Pon Khin. He and his wife, Sai, claim they can turn the *dirtiest, darkest things into gleaming white.*

KING: So?

NU: So, therefore, Your Highness, no doubt these washers can scrub gray elephants in your royal herd until they become white. (PA *turns aside to hide a smile.*)

KING: How extraordinary!

PA: It is indeed as my husband says. I have seen their marvelous work.

NU: And we have heard their loud boasts many times.

KING (*Rising*): Hm-m-m. Scrub gray elephants white. Messenger, find this washerman and his wife and bring them to the palace.

MESSENGER (*Bowing*): Yes, Your Highness. (*Exits left.* NU *and* PA *cross up left, chuckling and congratulating each other stealthily so* KING *does not see. Meanwhile,* KING *strides about with excitement.* SERVANT *follows, trying to keep umbrella over* KING's *head.*)

KING: Ah-h! At last I will have two white elephants, just like the King of Siam's white elephants. What is more, the washerman and his wife can scrub *all* my gray elephants into white ones. Imagine! (*Throwing arms into air, hitting umbrella, to alarm of* SERVANT) A herd of a thousand white elephants. I will be the richest king in the world. (MESSENGER *re-enters, followed by* PON *and* SAI, *who see* NU *and* PA *and react with surprise. The four exchange smiling, polite bows. Then* NU *and* PA *turn to face upstage.* KING *crosses to sit on throne.*)

PON (*To* SAI): What do you suppose Nu Aung and Pa Song are doing in the courtyard of the King?

SAI: I wonder, too. Their smiles make me uneasy. (PON *and* SAI *bow to* KING.)

KING: Pon Khin and Sai, is it true you can turn the *dirtiest, darkest things into gleaming white?* (PON *and* SAI *smile broadly.*)

SAI: Those are my very words, Your Highness.

PON: Do you wish us to scrub your royal laundry?

KING: No, I wish you to scrub my gray elephants until they turn white. (PON *and* SAI *look at each other in amazement.*) With your reputation, that should be easy.

PON *and* SAI (*Groaning*): Oh-h-h-h!

KING (*Rising, threateningly*): I trust you can do what you claim. Otherwise, it will be fearfully bad for your business (*Louder*) and terrible for your health.

PON *and* SAI (*Gulping and nodding*): Yes, Your Highness.

PON: Ah—er, Your Highness, may we have a moment to discuss the best way to handle this job?

KING: Of course. And whatever materials you will need shall be yours. (*Sits.* PON *and* SAI *cross down center.*)

PON: I do not see how we can possibly scrub an elephant white.

SAI: Nor do I. Now I understand why the potter and his wife are here. They repeated my words to the King. Forgive me, husband. This is what comes of my foolish bragging.

PON: Never mind, Sai. It is done. I will have to admit, it is a clever trick Nu Aung has played on us.

SAI: If only we could be clever, too.

PON (*Suddenly snapping fingers*): I have an idea. We shall be clever. (*Crosses to* KING, *bowing, followed by* SAI) Your Highness, we are ready to scrub our first elephant white.

KING: Excellent!

PON: However, we cannot take the elephant to the river, as our soapsuds would be washed away. It is most important to have a high concentration of suds. What we need is a giant bathtub.

KING: Ah, yes, a giant bathtub.

PON: A *pottery* one is best.

KING: Hm-m-m. The man who was just here is a potter. (*Gestures at* NU. PON *looks at* NU.)

PON (*In mock surprise*): Why, it is Nu Aung. Your Highness, he is just the one. I have often heard him say these words: *For me, no pottery job is too difficult.* (SAI *turns aside to hide a smile.*)

KING (*Calling*): Nu Aung. (*Beckons.* NU *crosses right, followed by* PA. PON *and* SAI *cross up left.*) Nu Aung, you have the honor of making the bathtub.

NU (*Shocked*): The bathtub? What for?

KING: To hold each elephant while it is being scrubbed white.

NU: But, I have never made a tub so large.

KING: Did you not say these words: *For me, no pottery job is too difficult?*

NU (*Nervously*): Yes, but . . . but . . . .

KING (*Rising, threateningly*): I trust you can do what you claim. Otherwise, it will be fearfully bad for your business (*Louder*) and terrible for your health.

NU (*Gulping and nodding*): Yes, Your Highness. One moment, please, while I discuss this job with my wife.

(*Backs into* PA *accidentally. They cross down center to confer.*) This is a dreadful situation. The washers have repeated my words just as I repeated theirs. This is what comes of my foolish bragging.

PA: Never mind, Nu Aung. It is done.

NU: I will have to admit, it is a clever trick they have played on me. Yet, how can I mold an elephant's bath-tub?

PA: With your hands, husband. It will be hard, but we will work together.

NU: You are right. (*Bows to* KING, *as does* PA) Your High-ness, we will start on the tub immediately.

KING: Excellent! (NU *and* PA *cross left, exchanging smiling bows with* PON *and* SAI. *Curtain starts to close as the four exit left.*) A herd of a thousand white elephants! I shall be the most powerful king in history. (*Curtain closes.*)

* * * * *

SCENE 3

BEFORE RISE: *Off left,* NU *and* PA *are shouting.*

NU *and* PA (*Offstage; ad lib*): Hurry. Yes, yes. Come on. Faster. (*Etc.* PON *and* SAI *peer out through curtain, at center, looking left.* NU *and* PA *enter, running, panto-miming carrying clay.*)

NU: More clay for the elephant's bathtub.

PA: More clay. More clay. (*They exit right.*)

NU (*Shouting from offstage*): More water to mix with the clay. (*They re-enter.*)

PA (*Shouting*): More water. More water. (*They rush across, exiting left.*)

SAI: The lazy lizards have turned into tigers.

PON: They are certainly not sleeping these days.

SAI: Husband, what would happen to us if, by some chance, they should succeed?

PON: One problem at a time, Sai. I wonder what sort of tub they are creating? (*They pull heads back inside curtain. Curtain opens.*)

*   *   *

SETTING: *The same as Scene 2.*

AT RISE: KING *sits on throne as before with* SERVANT *holding umbrella over his head.* MESSENGER *enters left and bows.*

MESSENGER: Most magnificent lord of a thousand elephants, the potters are approaching with the elephant's bathtub.

KING (*Rising*): Hurry to the royal compound and select the noblest of my gray elephants. (MESSENGER *bows and exits right.* NU *and* PA *enter left, pushing and pulling small tub, a cut-out, which they push into place at center stage.*)

NU: Your Highness, here is the tub for the elephant.

MESSENGER (*Re-entering, leading* GRAY ELEPHANT): Your Highness, here is the noblest of your elephants.

KING: Let the elephant step into the tub. (MESSENGER *prods* ELEPHANT. *It pantomimes trying to get into tub, but finds it too small, and finally sits and trumpets loudly, swinging head from side to side, trunk swaying, indicating no.* KING *grumbles.*) This tub is too small. (*Sits with frown*)

NU: Perhaps you have a smaller elephant?

KING (*Angrily*): No!

PA (*Hopefully*): Maybe the elephant will shrink in the hot water.

KING (*Bellowing*): Ridiculous! Take this little tub away and make a bigger one. (NU *and* PA *exit left, pushing tub, as curtain closes.*)

*   *   *   *

SCENE 4

BEFORE RISE: *From off left,* NU *and* PA *are heard shouting.*
PON *and* SAI *peer through curtain to watch as* NU *and*
PA *enter left, running, pantomiming carrying clay.*

NU: More clay.

PA: More clay. (*They exit right.*)

NU (*Offstage; shouting*): More water. (*They re-enter.*)

PA (*Shouting*): More water. (*They rush across stage, exiting left.*)

SAI: They are really working.

PON: What sort of tub are they making now? (*Pull heads
inside curtain. Curtain opens.*)

* * *

SETTING: *The same as Scene 2.*

AT RISE: KING *and* SERVANT *are in same positions.* MES-
SENGER *enters left and bows.*

MESSENGER: Most magnificent lord of a thousand elephants, the potters approach with another elephant's
bathtub.

KING (*Rising*): I hope it is better than the last one. Bring
the elephant. (MESSENGER *bows and exits right, running.*
NU *and* PA *enter left with second tub, a cut-out, which
they push into position at center.* MESSENGER *re-enters,
leading* GRAY ELEPHANT, *who pantomimes getting into
tub. There is a loud cracking sound, and tub falls apart
in two pieces.* NOTE: *Tub is made of cut-out in two
pieces, taped together.* ELEPHANT *gets into tub and pulls
off tape, unseen by audience, causing tub to fall apart.
After tub splits,* ELEPHANT *jumps out, sits, trumpets
loudly, and swings trunk, as before.* KING *is upset.*) The
pottery in this tub is too thin. (*Sits, scowling*)

NU: Perhaps I can hold the pieces together while the elephant sits inside.

KING (*Angrily*): No!

PA (*Hopefully*): Do you have any royal glue?

KING (*Bellowing*): Ridiculous! Take this broken tub away and make a thicker one. (NU *and* PA *exit left, running, each with half of the tub, as curtain closes.*)

* * * * *

SCENE 5

BEFORE RISE: *Off left,* NU *and* PA *shout ad libs from offstage, sounding frantic.* PON *and* SAI *again peer through curtain as* NU *and* PA *enter left, pantomiming carrying clay.*

NU (*Gasping*): Clay.

PA (*Wearily*): Clay. (*They exit right.*)

NU (*Offstage; shouting*): Water. (*They re-enter.*)

PA (*Shouting*): Water. (*They rush across stage and exit left.*)

SAI: I am beginning to feel sorry for them.

PON: So am I. They have been slaving for so long! What sort of tub will they create this time?

KING (*Bellowing from offstage*): No! No! (*From offstage,* ELEPHANT *trumpets loudly.*) This tub is too thick. Water will never heat up in here. (PON *and* SAI *shake heads sadly.*)

NU (*Re-entering, exhausted*): I am so tired. But I will not give up. I must create a perfect tub. (PA *re-enters, wiping sweat from face.*)

PA (*Wearily*): We will try again. (*They exit right.*)

SAI: Husband, I hope this time they succeed. They have worked so hard.

PON (*Nodding*): I was just thinking the same thing. However, if they do make the perfect tub, we will be in very hot water. (*Pull heads inside curtain. Curtain opens.*)

* * *

SETTING: *The same as Scene 2.*

AT RISE: KING *and* SERVANT *are in same positions.* MESSENGER *rushes in left and bows.*

MESSENGER (*Breathlessly*): Most magnificent lord of a thousand elephants, the potters approach with yet another tub.

KING (*Rising, glowering*): I am sick of bad bathtubs. If this one is no good, I will have these potters thrown into the river. (MESSENGER *dashes off right.* NU *and* PA *stagger on left, pushing third tub, which they set at center.* MESSENGER *re-enters, leading* GRAY ELEPHANT, *who walks around tub, trumpets loudly, then pantomimes climbing inside.* NU, PA, MESSENGER, *and* SERVANT *hide eyes, waiting fearfully for results.* ELEPHANT *trumpets approval, waving head up and down. All cheer.*) Ho, ho! This tub is just right. It is magnificent. Messenger, find the washers. Potters, fill the tub with water. Servant, build a fire to heat the water. (MESSENGER *exits left, running.* NU *and* PA *run off right and re-enter in a moment, pantomiming carrying heavy buckets of water and pouring them into tub.* SERVANT *starts to exit left, stops, waves umbrella, pointing to it, and* ELEPHANT *reaches out with trunk and takes umbrella, holding it over* KING's *head.* SERVANT *pantomimes bringing wood from off left and stacking it at base of tub. They continue to pantomime these actions, using speeded-up movements and ad libbing sounds such as "s-slurp" for pouring water and "f-ft, crackle, snap" for fire. Finally* SERVANT *pantomimes touching a torch to wood, and then retrieves umbrella from* ELEPHANT *and holds it over* KING, *who crosses to sit majestically on throne.* MESSENGER *re-enters, and* NU *and* PA *collapse with exhaustion at left of tub.*)

MESSENGER (*Bowing*): Most magnificent lord of—

KING (*Interrupting, impatiently*): All right, all right. Get on with it.

MESSENGER: The washers are here. (PON *and* SAI *enter nervously,* PON *with scrub brush and* SAI *with soap. They bow and begin vigorously scrubbing* ELEPHANT, *who enjoys the bath.*)

NU (*Observing* PON *and* SAI): Pa Song, we have at last created a fine pottery tub. (PA *nods.*) I thought this would be the happiest day of my life. But now I find myself wishing I had not played such a dirty trick on Pon Khin and Sai.

PA: I was just thinking the same thing.

NU: They are good people, these washers. They were right about how lazy we once were. See how hard they are trying to scrub the elephant white.

PA: What will happen to them? They cannot possibly succeed.

NU: If only a miracle would produce a white elephant, we could be happy together. (*Sound of elephant trumpeting off left is heard. All freeze with surprise.*)

KING (*Rising*): Messenger, see what is happening out there. (MESSENGER *bows and exits left, re-entering with scroll and leading* WHITE ELEPHANT.)

ALL (*Awed*): A white elephant!

KING: Great *acheik**! How did this rare white elephant come here?

MESSENGER: It is a gift from the King of Siam.

ALL (*Together*): The King of Siam?

MESSENGER: And he sent this message to you, Your Highness. (*Reading from scroll*) "I, the King of Siam, have two white elephants, while the King of Burma has none. To show the deep friendship between our two countries, I give the King of Burma one of my white elephants. May we always live side by side, on equal terms, in peace and harmony."

---

* *Acheik* means "dog's tooth."

KING (*Thoughtfully*): The King of Siam is most generous, and I am ashamed of my greedy thoughts. (*Rises*) Potters, you will be well rewarded for your fine tub. Washers, there is no need to scrub further. You will be well rewarded for your time. Since you wash so well, return to the palace each week to keep this beautiful elephant white. And now, you may all go home. Messenger, proclaim this great news throughout the land: King Binnya Dala does not need, nor does he want, any more white elephants. (*All cheer,* ELEPHANTS *trumpet, and curtain closes.*)

THE END

FIRE DEMON AND SOUTH WIND

FIRE DEMON AND SOUTH WIND

In contrast to Korea's rugged terrain and its history of domination by harsh invaders, Korean folklore is gentle in tone and beautiful in the pictures it evokes. The characters are patient and seldom cruel, poking good-natured fun at braggarts, at the pompous, and at self-styled intellectuals. In this play, Fire Demon, South Wind, and Deadly Dragon create problems, but they are amusing and fun to observe. Even the scary Stone Monster is more humorous than horrible.

Fire Demon and South Wind

A Korean tale

Characters

SOUTH WIND
FIRE DEMON
KING CHUNG-HU
PRINCESS SOON, *his daughter*
THREE VILLAGERS
OTHER VILLAGERS, *extras*
WISE WON ⎱ *King's*
MIGHTY MAGICIAN ⎰ *advisors*
MASTER WELL-DIGGER
DRAGON-TAMER
DEADLY DRAGON
STONE MONSTER

SCENE 1

TIME: *Long ago.*

SETTING: *Korean countryside. There is a rice paddy at center. Up right is a cardboard cut-out of mountains and a tall volcano. Behind volcano there is a stepladder for Fire Demon. Up left is a cardboard cut-out of the Silver Palace of King Chung-Hu.*

AT RISE: FIRE DEMON *is sitting on stepladder, asleep, with his head resting on top of the volcano.* SOUTH WIND *and* STONE MONSTER *are behind mountains, out of sight.* KING CHUNG-HU *and* PRINCESS SOON *are behind Silver*

197

Palace, out of sight. All VILLAGERS *stand at center, in rice paddy, pantomiming planting rice.*

VILLAGERS (*Chanting in unison*):
Between tall peaks (*Pointing to mountains*) and Silver
    Palace (*Pointing to Palace*)
Paddies of rice are growing, growing.
Near volcano, south of Seoul,
Stand monster stones.
(*They continue to pantomime planting rice. Suddenly* SOUTH WIND *bounds into view from behind mountains, blowing and howling.* VILLAGERS *cringe.*)
SOUTH WIND: Blo-o-o-ow! Blo-o-o-ow! Play tricks and games! (*Howls*)
1ST VILLAGER (*Calling*): Bad wind from South is here.
2ND VILLAGER (*Calling*): No use working in rice paddy.
3RD VILLAGER (*Calling*): Let us return to village. (*They cross right, moving in unison, pantomiming walking against a heavy wind. Each holds right arm in front of face. They exit down right.*)
FIRE DEMON (*Waking up*): Gr-r-rumble! Gr-r-rumble! Who is making all that noise? Who dares to wake up hungry Fire Demon?
WIND: It is I, South Wind.
FIRE DEMON: Gr-rowl! Gr-rump!
WIND: Stop growling and grumping and come out to play.
FIRE DEMON: *Me* play? I have not left this volcano for centuries.
WIND: Then it is about time you did.
FIRE DEMON (*Laughing*): I might if you had anything good to eat. Gr-r-rumble! Gr-r-rumble! My food supply is so low my stomach is growling.
WIND: I know where you can find something delicious to eat.
FIRE DEMON: Where?

WIND: Over there. (*Pointing*) The Silver Palace of King Chung-Hu.

FIRE DEMON (*Licking lips*): M-m-m! Gr-r-ruff! That does look good. (*He climbs down ladder and re-enters from behind mountains. He sneaks to Palace with* WIND *following, dancing about.* FIRE DEMON *pretends to "eat" Palace by "setting it on fire," as* WIND *puffs on walls.*) Cr-r-rackle, cr-r-rickle, lick, lap. Oo-o-o-o! Ah-h-h-h! (*Palace falls over backward.* KING CHUNG-HU *and* PRINCESS SOON *run out from behind palace, wailing, and cross center.*)

KING CHUNG-HU *and* PRINCESS SOON (*Wailing*): *Ai-goo! Ai-goo!* Alas! Alas!

KING (*Shouting*): Silver Palace is burning!

PRINCESS (*Shouting*): Roof is on fire! (FIRE DEMON *and* WIND *kneel and continue to devour Palace.* VILLAGERS *re-enter, running. They stop in horror, pointing to Palace, waving arms and jabbering excitedly.*)

VILLAGERS (*Ad lib*): Silver Palace! Burned to ashes! Gone! Hungry Fire Demon! Bad South Wind! Terrible! (*Etc.*)

FIRE DEMON (*Rising, patting stomach*): That was splendid meal. (*Laughs with* WIND *as they disappear behind mountains*)

KING (*Wringing hands*): Oh, oh, what shall I do? I must have palace to show how rich and powerful I am. Villagers, build new palace at once.

VILLAGERS (*Bowing*): Yes, King Chung-Hu. (*Chanting, they pantomime sawing and hammering to build a new palace. They replace supports and raise cut-out of Palace to standing position. Then they pantomime painting it.* KING *watches with superior air;* PRINCESS *flutters eyes.*)
Build palace out of ashes,
Hammer, hammer, bang, clang, bang.
Raise walls of shining shimmer.
Paint all with sparkling silver.

KING: Aha! New Silver Palace is ready.

PRINCESS: But Father, how will we keep Fire Demon and South Wind away?

KING: That is big problem. (*Scratches head*) I will call council meeting to decide solution. (*Calls right*) Wise Won! Wise Won! (WISE WON *enters right, carrying large scroll.*)

VILLAGERS (*Bowing and murmuring together*): Oh-h-h, many brains.

KING (*Calling left*): Mighty Magician! Mighty Magician! (MIGHTY MAGICIAN *enters left, pulling a scarf from each sleeve and waving scarves in mysterious manner.*)

VILLAGERS (*Bowing and murmuring together*): Oh-h-h, magic maker.

KING: This meeting is for purpose of advice. How do I keep Fire Demon and South Wind from destroying Silver Palace? Wise Won, what do you say? (WISE WON *unrolls long scroll, reads, then thoughtfully rolls it up and unrolls new sections, reading here and there. All watch with fascination.*)

WISE WON: Hm-m-m. Angle X, Y, Z, plus two, four, six, eight, pi R squared to sixth power, nine times nine equals eighty-one minus seven. . . . Now let me see. (*Rolls up scroll and squints at mountain, then Palace, using scroll as telescope*) Yes, yes. (*To* KING) I say we must import Master Well-Digger from Japan.

ALL (*Amazed*): Master Well-Digger from Japan?

WISE WON (*Nodding*): Since Fire Demon and South Wind come from this direction (*Points to mountains*), it is important to dig enormous well here. (*Points to right of Palace*)

PRINCESS (*Gesturing*): Then Fire Demon will fall into well. And everyone knows fire cannot live in water.

WISE WON: Exactly! (*All except* MAGICIAN *murmur approval.*)

KING: Fine solution. Do you agree, Mighty Magician?

MAGICIAN (*Miffed*): Well, that is not my idea, but go right ahead. (*Tucks scarves up sleeves in huff*)

KING (*To* WISE WON): Send for Master Well-Digger from Japan.

WISE WON: Just so happens I already have. Wise Won thinks ahead (*Taps head*), you know. (*Calls right*) Master Well-Digger! (WELL-DIGGER *enters right with shovel over shoulder and bows.*) Dig deepest, largest well in world right here. (*Points.* WELL-DIGGER *bows again. All stand back to watch as he pantomimes digging as fast as possible, huffing and puffing, occasionally wiping brow and heaving sighs. Finally, he finishes, bows, gestures to "well," and exits right, staggering with exhaustion.*)

KING: Now Silver Palace is safe. All go home. (VILLAGERS *exit right.* KING *and* PRINCESS *exit into Palace.* WISE WON *and* MAGICIAN *bow to each other and exit same way they entered. Just before exiting,* MAGICIAN *jeers and sticks out tongue at* WISE WON. *Then* WIND *and* FIRE DEMON *re-enter, crossing toward Palace as before.* WIND *suddenly stops, holding* FIRE DEMON *back with one arm and pointing to "well" with other arm.*)

WIND: Look! Huge well is now in our path.

FIRE DEMON: What? Water! (*To* WIND) One puff from you and I might fall in and drown. (*Turns back toward mountains*) Gr-rump! Now I will have to chew hard old hunk of lava instead of delicious Silver Palace.

WIND: Wait! We can travel East and blow into Palace that way. I will hold my breath until we get past well. (*Sucks in breath as they tiptoe down to left of Palace. Then* WIND *lets out breath and begins puffing at Palace walls, while* FIRE DEMON *gives wild yell and leaps at Palace, eating and setting fire to it as before.*)

FIRE DEMON: Cr-rackle, cr-rickle, l-lick, l-lap. Oo-oo, ah-h-h!

(*Palace falls over and* KING *and* PRINCESS *run up center, shrieking.*)

KING *and* PRINCESS: *Ai-goo! Ai-goo!*

KING (*Shouting*): Silver Palace is burning!

PRINCESS (*Shouting*): Roof is on fire! (VILLAGERS *re-enter, running.*)

VILLAGERS (*Ad lib*): Silver Palace! Burned to ashes! Gone! Hungry Fire Demon! Bad South Wind! Terrible! (*Etc.*)

FIRE DEMON (*Rising, patting stomach*): This meal even better than last. (*Laughs with* WIND *as they disappear behind mountains*)

KING (*Wringing hands*): Oh, oh, I must have beautiful Palace again. Villagers, build new Palace at once.

VILLAGERS (*Bowing*): Yes, King Chung-Hu. (*Chant and pantomime as before*)

Build basement out of ashes.
Hammer, hammer, bang, clang, bang.
Raise walls of shining shimmer.
Paint all with sparkling silver.

PRINCESS: Father, Silver Palace has been eaten *twice*. (*Holds up two fingers*) Hungry Fire Demon and South Wind surely will return to eat *thrice*. (*Holds up three fingers*)

KING (*Nodding*): I will call council again. (*Calls right*) Wise Won! (WISE WON *re-enters, with scroll, and stops to stare in dismay as he sees* VILLAGERS *rebuilding Silver Palace.* KING *calls left.*) Mighty Magician! (MAGICIAN *re-enters as before, also stopping in surprise, then chuckling aside.*) Master Well-Digger from Japan dug well, but Silver Palace still eaten up. What is your idea, Mighty Magician?

MAGICIAN (*With dramatic gestures*): I say, rent Deadly Dragon from China.

ALL (*Amazed*): Deadly Dragon from China?

MAGICIAN (*Nodding*): Complete with Dragon-Tamer.

Have them live in swamp at foot of mountains. (*Gestures*)

PRINCESS (*Indicating*): Dragon will keep Fire Demon inside volcano and South Wind inside mountains.

MAGICIAN: Exactly! (*All except* WISE WON *murmur approval.*)

KING: Fine solution. Do you agree, Wise Won?

WISE WON (*Miffed*): No! Only reason my idea did not work was slight miscalculation. (*Sighting through scroll at mountains*) Maybe should have pi R tripled to tenth power with angle A, B, C, plus eight times eight equals sixty-four and. . . . (*Voice trails off as all shake heads in disbelief. He shrugs and peeks into scroll as* KING *speaks.*)

KING: Mighty Magician, send for Deadly Dragon and Dragon-Tamer.

MAGICIAN (*Raising arms dramatically*): Sh-h-h! Must have absolute quiet. (*All freeze as* MAGICIAN *closes eyes.*) I shall communicate with ancient ancestors. China, China, calling spirits in China. Please locate Deadly Dragon and Dragon-Tamer. (*Waves scarves in magical motions, then chants magic words*) Kim-chi, chu-chon-ja. Ko-map-sum-ni-da.* (*Opens eyes and lowers arms. Sound of drumbeat is heard from off left.* DRAGON-TAMER *enters, carrying whip, leading* DRAGON *on leash, both walking in time to drumbeat. Others watch fearfully, heads and eyes moving in unison, as* TAMER *leads* DRAGON *to mountains. Then* TAMER *cracks whip and points to ground. Drumbeat ceases.* DRAGON *snarls and hisses, clawing at whip, finally gives a big hiss and meekly sits.* TAMER *bows as others clap and murmur approval.*)

DRAGON-TAMER: I promise to keep Dragon here in swamp.

---

* These "magic words" are actual Korean words and phrases: *kim-chi* is a favorite Korean food made of highly spiced vegetables, mostly cabbage; *chu-chon-ja* means kettle; and *ko-map-sum-ni-da* means thank you.

However, Villagers must furnish turnips, rice, and plenty of hot tea. (VILLAGERS *look at each other in terror.*) Hurry! Bring food for Deadly Dragon. (1ST VILLAGER *pantomimes carrying bowl of food to* DRAGON *and placing it near him.* DRAGON *hisses at* 1ST VILLAGER, *who runs off right.* 2ND VILLAGER *repeats business and exits.* 3RD VILLAGER, *who is last, pantomimes carrying large teapot and cup to* DRAGON, *then pouring tea for him.* DRAGON *gulps tea and holds out cup, demanding more. They repeat action until nervous* 3RD VILLAGER *starts to pour tea, stops, lifts lid of imaginary teapot, peers in, and, realizing tea is gone, bows to* DRAGON, *backing away, then drops teapot and races for right exit.* DRAGON *laughs in hissing manner until* TAMER *cracks whip for silence.*) Enough tea for now. Eat turnips and rice. (DRAGON *pantomimes gobbling food, bowls and all.* WIND *puts head around edge of mountains, puffing;* FIRE DEMON *puts head over top of volcano, growling.* TAMER *sees them, taps* DRAGON *and points to them.* DRAGON *roars furiously.* FIRE DEMON *and* WIND *disappear. All cheer, onstage and offstage.*)

KING (*Happily*): Good show! Fine act! Now Palace is safe. Council dismissed. (*Exits into Palace, followed by* PRINCESS. WISE WON *and* MAGICIAN *bow to each other, then start to exit. Just before exiting,* WISE WON *jeers and sticks out tongue at* MAGICIAN. TAMER *and* DRAGON *yawn, stretch, and sit,* TAMER *leaning against* DRAGON. *They fall asleep, snoring loudly,* DRAGON *hissing at end of each snore.* WIND *and* FIRE DEMON *re-enter, crossing down left of Palace. They repeat eating and blowing on Palace as before. Palace falls over.* KING *and* PRINCESS *run shrieking to center.*)

KING *and* PRINCESS: *Ai-goo! Ai-goo!* (DRAGON *and* TAMER *wake in surprise.* VILLAGERS *rush on, ad libbing as before.* FIRE DEMON *and* WIND *laugh and disappear behind mountains.*)

KING (*Jumping up and down, yelling*): Wise Won! Mighty Magician! Wise Won! Mighty Magician! (WISE WON *and* MIGHTY MAGICIAN *re-enter, stopping in surprise at sight of Palace.* MAGICIAN *holds hand over mouth in dismay;* WISE WON *chuckles aside.* KING *glowers at them.*) Council members have bad ideas. Dragon-Tamer and Deadly Dragon fell asleep. They are bad, too. You are all fired! (DRAGON *angrily leaps up, thrashing, hissing, and clawing air.* TAMER *frantically tries to hold onto leash. Others scream and back away.* KING *bellows to* MAGICIAN.) Send Dragon home to China. Quickly, before he causes flood with so much steam.

MAGICIAN (*Shouting*): Calling China. Calling China. Please come in, China. Take Dragon and Tamer home. (*Closes eyes, waves scarves, and chants as before*) Kimchi, chu-chon-ja! Ko-map-sum-ni-da! (*Drumbeat starts. He opens eyes and lowers arms, relieved. At drum sound,* DRAGON *is immediately quiet.* TAMER *leads* DRAGON *off left, walking in manner in which they entered. During exit,* VILLAGERS *pantomime rebuilding Palace to rhythm of drum.*)

KING (*Sadly*): Ai-goo! Three times Silver Palace was destroyed. I give up. Maybe I will hide in well (*Points to well*) or sit in swamp. I am sick of all this.

PRINCESS: Excuse me, Father. I have suggestion. Ask Villagers how to keep Silver Palace in one piece.

KING (*Startled*): But I am rich, powerful King. Villagers work for me. It is embarrassing to ask them.

PRINCESS: Father, has it not been said (*Posing with finger under chin*), "He who builds house knows best how to keep it up"?

KING (*Thoughtfully*): Ah-h-h! That is very smart saying. Since villagers built my Palace, perhaps they know what to do. (*Crossing to* VILLAGERS) Excuse me, but do you know how to keep Silver Palace safe? (VILLAGERS *huddle, whispering with heads bobbing up and arms waving at different times. Finally,* VILLAGERS *turn and bow to* KING.)

1ST VILLAGER: Solution is to go to mountains (*Points*) and cut giant granite stone. This stone is very strong.

2ND VILLAGER: It should be carved into fierce monster, one-third alligator, one-third water tortoise, and one-third salamander. Then stone will be frightful to see.

3RD VILLAGER: We whisper into stone monster's ear. (*Others lean forward to hear as* VILLAGERS *whisper loudly.*)

THREE VILLAGERS (*Together*): "You are here for *one* (*Hold up index fingers in unison*) purpose—to guard Silver Palace."

KING: What are we waiting for? This time, I will help, too.

PRINCESS: Father has big change of heart. (*All run behind mountains. Sounds of pounding, clanging, chipping, clanking. All re-enter, bowing, moving backwards to down left. Crash of cymbals is heard.* MONSTER *enters, walking like Frankenstein. He crosses to front of Palace.* WIND *and* FIRE DEMON *re-enter and head for Palace. All but* MONSTER *hide eyes to await outcome. Just as* WIND *and* FIRE DEMON *reach Palace and prepare to leap at it,* MONSTER *raises arms, spreads legs, and roars loudly. Cymbals crash; lights blink.*)

FIRE DEMON (*Exclaiming*): Gr-r-reat cinder cones! I cannot eat this stone. It is too hard.

WIND (*Blowing hard*): This hideous creature is too heavy for me to move. (*Exclaiming*) May the monsoons protect me! I had better blow away to Siam. (WIND *exits right, howling.* MONSTER *roars at* FIRE DEMON, *who quickly exits behind mountains.* FIRE DEMON *reappears on top of volcano.*)

FIRE DEMON (*Sadly*): Oh, well. (*Yawns*) Three good meals each century is all that any Fire Demon can expect. (*Falls asleep. Others look at Palace.*)

KING *and* PRINCESS (*Together*): Stone Monster saved Silver
Palace. Hurrah!

WISE WON *and* MAGICIAN (*To each other*): Villagers are
pretty smart. (*All cheer and dance around* MONSTER.)

ALL (*Chanting*):
Between tall peaks and Silver Palace
Paddies of rice are growing, growing,
Near volcano, south of Seoul,
Stand monster stones.

(*Curtain closes as dance ends.*)

THE END

AH WING FU AND THE GOLDEN DRAGON

AH WING FU AND THE GOLDEN DRAGON

The dragon is a mythical creature found in the folklore of most cultures, and though the physical characteristics of dragons vary, depending upon the country or area, basically they are all related to the snake or crocodile, with scales and the head of a lion, eagle, or hawk. In Chinese folklore, though the dragon is capable of causing widespread destruction if not treated with proper respect, it is basically a good creature—contrary to the Western view of dragons as fearful monsters which must be destroyed or slain by a great hero.

"Ah Wing Fu and the Golden Dragon" is in the Chinese tradition, to be performed with the conventions of the Chinese theater—a combination of songs, dances, pantomimes, acrobatics, and stylized acting. Properties are often pantomimed; chairs and tables represent whatever is necessary to set the scene—a building, mountain, etc. The elaborate, colorful costumes and fantastic makeup used provide sharp contrasts to the simple staging. Colors and patterns are symbolic: red for honesty and loyalty; green for devils; yellow for strength and cleverness; blue for ferocity; white for strength or evil. Leading female characters wear white powder base, with exaggerated black eye lines, rouge on cheeks, and bright lipstick.

To give an authentic feeling to the production of this play, actors should think of it as a dance which tells a story, using movements which suggest the characters: dainty and flowing for Chin Li; abrupt and stern for Chu Yu, the tiger; and so forth. Voice tones should indicate the characters and emotions.

The following stylized gestures and actions from Chinese theater may be used: *Weeping*—bend head slightly and raise arm to wipe away tears. *Despair*—turn palms outward, thumbs pointing down. *Anger, dismay*—stagger back, flinging arms forward. *Happiness*—raise hands chest high, palms down, then turn hands up and thrust arms forward. *Thinking*—hold up index finger near temple. *Rowing*—arms in air, imitate motion of oars. *Speaking aside*—raise hand to cheek and turn to side.

Ah Wing Fu and the Golden Dragon

A folktale in Chinese theater style

Characters

POET
AH WING FU
CHIN LI, *his wife*
SO SAN, *their daughter*
GRANDFATHER
CHU YU, *the tiger*
HEAD OF DRAGON ⎫
MIDDLE OF DRAGON ⎬ *Golden Dragon*
TIP-OF-TAIL ⎭
PROPERTY MAN
MUSICIANS, *4 or more*

TIME: *Long ago in spring.*

SETTING: *Ancient China. Large "tapestry" (sheet painted with scene of Chinese garden in spring) is up center. No front curtain is used.*

AT RISE: *As lights go up, stage is empty. Sound of gong is heard.* POET *enters right, followed by* MUSICIANS, *carrying instruments, who sit on floor down right facing stage.*

POET (*To audience*): I am poet of small village in province of Hunan, China, which is where our play takes place. (PROPERTY MAN *enters right with chair labeled* WELL, *and places it at center.*) If you please, pretend this person (*Indicates* PROPERTY MAN) is invisible. It is his

211

honorable duty to change our scenes and give you hints about conditions of weather. (PROPERTY MAN *exits. MUSICIANS play large drum, clappers and cymbals, as three actors playing the part of Golden Dragon enter left, curving back and forth, doing dance. HEAD OF DRAGON and MIDDLE OF DRAGON pantomime diving into "well." TIP-OF-TAIL, who has been observing sky, is roared at by HEAD and MIDDLE. He quickly "dives" after others.*) That was Golden Dragon, who lives in bottom of village well. We are most grateful to him, for he flies into clouds (*Gestures*) and brings down rain. (*Pantomimes rain falling*) And when our good earth is watered, Golden Dragon blows away clouds and comes home, living quietly in bottom of village well. (*MUSICIANS play peaceful flute music as POET crosses to center.*) As our play begins, it is first full moon of spring. I have written poem on silk (*Unrolls imaginary scroll*) about flowering plums and sweet-smelling jasmine. It is small gift for great Golden Dragon. (*Pantomimes rolling up scroll and dropping it into well*)

HEAD OF DRAGON (*In deep booming voice, from behind well*): Thank you, kind poet. (*POET bows, backing up right, where he strikes a pose. CHIN LI and SO SAN enter left, dancing with small steps. CHIN LI waves her fan. They move around well singing "ah-h-h" as MUSICIANS play bell accompaniment. After dance, CHIN LI and SO SAN cross down center to speak to audience.*)

CHIN LI (*In musical voice*): My name is Chin Li, and this is my little daughter, So San. (*SO SAN flashes big smile.*) We have come to village well to honor Golden Dragon. I bring lotus blossom from quiet pond (*Holding up imaginary flower*) as gift for good dragon.

SO SAN: And I give pretty poppy, as orange as sun. (*Pantomimes taking flower from hair and holding it up. As MUSICIANS play bells, CHIN LI goes to right of well, and*

So San *goes to left. They pantomime dropping in flowers.*)

HEAD OF DRAGON: Thank you, Chin Li. Thank you, So San. (CHIN LI *and* So SAN *bow, backing away upstage, and striking poses. As* MUSICIANS *softly play gong,* GRANDFATHER *enters left, slowly, with cane, and crosses down center to speak to audience.*)

GRANDFATHER (*In "old" voice*): I am ancient Grandfather, wise in head from much study and many years of living. I bring humble gift to Golden Dragon. It is small painting of fox barking at moon. (*Unrolls imaginary scroll for audience to see, then rolls it up. He crosses to left of well.*) Here, Golden Dragon. May it please you *well*. (*Points to well, chuckling at his play on words, then drops in scroll*)

HEAD OF DRAGON: Thank you, Grandfather. (GRAND-FATHER *bows, backing upstage, and strikes pose.* MUSI-CIANS *play stringed instrument and clappers as* AH WING FU *enters left, leaping about in fast dance. He stops down center, feet apart, hands on hips, to speak to audience.*)

AH WING FU: I am Ah Wing Fu. (*Pointing to each as he mentions their names*) Chin Li is my wife, So San is my daughter, Poet is my friend, and *there* is old Grandfather. All are nice people, but (*Crosses left, folding arms*)—I am tired of this village.

OTHERS (*Sadly*): Ah-h-h.

AH WING: I am sick of working in rice fields.

OTHERS (*Sadly*): Oh-h-h.

AH WING: Furthermore, I am handsome, charming and brave, and I wish to see whole world.

OTHERS (*Stunned*): E-e-e-e.

CHIN LI (*Crossing tearfully to him*): Husband, your daughter and I work beside you. We never complain. Do you not care for us?

AH WING: Of course, but I am bored. Life here is very dull.

GRANDFATHER (*Crossing down to him*): Shame on you, Ah Wing Fu!

AH WING (*Not listening; leaping about*): I want to be brilliant as butterfly. I want to see other side of mountains. I want to visit lovely gardens. I want to do nothing but enjoy many beauties of world.

GRANDFATHER: It is wise to be still about your wants. It is wiser still to sing *well* (*Indicates well*) of what you have.

AH WING: Honorable Grandfather, I cannot help singing *well* for what I have not.

GRANDFATHER: Grandson should learn old Chinese lesson: Better to be satisfied here (*Points to ground*) with little, than there (*Points to sky*) with nothing. Give gift to Golden Dragon and be content.

AH WING (*Turning away*): Old Dragon is not important at all. (*Others fall back with gasps of horror.* AH WING *pantomimes pulling imaginary scroll from belt and unrolling it.*) Here is message for Golden Dragon.

CHIN LI: What does husband's message say?

AH WING (*Strutting to right of well and reading loudly*): "Dumb Golden Dragon not as wise as butterfly. So pooh to you, from Ah Wing Fu." (*Pantomimes rolling up scroll and tossing it into well, then folds arms defiantly.* GRANDFATHER *drops cane in astonishment, then grunts as he tries to pick it up.* POET *rushes to assist him.* CHIN LI *gives little cry, waves fan in air, and takes pose of sorrow.* SO SAN *runs to* CHIN LI, *hiding face in sleeve.* AH WING *shrugs at commotion.*)

SO SAN (*Looking up at audience*): O sad day in spring! (*HEAD OF DRAGON growls from well, voice swelling into loud roar, until Dragon bursts from behind well, snorting wildly, clawing air.* TIP-OF-TAIL *gets stuck in well*

and has to be yanked out by HEAD OF DRAGON. GRAND-
FATHER *strokes beard and looks at Dragon with interest,
but others shrink away.*)

HEAD OF DRAGON (*Loudly*): I am angry, Ah Wing Fu.
(*Points claw at him; commanding*) *Be* a butterfly, and
pooh to *you.* (AH WING *pantomimes flapping wings,
happier each moment, while Dragon watches, seething.*)

AH WING (*Happily*): I have grown butterfly wings! Oh,
what beautiful flowers out there. (*Gestures at audience*)
Ah, what fragrant smells they must have. Ho, I shall
visit all gardens in world. Goodbye, family. Goodbye,
Golden Dragon. Whee! (*He circles stage, flying, pursued
by* SO SAN, *hands out, trying to catch him,* CHIN LI,
fanning herself in distress, and GRANDFATHER, *hobbling
and waving cane at him.* POET *watches in astonishment.*)

CHIN LI, SO SAN *and* GRANDFATHER (*Calling*): Come back,
butterfly. Come back. (AH WING *exits right, followed by*
CHIN LI, SO SAN *and* GRANDFATHER. POET *crosses right
and peers after them.*)

HEAD OF DRAGON (*To audience; furiously*): I am horribly
upset. Ah Wing Fu rubbed dragon scales wrong way. I
am so fired up, only drinking giant flood will cool me
down. (*Dragon circles stage, coiling, roaring, and clawing air.* POET *fearfully runs down left to escape him.
Just before Dragon exits right,* TIP-OF-TAIL *falls down.*
HEAD OF DRAGON *snarls in rage at* TAIL *who then
scrambles up. Dragon exits right.* PROPERTY MAN *re-
enters left with table labeled* MOUNTAIN *which he places
center. He puts chair on top of table, removing* WELL
sign, then exits. Sound of gong is heard.)

POET (*To audience*): Off flew Golden Dragon, raging
through sky, grabbing clouds, thrashing tail, till mighty
typhoon shook all of China. (PROPERTY MAN *re-enters,
running, holding "Wind" banner, followed by roaring
Dragon.* MUSICIANS *create sound effects.* PROPERTY MAN

and Dragon exit left.) Giant winds threw Ah Wing Fu high into air (AH WING *re-enters right, leaping wildly.*), blowing this way (AH WING *leaps*), that way (*Leaps*), and every way (*Leaps*).

AH WING: Hel-l-lp! Where are garden flowers? Sweet smells have blown away. And I am too weak and fragile to fly against such frightful winds. (*Grabs table leg and holds on with effort*)

POET: Then Golden Dragon opened up gates of water in sky. Down rushed rain—down, down—flooding land. (PROPERTY MAN *re-enters, running, holding "Water" banner, followed by hissing Dragon.* MUSICIANS *create sound effects.* PROPERTY MAN *and Dragon exit right.*) Ah Wing Fu crawled up sacred mountain of Heng Shan to escape great flood. (AH WING *climbs up end of table and onto chair.*)

AH WING: Where is shelter on Heng Shan Mountain? Each leaf I hide beneath is swept away. Help, help!

POET: At last droopy butterfly found cave. But, wait! Deep, dark cave is home of frightful *tiger.* (POET *exits right.* MUSICIANS *play sandblocks and little drum as* CHU YU, *the tiger, enters left, leaps on table, and snarls ferociously.*)

CHU YU (*Speaking in snarling manner*): Gr-r-r. I am Chu Yu, fierce tiger of Heng Shan Mountain. Right now I have problem of ter-r-rible hunger. (*Looking below*) Flood water carried my food away. So, I will eat anything I can find. Gr-r-r.

AH WING (*Removing cap and wringing it out*): Shelter of cave will protect me from angry storm. (*Sees* CHU YU) Oh, no! Tiger is in cave. What to do? Outside I will drown—inside I will be eaten. Perhaps if I am very still, tiger will not notice me. (*He huddles as if hiding in corner, and watches* CHU YU *with fear.* GRANDFATHER, CHIN LI, *and* SO SAN *re-enter right, close together, mov-*

*ing across stage with small steps, pantomiming riding in
boat on choppy water.* GRANDFATHER *is rowing with
cane to which his straw hat has been tied.* CHIN LI *is in
pose of sorrow, holding umbrella over them, and* SO SAN
*bends as if holding sides of boat. All three are bare-
headed.* CHU YU *sees them.*)

CHU YU (*Excitedly*): Gr-r-reat, gr-r-reen bamboo! Here
comes my dinner in that boat. (*Points to them*) Mm-m,
old one may be tough to eat, but other two look delicious. Gr-r-r. (CHU YU *prepares to spring on them when
they come by.* AH WING *suddenly sees* CHIN LI, SO SAN,
and GRANDFATHER.)

AH WING (*Realizing with horror what* CHU YU *plans to
do*): Alas! Family approaches in small boat. Fierce
tiger is ready to spring on them. What can butterfly do?
Awful situation is my fault. If I had not insulted Dragon,
Dragon would not have caused flood, I would not
be weak butterfly, and tiger would not be planning to
eat my family. (HEAD OF DRAGON *appears right, one claw
held up to ear, listening to* AH WING.) Oh, why was I
so disrespectful? If only I had second chance. (*Dragon
enters quietly, unseen by others, and sneaks upstage of
mountain.*) I must do something to save my family.
Only one thing I can do—sacrifice myself. (*Jumps off
chair onto right side of table, fluttering wings at* CHU
YU.) Tiger, tiger! Eat me instead.

CHU YU (*Sitting up to inspect* AH WING): You? Eat *you*
instead? (*Laughs uproariously*) You are so tiny, you
wouldn't even be a mouthful.

AH WING: I may be tiny, but I am delicious delicacy.

CHU YU: Mm-m. I did not know that.

AH WING: Have you not heard that our highly exalted
and illustrious Emperor has butterfly wings for breakfast? (*Meanwhile,* GRANDFATHER, CHIN LI *and* SO SAN
move past mountain and toward left exit.)

CHU YU (*To* AH WING): My, my, how interesting! Butterfly wings for breakfast. . . .

AH WING: Indeed, truly excellent gourmet dish. (GRANDFATHER, CHIN LI *and* SO SAN *exit left.*)

CHU YU: Then I shall be most happy to chew you up. But first I will eat people in boat. (*Looks down*) Where are people? Gr-r-r. I wasted time talking to butterfly and lost big dinner. (*Crosses left on mountain, peering off left into distance.* AH WING *flutters right on mountain.*) Gr-r-reat, gr-r-reen pussywillows! Now I only have butterfly to eat. (*He prepares to spring on* AH WING, *who kneels and covers eyes with wings, waiting in resignation. Dragon suddenly pokes head up from behind mountain, roaring at* CHU YU, *who freezes in astonishment.* AH WING *looks up in surprise.*)

HEAD OF DRAGON: Fear not, Ah Wing Fu. Chu Yu will not chew you. (*To* CHU YU) Ho, ho, fierce tiger of Heng Shan Mountain, do you wish to fight powerful Golden Dragon of China? (*Starts crawling onto mountain.* CHU YU *backs away to edge, fearfully, looking down and then at Dragon.*)

CHU YU: Terrible decision to make. Shall I leap into flood and try to swim to other mountain? Or shall I leap at Golden Dragon and maybe suffer humiliating defeat? (*Dragon roars and hisses loudly, frightening* CHU YU.) Oo-oo! Decision is made. I leap into flood at once. (*He jumps off mountain and pantomimes swimming left, puffing and snarling unhappily, and finally exiting.*)

AH WING (*Humbly*): Magnificent Golden Dragon, why did you save small, miserable butterfly? (*Dragon crawls off mountain and crosses left, one claw raised in pose of thinking.*)

HEAD OF DRAGON (*Turning to* AH WING): Partly because butterfly was brave and willing to give self to save family. And partly because I am sick of whole silly typhoon. I am not mean dragon, you know.

AH WING: I *do* know. You have always been good to our village, watering fields with gentle rain.

HEAD OF DRAGON: But in hot anger I caused much damage. Then I drank too much water. And now I have worst stomachache in three thousand years. (MIDDLE OF DRAGON *hiccups to* HEAD OF DRAGON's *surprise.* TIP-OF-TAIL *sighs and falls asleep.*)

AH WING: My humble apology for being cause of damage and indigestion. It will not happen again. (*Bowing*) You are most honorable dragon in all China.

HEAD OF DRAGON: Well, that is more like it. (*He crosses right.* MIDDLE OF DRAGON *wakes* TIP-OF-TAIL *with a poke, and they follow.*) Flood is over. (*Waves claws in sweeping gestures*) Water, return to sky. Golden Dragon goes home to village well. (*Turns and points to* AH WING) And *you* are no longer dumb butterfly. (AH WING *puts on hat, jumps off mountain, and bows low to Dragon.*)

AH WING: My eternal gratitude. (HEAD *nods approval, then starts to exit right.* TIP-OF-TAIL *has to be awakened again. Dragon exits.* AH WING *holds bowing position while* PROPERTY MAN *removes mountain.* CHIN LI, SO SAN *and* GRANDFATHER *re-enter left, still pantomiming rowing in boat.* GRANDFATHER *pantomimes getting oar stuck in mud.*)

GRANDFATHER (*Struggling*): Water has gone, Chin Li, and we are stuck in mud. (*He suddenly pulls oar out, almost falling over, then removes hat from cane, shakes it, and replaces it on head.*) Better to have mud *on* head than *in* head. (*He pantomimes wiping mud from face and shaking it off hand.* CHIN LI *lowers umbrella and replaces headdress.* SO SAN *replaces flowers in hair.*)

CHIN LI (*Seeing* AH WING): Look, there is my husband. (AH WING *looks up, then joyfully hurries to help* GRANDFATHER, *then* CHIN LI, *as they pantomime getting out of boat.*)

AH WING: I am thankful to see my family safe.

CHIN LI: It is good to have you home, Ah Wing Fu.

AH WING: It is good to be home, Chin Li. I have learned many lessons since I flew away.

GRANDFATHER (*Aside*): It's about time he learned something.

AH WING: One important lesson was this: Butterflies find distant gardens beautiful, but a wise man finds as much beauty at home. (*Gestures to* CHIN LI *and* SO SAN)

SO SAN (*Jumping out of boat with big smile*): Oh, happy day in spring. (*All exit, dancing happily, accompanied by* MUSICIANS, *as* POET *re-enters right, watching them with approval.*)

POET (*To audience*): Within dark hills, ancient ones say, dragon-backs may be seen today. And dragons are known to hide under waterfalls, in rushing streams, and deep in mountain lakes. But Golden Dragon lives in bottom of well in some small village of Hunan Province. If you find that well and stare into it long enough, you might see Dragon's eyes. (*Raises arms*) I hope you have good fortune to meet most honorable Golden Dragon. (*Sound of gong is heard.* POET *bows and exits left, followed by* MUSICIANS. *Lights dim.*)

THE END

JAPANESE TRIO

JAPANESE TRIO

Kyogen (meaning "mad words" in Japanese) is the name given to the short, funny plays presented between the classical dance dramas called No. There are usually two Kyogen to five No dramas on a program, and these comic interludes relieve the emotional tension in the plays that compose a No sequence.

The informal, often improvisational style of Kyogen is in sharp contrast to the serious, literary nature and rigid conventions of No drama. Like folktales, Kyogen had been passed down orally for several hundred years before appearing in written form. The actors usually perform in ordinary dress rather than the rich costumes and masks used in No plays.

Using farce and satire, Kyogen plays mock traditions, superstitions, and pretensions of feudal lords or public officials, and ridicule the rich and pompous, the impudent or dishonest, the boastful and the stupid. Kyogen has been called Japan's first drama of social protest.

Japanese Trio

Plays in Kyogen style based on Japanese folktales

I. Paying the Eel Broiler

Characters

YOKU, *the eel broiler*
TRAVELER
TARO, *a clever servant*
ANNOUNCER
STAGEHAND

SETTING: *On rear wall there is a painting in Japanese style of a large pine tree. A pillow is down left, for Announcer. There is no front curtain. Actors make entrances from up right, walking in comic, exaggerated heel-to-toe manner.*

AT RISE: *Sound of wooden clappers is heard from offstage. STAGEHAND enters carrying an open box made of bamboo poles lashed together in a rectangular shape, about 3' by 5'. Box represents eel broiler's stand. ANNOUNCER enters and sits on pillow, facing stage; he always speaks in loud, chanting voice.*

ANNOUNCER: Presenting Japanese folk-play number one, called, "Paying the Eel Broiler." (*Sound of gong is heard.*)
    Eels are good to eat,
    But here the broiler charges
    Far too much, we think.

(YOKU *enters, as fast drumbeat is heard from offstage. He carries two skewers with pieces of "eel" on them. He steps inside his stand and, using downstage edge of box as if it were a counter, pantomimes dipping eel into soy sauce and holding it over coals, as if broiling it.*)

YOKU (*Calling*): Broiled eels dipped in finest soy sauce. Fresh broiled eels. The best kabayaki in all Izu. (*To audience*) My name is Yoku. Villagers say my price is too high. Yet I say my eels are so delicious their price should be even higher. Besides, I intend to get rich in this business. (TRAVELER *enters, carrying small flat wooden lunch box containing chopsticks. He mops sweat from face.*) Here comes a hungry-looking traveler. I'll make sure he buys eels from me.

TRAVELER (*To audience*): I am exhausted, for I have walked all the way from Kamakura. First I must find relief from that fiery sun. Then I will eat my small lunch of rice. (*Looking about, then spying shop*) Ah, beside that shop is a shady spot. (*Crosses and sits, then sniffs air*) M-m-m, I have chosen to rest where wonderful cooking smells fill the air. (*Opens box and pantomimes eating rice with chopsticks*)

YOKU: Traveler, why do you sit there eating plain rice? You must buy my broiled eels.

TRAVELER: Indeed they do smell good and would go well with my lunch. How much are they?

YOKU (*Aside*): I'll charge him well. (*To* TRAVELER) Tell me, sir, how much money do you have?

TRAVELER: Two coins. Surely one coin will be enough for those two pieces of eel you are broiling.

YOKU: Hah! Your two coins wouldn't even pay for *one* piece of eel.

TRAVELER: Not even one? You are much too expensive.

YOKU: To get the best eels in Izu, you must pay more.

TRAVELER: That may be, but they are not worth it to me.

I shall sit here and smell your eels, instead, and pretend I am eating them with my rice. (*Eats and sniffs*) M-m-m, how delicious! (YOKU *snorts angrily.* TARO *enters, crossing down.*)

TARO (*To audience*): My name is Taro, clever servant to Sanjo, the feudal lord of the nearby castle. (*Sniffing*) M-m-m, eels broiling. Ho, it's Yoku, the haughty eel broiler who is out to make his fortune by cheating others. I wonder why he looks so angry. (*Crossing to stand*) Excuse me, Yoku. Why does your face look as red as your glowing coals?

YOKU: Because this traveler sits here smelling my food.

TARO: So he does. What is wrong with that?

YOKU: Half the enjoyment of eating is smelling the food. I shall insist he pay me two coins, half the price of a lunch of eels, for the privilege of smelling the food. (*Extends hand for payment*)

TRAVELER (*Scrambling up*): What? Pay for smelling the air? That's ridiculous! Terrible!

TARO (*Interrupting*): Wait, wait, good traveler. What the eel broiler says makes sense. To show you both what a generous fellow I am, I will pay the price. (*Takes two coins from purse and holds them up before* YOKU's *eyes*) Do you see these two coins, Yoku?

YOKU: Yes, yes, I see. Give them to me. (*Grabs at coins, but* TARO *waves them about so* YOKU *is grabbing at the air several times.*) Give me. Give me. (TARO *replaces coins in purse.*)

TARO: Now then, Yoku, you have been paid in full. (*Crosses away*)

YOKU (*Following, angrily*): I haven't been paid at all. You put the coins back into your purse.

TARO: But of course. Did you not want payment for eels that were *smelled*?

YOKU: Yes.

TARO: Then you were paid with money you *saw. Sayonara,* greedy merchant. I doubt if you'll ever get rich. (*Bows and exits while* TRAVELER *laughs and* YOKU *looks stunned.*)

YOKU (*To audience*): *Tasukete!* Help! I've been tricked. Catch him! Catch him! (*Drumbeats are heard, accompanying* YOKU *as he exits, running after* TARO, *followed by* TRAVELER, *trying to stop* YOKU.)

* * * *

II. The Most Fearful Thing

Characters

SANJO, *a feudal lord*
TARO, *his clever servant*
WOLF
THIEF
DEVIL
ANNOUNCER
STAGEHAND

SETTING: *Same as Scene 1.*

AT RISE: STAGEHAND *enters and turns box upright onto short end, places cardboard roof on top, and then exits. Box now represents castle.* ANNOUNCER *still sits on pillow.*

ANNOUNCER: Presenting Japanese folk-play number two, called, "The Most Fearful Thing." (*Sound of gong is heard.*)
When cold sweeps the land,
Even the great feudal lords
Spend their days inside.
(SANJO *enters to sound of slow drumbeat, followed by* TARO. *They sit inside box.*)

SANJO (*To audience*): I am Sanjo, magnificent feudal

lord, living in magnificent castle on magnificent hill.

TARO: And I am Taro, his clever servant. On this cold winter day my master calls me to sit with him. We huddle around this small pit (*Indicating imaginary pit of coals*) where coals glow red and keep us warm. No doubt my lord is bored and wishes to fill time with conversation.

SANJO: Tell me, Taro, of what things are you most afraid?

TARO: Let me think. (*Pauses*) Well, to begin with, master, I am afraid of a wolf.

SANJO: Because a wolf might eat you up?

TARO: Oh, no. Only because a wolf might sneak into your castle and attack you.

SANJO (*Nodding*): Loyally spoken, Taro. (WOLF *enters, downstage, growling, unseen by* SANJO *and* TARO)

WOLF (*To audience, snarling*): I'm a hungry, man-eating (*Pantomimes grabbing a person's leg and chewing on it*), flea-bitten (*Scratches*) wolf. The well-fed lord of this castle would make a juicy meal for me. But before I pounce upon him for my dinner, I must get rid of some of these fleas. (*Sits, hunting for fleas*)

TARO: Furthermore, Lord Sanjo, I am afraid of a thief.

SANJO: Because a thief might steal your food?

TARO: Oh, no. Only because a thief might sneak into your castle and steal your valuable swords.

SANJO (*Nodding*): Loyally spoken, Taro. (THIEF *enters, with sack over shoulder, and sneaks downstage center, unseen.*)

THIEF (*To audience, speaking in nasal voice*): I am a thief with a bad allergy. This castle contains gold, jewels, and old swords worth a fortune. I plan to steal these things, sell them to the merchants in Osaka, and sail away to India to find a cure for my runny nose. (*Sits, opening sack*) Now where did I put my handkerchief? (*Hunts*)

TARO: And also, Lord Sanjo, I am very much afraid of a devil.

SANJO: Because a devil might run away with you?

TARO: Oh, no. Only because a devil might fly into your castle and grab your soul, and maybe your head, too.

SANJO: Loyally spoken, Taro. (DEVIL *enters, laughing evilly, and crosses downstage, unseen.*)

DEVIL (*To audience*): You are looking at the most fiendish devil in Izu. I spend my time flying about snatching parts of people and throwing them so high into the sky they disappear. (*Jumps closer to audience and hisses*) Sometimes I snatch boys and girls, too. (*Laughs evilly and sneaks behind castle.* THIEF *sneaks up to left of castle, and* WOLF *pads up to right of castle. They are preparing to enter when* WOLF *scratches loudly, causing others to freeze.*)

SANJO: What was that noise?

TARO (*Shrugging*): I shall investigate. (*Crawls right, coming eye to eye with* WOLF, *gasps and backs away.*) My lord, a wolf is outside.

SANJO (*Mildly surprised*): A wolf? My, my, how peculiar! (THIEF *sneezes. Again all freeze.*) What was *that* noise?

TARO: I shall investigate. (*Crawls left, coming to legs of* THIEF, *then looks slowly up to* THIEF's *face, gasps, then backs away.*) My lord, a thief is outside.

SANJO (*As before*): A thief? My, my, how peculiar! (DEVIL *bursts into laughter. Again all freeze.*) And what was *that* noise?

TARO: I shall investigate. (*Rises, sees* DEVIL *eagerly wiggling fingers at him, then collapses to knees, shaking fearfully.*) My lord, a devil is here.

SANJO (*As before*): A devil? My, my, how peculiar!

TARO (*Suddenly*): Lord Sanjo, I have an idea to save us both. As I talk loudly now, agree with all I say. Answer yes to all my questions.

SANJO: All right. (*To audience*) I am not worried about

these creatures, because my loyal servant is more clever than they.

TARO (*Loudly*): Lord Sanjo?

SANJO (*Loudly*): Yes, Taro?

TARO: Are you afraid of a wolf?

SANJO: Yes, Taro.

TARO: Are you afraid of a thief?

SANJO: Yes, Taro.

TARO: Are you afraid of a devil?

SANJO: Yes, Taro.

TARO: But are you not *most* afraid (WOLF, THIEF *and* DEVIL *lean forward to listen.*)—most afraid—of a terrible leak? (*Points to roof*)

SANJO: Oh, yes, Taro. Nothing is worse than a terrible leak.

WOLF: A terrible leak? What sort of creature is that?

DEVIL: It could be related to a dragon.

THIEF: Or a giant.

TARO (*Continuing*): Terrible leaks can destroy houses.

SANJO (*Nodding*): True, true.

WOLF (*Scratching head*): It must be a horrible thing. (TARO *suddenly jumps up with hands outstretched, palms up, looking at roof.*)

TARO (*Shouting*): Look out! Here comes the terrible leak. (WOLF, THIEF, *and* DEVIL *freeze in terror.* SANJO *shouts, leaps to feet and holds up robe, looking at roof.* WOLF, THIEF *and* DEVIL *shriek and fall over each other trying to exit.*)

WOLF, THIEF *and* DEVIL (*Ad lib*): The terrible leak! It's after us! (*Etc. They exit.*)

SANJO (*Yelling, excitedly*): Where? Where? (TARO *peers out of castle, then nods as he sees that* WOLF, THIEF *and* DEVIL *are gone. He turns and notes with surprise that* SANJO *is still holding up robe and looking up in alarm.*) Where is the leak?

TARO: The leak, my lord? There is no leak.

SANJO: No leak?

TARO: I merely said that to frighten away the wolf, the thief, and the devil.

SANJO (*Relieved*): Oh, I am so glad there is no leak.

TARO (*Crossing downstage; to audience*): Hm-m-m. I was most afraid of those three creatures, but it appears my master was most afraid of getting his robes wet. (SANJO *and* TARO *exit quickly to sound of drum.*)

*   *   *   *   *

III.   Why We Cannot Lend

Characters

SANJO, *a feudal lord*
TARO, *his clever servant*
BUSO, *his stupid servant*
PRIEST
TRAVELER
FUJIKO, *lady from a neighboring castle*
ANNOUNCER
STAGEHAND

SETTING: *Same as Scene 1.*

AT RISE: STAGEHAND *enters and attaches spray of cherry blossoms to right side of box, then exits.* ANNOUNCER *still sits on pillow.*

ANNOUNCER: Presenting Japanese folk-play number three, called, "Why We Cannot Lend." (*Sound of gong is heard.*)

> Lo, the cherry blooms
> Have fallen in the garden
> Pushed by April's rain.

(SANJO *enters to slow drumbeat and stands inside castle.*)

SANJO: Today I shall relax in my garden teahouse with the shoji screens open and watch cherry blossoms falling in the rain. (*Calling*) Taro, Taro!

TARO (*Entering, running*): My master, Lord Sanjo, calls. (*Bows to* SANJO)

SANJO: I am going to my garden. Run the castle, and do not disturb me with problems.

TARO (*Bowing*): Yes, master. (SANJO *leaves castle, smelling blossoms, and crosses right, where he sits.* PRIEST *enters and crosses downstage.*)

PRIEST (*To audience*): I am a priest, making the long journey to Hakone Shrine. (*Pantomimes feeling rain falling*) Alas, a rain shower! I'll hurry to this castle. (*Crosses to castle*)

TARO (*Seeing* PRIEST): Do you wish shelter?

PRIEST: No, but I would appreciate the loan of an umbrella. Of course, I would return it on my way home.

TARO: One moment, please. (*Crosses upstage, back to audience.* STAGEHAND *enters with umbrella, giving it to* TARO, *who crosses back to* PRIEST.) Here. This is the best umbrella my master has.

PRIEST: Most kind. (*They bow.* PRIEST *opens umbrella and exits, walking under it.* SANJO *sees umbrella as* PRIEST *passes, and hurries to castle, startled.*)

SANJO: Taro, was that my best umbrella passing out the castle gate?

TARO: Yes, I lent it to a priest.

SANJO (*Horrified*): You lent my umbrella? *My* umbrella? I cannot bear the thought of losing anything.

TARO: But the priest will return it.

SANJO (*Interrupting*): Go away! (*Pantomimes striking him.* TARO *retreats to left of castle.*) Since Taro does not know how to take care of my possessions, I shall put another servant in charge. (*Calling*) Buso, Buso! (BUSO *enters in shuffling, stupid manner. He always has a foolish grin.*)

BUSO (*Bowing*): Yes, Lord Sanjo?

SANJO: Taro has lent my best umbrella. Therefore, I put you in charge. See to it that no umbrella is lent.

BUSO (*Nodding*): I understand. Tell me what to say.

SANJO: Simply say, "It got caught in a windstorm, the ribs were torn out, and it is presently hanging from the ceiling until it dries."

BUSO: All right, then, that's what I'll say.

SANJO: I shall return to my teahouse and try to find peace again.

BUSO: No finer occupation, my lord. (SANJO *returns to garden, right.* TRAVELER *enters, limping wearily, and crosses downstage.*)

TRAVELER (*To audience*): I am a weary traveler going to Odawara. A moment ago my horse stepped in a mud hole, threw me off, and ran away. At this castle I shall try to borrow a horse. (*Approaches castle*)

TARO (*To audience*): Someone else approaches. I'd better listen to make sure Buso lends nothing. (*Listens*)

TRAVELER (*To* BUSO): I am in desperate need of a horse.

BUSO: Oh, what a pity! We had one but it got caught in a windstorm, the ribs were torn out, and it is presently hanging from the ceiling until it dries. (TRAVELER *draws away, frightened.* TARO *bursts into laughter, frightening* TRAVELER *more.*)

TRAVELER (*In alarm*): The people here must be insane. I'd better search for a horse elsewhere. (*Exits, running with limp, and glancing back nervously*)

TARO (*Running to* SANJO): Master, a traveler tried to borrow a horse, and Buso told him it was hanging from the ceiling to dry.

SANJO: What? (*Crosses to* BUSO. TARO *returns left of castle to listen.*) Buso, that was *not* what you should have said. It's different for a horse.

BUSO (*Bowing*): Oh? Forgive me. Tell me what to say next time.

SANJO: You simply say, "He was out eating grass one day when suddenly he lost his mind, jumped the fence, broke his hip, and is presently lying in the stable under a pile of straw."

BUSO: All right, that's what I'll say.

SANJO: I shall return to my teahouse and try to calm down.

BUSO: No finer occupation, my lord. (SANJO *returns to garden.* FUJIKO *enters, crossing daintily down stage.*)

FUJIKO (*To audience*): I am Fujiko, a lady serving the lord of the neighboring castle. I come bearing an important invitation, (FUJIKO *crosses to castle.* BUSO, *seeing her come, holds finger to lips.*)

BUSO: Sh-h-h. My master must not be disturbed. What do you wish to borrow?

FUJIKO (*Flirtatiously*): My Lord Ichido invites Lord Sanjo to attend the great annual Cherry Blossom Festival. (*Flutters eyelids coyly*) It is your master we wish to borrow.

BUSO: Oh, what a pity! We had one, but he was out eating grass one day when suddenly he lost his mind, jumped the fence, broke his hip, and is presently lying in the stable under a pile of straw. (FUJIKO *shrieks, terrified.* TARO *laughs as before, frightening* FUJIKO *even more.*)

FUJIKO (*Fanning herself to keep from fainting*): Amida protect me! I must tell Lord Ichido at once. (SANJO *turns and sees* FUJIKO *and crosses to greet her.* FUJIKO, *backing away from* BUSO, *collides with* SANJO, *turns, shrieks in recognition, and exits, running.*)

SANJO (*Yelling*): Wait! Come back! What is wrong? (*Exits, running*)

FUJIKO (*Offstage; screaming*): *Tasukete! Tasukete!* Help! Help!

BUSO (*Shocked*): Lord Sanjo is running after a lady.

TARO (*Grinning*): No finer occupation for our Lord Sanjo. (BUSO, *scratching head, and* TARO, *laughing, exit, running after* SANJO, *as sound of drumbeat is heard.*)

ANNOUNCER (*Standing*): This concludes our Japanese Trio. *(Sound of gong is heard.* ANNOUNCER *bows and almost collides with* STAGEHAND, *who rushes onstage. They bow to each other several times. Then both exit,* STAGEHAND *carrying box.)*

THE END

FOLLOW THE RIVER LAI

FOLLOW THE RIVER LAI

The tale on which this play is based comes from Vietnam, although there are several themes in the play common to many Asian countries. One concerns the person who goes in search of a perfect place, a utopian land, and, finding it, decides to live there. After a time, he returns home to discover that a century has passed. Another related theme in folklore has to do with lost time, as in such well-known tales as "Rip Van Winkle" and "Sleeping Beauty," in which a person falls asleep and awakens many years later.

Because China ruled Vietnam for a thousand years, there are close cultural ties between the two countries. As a result, many Vietnamese folktales have Chinese roots. The Vietnam stories, however, show the influence of the unique problems and environment of Southeast Asia.

Though "Follow the River Lai" is basically a Chinese tale, with such characters as the Mandarin (Chinese public officer) and the bonze (Chinese Buddhist priest), the theme and setting are definitely Southeast Asian in character: the inner struggle, the deep feelings and emotions, the dreams of Tu Khiem and Le Vang are definitely Vietnamese. There is a saying in Vietnam when a man sees a beautiful woman—"she must come from the Land of Bliss."

Follow the River Lai

A Southeast Asian legend

Characters

Tu Khiem, *a young mandarin*
Le Vang, *his merchant friend*
Duc, *Le Vang's son*
Housekeeper
Chief Bonze
Sweeper
Grotto Queen
Giang Huong, *her daughter*
Two Grotto Maidens
Servant
Soldier
Bystanders
Voice, *offstage*

Scene 1

Time: *A summer afternoon, long ago.*

Setting: *The home of Tu Khiem. At center is a low table covered with scrolls, maps, and old books, which are also scattered on floor. There are cushions on floor. At rear is screen, and behind it, a potted plant is seen in silhouette.*

At Rise: Tu Khiem *is poring over a map. He shakes his head, sighs, mutters, and looks off into space. The tinkle of a bell is heard from offstage.* Housekeeper *enters and bows.*

HOUSEKEEPER: Learned master, your friend, Le Vang, comes through the gate.

TU KHIEM: Good! Bring us tea and cakes. (*Pushes maps aside and rises.* HOUSEKEEPER *bows and exits left.*)

LE VANG (*Entering left, carrying book*): Well, Khiem, your books are all about as if a great dragon had blown them upon you. (*Holds his book up*) Look! I brought you a small book of poetry to add to your enormous collection.

TU KHIEM (*Accepting book*): You are kind. (*Opens book*) Ah, you have written here.

LE VANG: I took great care with those words.

TU KHIEM (*Smiling*): Your inscription is quite—accurate. (LE VANG *bows.*) Sit down, my friend.

LE VANG (*Sitting on cushion*): Why must you have so many books? It puzzles me.

TU KHIEM: In them I can find most of the knowledge of the world.

LE VANG: What do you plan to do with this knowledge?

TU KHIEM: I am not certain. I do not have the patience to become a teacher, and my position as a mandarin gives me little pleasure.

LE VANG: Yet the peasants seem to think you fair. (HOUSE-KEEPER *re-enters with tray containing two cups, a pot of tea, and a plate of cakes. As men talk, she pours tea and gives each man a cup, then exits.*)

TU KHIEM: That is because they have learned to expect so little. (*Paces about*) There must be something better.

LE VANG (*Eating a cake*): In this world we learn to accept the evil with the good, my friend.

TU KHIEM: So much is evil. There seems to be little else.

LE VANG: Your difficulty, Khiem, is that you want everything to be beautiful. (*Eats another cake*)

TU KHIEM: And why should it not be so?

LE VANG: There must always be contrasts. How would

I know that this cake is so good unless I had eaten frightfully bad ones?

TU KHIEM: You would know.

LE VANG: I insist that I would not have as much appreciation. (*Sips tea*) Did you ask me here today to argue about cakes?

TU KHIEM: I asked you to come because—you will laugh when I explain.

LE VANG: Perhaps.

TU KHIEM: No matter. (*Sits. Picks up cup and nervously puts it down again*) Have you ever heard of the Land of Bliss?

LE VANG (*Snorting*): A place of eternal youth where all the women are lovely and life is full of laughter, music, and dancing. (*Eats another cake*)

TU KHIEM: Since my childhood I have longed to go there. (*Gestures to books*) I have searched through a hundred times as many books as you see here. I have examined every map and chart in existence, but I have found nothing about the location of the Land of Bliss.

LE VANG: It is a fairy tale. No such place exists!

TU KHIEM: I believe it does. Lately, I have been so bothered by my desire to go there that I cannot sleep at night. I find I am speaking aloud to no one—my mind is filled. I feel I shall go mad.

LE VANG (*Staring thoughtfully at* TU KHIEM): You need a change. I know an old pagoda where the red peonies are blooming. It will do you good to leave your books for a while.

TU KHIEM: You are right. We will go tomorrow. (*Notices tea tray and laughs*) Each day you enjoy your food more. You left no cakes for me.

LE VANG (*With a shrug*): You appeared too upset to eat, and I am not a man to let good opportunities pass. I will come for you at sunrise.

TU KHIEM: We shall watch nature waken herself in splendor.

LE VANG: And listen to the discordant cries of the fish peddlers. (*Exits*)

TU KHIEM: I am weary tonight. (*Shakes his head, then takes another map and studies it, muttering to himself, as curtain closes.*)

* * * * *

SCENE 2

TIME: *The next morning, at sunrise.*

SETTING: *The old pagoda. A large drawing of the pagoda is at rear, and brilliant red flowers and bushes surround it. This scene may be played in front of the curtain.*

AT RISE: CHIEF BONZE *stands beside pagoda with his arms folded.* SWEEPER *is raking leaves left.* BYSTANDERS *walk about, admiring flowers. From offstage,* VOICE *of fish peddler is heard, calling his wares, and a gong sounds.* TU KHIEM *and* LE VANG *enter.*

LE VANG: Is this not better than studying your books, my friend?

TU KHIEM: How beautiful! The peonies are touched with fire. If only the whole world could be this lovely!

CHIEF BONZE (*Bowing*): Good morning, honorable gentlemen. (LE VANG *and* TU KHIEM *bow respectfully.*) I am glad that you enjoy the blossoms, but I must caution you not to pick them. The fine is high for causing even a single flower to fall.

TU KHIEM: Since I brought no money, I shall admire them from afar.

LE VANG: And I, being a merchant, can think of more useful places to invest my money. I shall certainly go no closer. (GIANG, *a young woman, enters, and runs over to blossoms, exclaiming in delight.*)

Tu Khiem: That lovely lady makes the picture even more of a delight to the eyes.

Le Vang: Indeed! I wonder who she is? A visitor to our village, I suppose. (Giang *pulls a branch closer to her. It breaks, and falls to the ground.*)

Giang: Oh! I did not mean to break it.

Chief Bonze (*To* Sweeper): Arrest that woman! She has destroyed the sacred flowers. (Sweeper *drops broom, runs to* Giang *and pulls her to* Bonze. Bystanders *murmur in concern.*)

Giang (*Kneeling*): Forgive me. It was an accident.

Chief Bonze (*Gesturing for her to rise*): I know it was not an evil deed, yet I must fine you. It is the law, which must be obeyed.

Giang: I have no money.

Chief Bonze: Then I am afraid you will have to go to prison.

Tu Khiem (*Stepping forward*): How much is the fine?

Chief Bonze: Ten golden coins. (Bystanders *and* Giang *gasp.*)

Tu Khiem: I do not have the money, but (*Removing coat*) take this brocade coat. It is made of the finest silk, embroidered with gold and silver. (*Gives it to* Bonze)

Chief Bonze (*Examining coat*): This is worth more than ten golden coins. Surely you would not wish to part with it.

Tu Khiem: Set the woman free.

Chief Bonze: Very well. (Giang *moves quickly away.*) I am sorry, but I must do my duty.

Tu Khiem: I am well acquainted with the law. (*He bows to* Bonze, *who bows in return and exits with coat. Murmuring,* Bystanders *exit, and* Sweeper *picks up broom and exits.* Giang *smiles at* Tu Khiem *and looks shyly down.*)

LE VANG: That was a noble deed, Khiem. You are good-hearted but impulsive. You lack discipline of your emotions.

TU KHIEM (*Ignoring him and crossing to* GIANG): Is there anything else I may do to help you?

GIANG: No. You are very generous, honorable sir.

TU KHIEM: I could not see such a beautiful lady go to prison.

GIANG: How may I repay you?

TU KHIEM: Let me see you again.

GIANG: I come from a land far away.

TU KHIEM: There is no place too far.

GIANG (*Looking at him curiously and smiling*): Have you ever been to Tong-Son, where there are many crystal springs and deep grottoes?

TU KHIEM: No, but I have read about it.

GIANG: If you should go there, walk into the forest, follow the River Lai, and rest where the river meets the sea. (*Exits*)

TU KHIEM (*Starting to follow*): Wait! Tell me your name. (*Staring off*) Strange! She has vanished.

LE VANG (*Dramatically*): In the shadow of an old pagoda, where brilliant peonies burst the dawn, Tu Khiem gave his brocade coat for the freedom of a gentle lady whose eyes were deep as the forest. See, you move me to poetry. (*Pats stomach*) I am hungry. Let us go for breakfast.

TU KHIEM (*Suddenly*): I resign my office as mandarin chief of this district.

LE VANG (*Shocked*): What?

TU KHIEM: My friend, I give you my house and my wealth. I am going away, and I do not know if I shall return. (*Exits right*)

LE VANG (*Shrugging*): Poor Khiem. He flies off into the

wind, pursuing some vision. I am afraid he will go mad in his flight. (*Curtain*)

* * * * *

SCENE 3

TIME: *Many days later.*

BEFORE RISE: TU KHIEM *enters left in front of the curtain, carrying a book of poetry. On his back is a small pack with a gourd cup tied outside it.*

TU KHIEM (*Gesturing overhead*): This great forest weaves a canopy over my head. (*Looking over edge of stage*) And the River Lai whispers secrets which I can almost hear. (*Looks into audience*) At last, here is the sea. (*Takes off pack and sets it down*) The journey has been long, and I am tired. (*Gesturing to curtain*) At the foot of this great mountain I shall rest and read a poem from my friend's book. (*Lies down, resting against pack, and reads. Curtain slowly opens.*)

* * *

SETTING: *The Land of Bliss. A carved throne is at center, surrounded by ferns, flowers, and trees. At right, a drawing of a bridge stands over a lotus pool.*

AT RISE: GROTTO QUEEN *sits on throne. Music is heard from offstage, and* MAIDENS *begin to sing the song below, offstage.* TU KHIEM *sits up and watches as* MAIDENS *come dancing in, singing and carrying incense.* NOTE: MAIDENS *may enter through audience if desired.*

MAIDENS (*Singing to an Oriental melody*):
> Lotus blossoms
> Floating gently
> Underneath the Chi-Nan Bridge.
> Incense burning
> In the garden.

There is beauty all around.
Softly, softly
Blows the east wind,
Breathing clouds across the sky.
Lotus blossoms
Floating gently.
There is beauty all around.

TU KHIEM (*Rising*): The mountain opened. Am I asleep?
(MAIDENS *giggle*.)

QUEEN (*Smiling*): We welcome you, learned scholar and
gentle poet. Do you know where you are?

TU KHIEM: It appears to be a wonderful place.

QUEEN: You are in the sixth of thirty-six grottoes of Phi
Lai Mountain. This mountain floats on the sea and
appears and vanishes according to the winds. I am the
Grotto Queen. (*Motions to* MAIDENS) You may tell her
that he is here. (MAIDENS *exit, giggling*.)

TU KHIEM: Is this the Land of Bliss?

QUEEN (*Laughing*): That is the name you Earth people
have given it. You see, we know all about the things
that go on in your world, for we visit it often. It is
seldom, however, that we allow anyone to come to our
world. (MAIDENS *re-enter, ushering* GIANG, *who looks at*
TU KHIEM *shyly*.)

TU KHIEM (*Crossing to* GIANG): You are the lady at the
pagoda. (GIANG *nods*.)

QUEEN: This is my daughter, Giang Huong. We have not
forgotten how you helped her when she was in trouble.
To show our gratitude, we have brought you to this
land which you have searched for and dreamed of for
so long.

TU KHIEM: The Land of Bliss!

QUEEN: You will find that life here is easy. There are no
problems to solve, no sadness to bring you tears, and

no work to make you weary. It is a land of eternal youth. All that you wish will be given to you. Stay with us as long as you desire—forever, if you like.

Tu Khiem: I am full of gratitude, but I cannot express it in words. It is more than a poet can tell.

Queen: We understand. (*To* Maidens) Come—let us prepare a great celebration feast. (*Exits right with* Maidens *following*)

Tu Khiem (*To* Giang): I was afraid that I might not find you—so many days have passed.

Giang: Remember the branch of peonies? I broke it to test you. We have been watching you for a long time. When you proved your kindness, I knew that you would be allowed to visit us.

Tu Khiem: I am the happiest man in the world.

Giang (*Moving away, thoughtfully*): But you are not *in* the world. (*Turns back to him*) Today you are happy. There will come a time when you will tire of this land— when you will wish to return to your world of mixed blessings.

Tu Khiem: Never!

Giang: We shall see. Earth people were not created for eternal pleasure, although this is what they constantly desire.

Tu Khiem: I cannot believe—

Giang (*Gently placing her hand over his mouth*): Sh-h! Let us not speak of it now. Come, Tu Khiem. I will show you many wonders. Soon the celebration will begin. You will see dancing and hear music finer than anything you have in your world. (*Exits right, followed by* Tu Khiem. *Music and* Maidens *singing are heard in the distance. Curtain slowly closes as music grows louder.*)

*   *   *   *   *

Scene 4

SETTING: *Same as Scene 1, except books and maps are gone, and furniture is arranged differently. Potted plant is moved farther away from screen to cast the shadow of a much larger plant than in Scene 1.*

AT RISE: DUC, LE VANG'S *son, is sitting at table writing. He wears modern clothes, Oriental smoking jacket.* SERVANT *enters.*

SERVANT (*Bowing*): There is a stranger at the door who insists on seeing the owner of this house. He claims to be a good friend of yours. As far as I can tell, he is unarmed.

DUC: We cannot be too careful. I will see him, but stay just outside. If there is difficulty, I will give you a signal to run to the general for help. (SERVANT *nods and exits.*)

TU KHIEM (*Entering cheerfully*): My friend, it is good to see you again. You look well. (*Indicates* DUC'S *stomach*) You are eating less these days? I thought surely you would be as wide as the Eastern Bridge. Tell me, what has happened to our village? It appears as if an earthquake has struck. It is all so different that I could scarcely find my way here. And, I have not seen a familiar face until yours. (*As he speaks,* DUC *secretly opens drawer, takes out gun and conceals it in his pocket, keeping his hand on it.*)

DUC: I do not know you. Tell me your name.

TU KHIEM: Have you forgotten so soon? (*Laughs*) You always were dramatic. Stop this! You most certainly do know me.

DUC: Perhaps if you will tell me where you think we met—

TU KHIEM (*Annoyed*): You are joking with me. Is this the way you welcome home your best friend? (*Silence from* DUC) What is the matter with you? I gave you this house and all of my wealth. (*Silence*) This is ridiculous! (*Crosses to table and indignantly strikes it with his fist*) Has all of your importance gone to your head? (Duc *rises and backs away.*) I am Tu Khiem, the former mandarin chief of this district. I have returned. (*Looks left*) Where is my housekeeper? (*Looks at screen*) What have you done to my potted bamboo to make it grow so large? (Duc *backs around table and crosses slowly left as* Tu Khiem *crosses right.*) This house is entirely different. (*Whirls around and faces* Duc) What is the matter with you? Your clothes are strange. Why do you move away from me? I have not come back to take the house away from you. Do you really not remember me, Le Vang?

Duc: I am not Le Vang. (*Gestures behind his back to* Servant *offstage*)

Tu Khiem: Something is terribly wrong here. I do not understand. You look like my friend.

Duc: I am the son of Le Vang.

Tu Khiem: His son!

Duc: My father died thirty years ago, an old man of ninety-two.

Tu Khiem (*Stunned*): Please, may I sit down? (*Sinks onto cushion*) My friend is dead. So that is it. The time—I had forgotten about it. The time is not the same.

Duc (*Crossing warily toward him*): How can you be Khiem? He left this village a hundred years ago. They say he went mad, drowned in the River Lai, and was washed out to sea. I do not know who you are. (*Draws gun and points it at* Tu Khiem) Our country is at war, sir, and we can trust no one. You are either a spy or a madman. I have sent for the soldiers. They will be here soon.

Tu Khiem (*Dazed*): A year on Earth is only a day in the Land of Bliss. I have lost my generation. (*Looks at* Duc *and then at gun*) My story is too strange to believe. But put away the weapon—I am harmless. Did your father tell you why I left? (Duc *shakes his head*.) I went to look for the Land of Bliss, son of Le Vang, and I found it— but I grew tired of its perfection. Your father would understand. (*Looks about*) My memories of Earth would not go away, but this is not the world I left. I find it bewildering. (*Looks back at* Duc) I will show you what your father gave me the day before I left. Perhaps that will make you believe. (*Starts to remove pack*)

Duc: Stop! (*Keeping gun on him*) Put the pack on the floor. (Tu Khiem *does so.* Duc *carefully takes it and moves back.*)

Tu Khiem: Inside you will find a small book of poetry. (*Keeping an eye on* Tu Khiem, Duc *takes out book.*)

Duc: Is this what you mean?

Tu Khiem: Yes. (Duc *feels pack to make certain there is no weapon in it, places pack on floor, and kicks it back to* Tu Khiem.) Look on the first page. You will find some writing by your father.

Duc (*Quickly glancing at first page and reading*): "To my good friend, Tu Khiem, who searches for only the beautiful, from Le Vang, who accepts life for what it is." (*Their eyes meet, and* Duc *lowers the gun. From offstage comes the sound of running feet and excited voices.*)

Soldier (*From offstage*): Where is he?

Servant (*From offstage*): In there. Careful! He may be dangerous, and my master is with him.

Duc (*Pointing to screen*): Quickly, go! (Tu Khiem *picks up pack and runs to screen. Just before* Tu Khiem *slips out,* Duc *gives book to him. For a moment they exchange smiles, then* Tu Khiem *exits behind screen.* Duc *puts gun into drawer and sits.*)

SERVANT (*From offstage*): Look! There he goes—across the garden. (*Sounds of running are heard*)

SOLDIER (*From offstage*): I don't see him. Where did he go? (*Yelling*) You men take the gate and try to head him back this way. (*Enters behind screen, running close to it so that he is in sharp silhouette*) I see him. (*Kneels and raises rifle. A shot is heard, then he runs offstage. DUC sits tensely, waiting. After a moment of silence, running footsteps are heard and SERVANT enters, breathless.*)

SERVANT: The man has escaped into the forest. He headed in the direction of the River Lai. The soldiers think it useless to pursue him any further. They will be watching in case he returns.

DUC: I do not think he will be back.

SERVANT: I wonder if he was a spy.

DUC: I doubt if he was from the enemy. (SERVANT *bows and starts to exit.*) Wait! (*Picks up paper from table*)

SERVANT: Do you wish me to take a message to the general?

DUC (*Thoughtfully*): Yes. (*Crumples paper*) I have decided not to leave. Tell the general that, with his kind permission, I would rather stay in my village.

SERVANT: It is dangerous, sir.

DUC: I know, but perhaps I can be of help to our people here. Tell him that I do not condone his presence, but I refuse to run to a safer place.

SERVANT: I do not believe I understand you.

DUC (*Smiling*): I do not fully understand myself, but I would like to try. (*Crosses to table and sits. SERVANT exits. Curtain.*)

THE END

LITTLE MOUSE-DEER

LITTLE MOUSE-DEER

Off the Southeast Asian coast lies Indonesia, a country composed of many islands, with the fifth largest population in the world (the United States is fourth). On some of these islands there are modern cities, but most of Indonesia is farm country and wilderness. Deep in the forests lives the antelope-like animal, about a foot high, called mouse-deer, and the folklore of Indonesia abounds in stories of this clever little creature, called Kancil (Kant'chil).

Some of these folktales were brought to Indonesia by Moslems and Malays and include familiar themes but in exotic settings. Children in Indonesia begin at an early age to learn the folklore and history of their country, and with their parents participate in the dances and dance dramas which depict these tales. Accompanying the festival activities are orchestras made up primarily of different kinds of gongs.

Wooden puppets dressed in elaborate costumes and shadow puppets made of the skins of water buffalo and cut into lacelike patterns are used in presentations in many parts of Indonesia. In shadow puppet performances, a single puppeteer manipulates all of the puppets and narrates the story, assisted by a small background orchestra. The puppets are held and operated behind a sheet-like screen, in front of a light or hanging lantern which casts the shadows of the puppets onto the screen. Presentations using wooden puppets require a number of puppeteers who manipulate puppets on slender sticks in full view of the audience.

Little Mouse-Deer

A dance drama from Indonesia

Characters

1ST STORYTELLER (*xylophone*)
ORANG, *a man*

2ND STORYTELLER (*bells*)
KANCIL, *the mouse-deer**

3RD STORYTELLER (*drum*)
HARIMAU, *the tiger**

4TH STORYTELLER (*sticks*)
MONYET, *the monkey*

5TH STORYTELLER (*gong/drum*)
KERBAU, *the water buffalo*

6TH STORYTELLER (*gong set*)
BABI, *the pig*

I. How Mouse-Deer Fools the Tiger

SETTING: *Indonesian rain forest, shown on backdrop. There is no front curtain.*
AT RISE: 1ST, 2ND *and* 3RD STORYTELLERS *enter with their instruments and sit on floor at one side, facing stage.*

---

* Kancil is pronounced *Kant'-chil.* Hariman is the Indonesian word for tiger and means "the will of the day," for the tiger takes whatever he wants.

NOTE: STORYTELLERS *play instruments to accompany the actions of the particular character with whom each is associated, as indicated in text. They do not play during the characters' speeches. Actors perform all movements and pantomimes in exaggerated dance-like style.*

1ST STORYTELLER: In the rain forest of Indonesia, there lives a tiny animal with the face of a mouse and the legs of a deer. It is Kancil, the mouse-deer. This story tells how Kancil fools the tiger. (2ND STORYTELLER *plays bells for a moment.*)

2ND STORYTELLER: Sly little Kancil scurries through the forest. (KANCIL, *carrying bag, enters, darting about, sniffing, with abrupt movements. Bells play.*) He stops to drink at a clear, deep pool of water. (KANCIL *pantomimes drinking, head bobbing close to floor.*)

3RD STORYTELLER: Not far behind prowls mean Harimau, the tiger. (HARIMAU *enters, slinking close to floor, snarling softly. 3RD STORYTELLER plays drum.*)

2ND STORYTELLER: Kancil finds some mango trees and starts to eat. (KANCIL *jumps, pantomimes grabbing fruit, then nibbles with enjoyment.*)

KANCIL: M-m-m, delicious. I'll pick more of this fruit to take home with me. (*Pantomimes picking fruit and filling bag*)

HARIMAU: Ho, those mango trees are mine. How dare you take my fruit! (KANCIL *whirls, startled.*) Oo-o, I'm getting angrier and angrier. (*Puffs himself up with snorts, then raises front claws, preparing to pounce on* KANCIL. *Drum and bells play rapidly.*)

KANCIL (*Gathering courage*): Er, ah, good morning, friend Harimau. A nice day, don't you think?

HARIMAU (*Snarling*): Not nice at all. The monsoon swept away my dinner last night, so this morning I'm terribly hungry.

KANCIL: Dear me, I'm sorry to hear that.

HARIMAU: Yes, I'm hungry for the one who eats mangoes from my trees.

KANCIL (*Glancing about*): Oh, dear, dear, you must mean me. (HARIMAU *nods slowly, examining claws, pulling them in and pushing them out.*)

3RD STORYTELLER: While Harimau makes sure his claws are in working order—

2ND STORYTELLER: Kancil is trying to think of a trick—a trick to stay alive. (KANCIL *suddenly jumps in air, clapping hooves.*)

KANCIL (*Aside*): I know. I know what to do. (*To* HARIMAU) Tiger, you mustn't eat me.

HARIMAU: Why not?

KANCIL: Haven't you heard? I can turn one into two.

HARIMAU (*With disbelief*): *Barongs!* Nobody can do that.

KANCIL: Say what you like, but I've been working all morning making two of one. That's why I was picking your mangoes—to double them.

HARIMAU: Double my mangoes?

KANCIL: Of course. Why, at sunrise I turned one monkey into two. Then I helped two farmers grow twice as much rice. And this afternoon the Raja wants me to make two of him.

HARIMAU (*Aside*): If there were two of me, I could hunt faster and sleep longer. (*Taps* KANCIL *on head*) Mouse-deer, make two of me.

KANCIL (*Shaking head*): No, no, you wouldn't want to go through all the necessary complicated magic.

HARIMAU: Yes, I would. Please! I'll do anything.

KANCIL: Sorry, my time is limited. I mustn't keep the Raja waiting.

HARIMAU: Please, Kancil, please fit me into your schedule!

KANCIL: Well, all right. However, you must follow my instructions carefully.

HARIMAU: Yes, yes.

KANCIL: First, close your eyes. Now, put this sack over your head. (*Pantomimes emptying fruit from sack, then gives it to* HARIMAU, *who puts it on head*) Next, count backwards from twenty to one. (KANCIL *laughingly exits on tiptoe as* HARIMAU *counts.*)

HARIMAU: Twenty, nineteen, eighteen (*Counts backward*), . . . three, two, one. (*Pause*) Kancil, what do I do now? (*Pause*) Kancil, where are you? (*Pause*) Kancil? (*Flings off bag and peers around*) Barongs! Mouse-deer's gone! He tricked me. (*Stomps on bag, growling fiercely*) I'm still only *one* tiger, and I'm still hungry.

1ST STORYTELLER: At that moment, Orang, the man, comes wandering through the forest. He's gathering flowers for the temple. (ORANG *enters, pantomiming happily picking flowers from trees and bushes.* 1ST STORYTELLER *plays xylophone.*) When Orang sees Harimau, he's frightened. (ORANG *starts to exit on tiptoe, but freezes when* HARIMAU *growls.*)

HARIMAU (*Growling*): Ho, ho, Kancil may fool me, but Orang won't. He's a bigger, better meal anyway.

ORANG (*Shaking*): H-how did Kancil f-fool you?

HARIMAU: He promised to turn me into two and didn't.

1ST STORYTELLER: Orang quickly thinks of a way to stay alive.

ORANG: Harimau, there *are* two of you.

HARIMAU: Two of me? (*Looking about*) Where?

ORANG: Take a look in that pool of water over there. (*Points to same pool where* KANCIL *drank*) Then you'll see the other tiger. (HARIMAU *bounds to "pool" and stares into it.*)

3RD STORYTELLER: When Harimau stares into the clear, still water, he sees himself. (ORANG *stealthily picks up bag, quickly pantomiming refilling it with mangoes, and exits on tiptoe.*)

HARIMAU (*Excitedly*): By all the rice paddies in Indonesia, there *is* another tiger here just like me. (*Scratches head and looks at audience*) Kancil did make two out of one. I believe that mouse-deer is almost as clever as I. (*Exits, prancing proudly. A minute of music ends the scene.*)

* * * * *

II. How Mouse-Deer Escapes from the Pit

SETTING: *Indonesian rain forest.*

AT RISE: 1ST, 2ND *and* 3RD STORYTELLERS *sit on one side of stage with instruments.* 4TH, 5TH *and* 6TH STORY-TELLERS *enter with their instruments and sit on opposite side, facing stage. As before,* STORYTELLERS *play instruments for actions of characters with whom they are associated.*

1ST STORYTELLER: This story tells how Kancil, the little mouse-deer, escapes from a deep pit. (2ND STORYTELLER *plays bells.*)

2ND STORYTELLER: Little mouse-deer doesn't always look ahead. (KANCIL *enters, eating and fanning himself with banana leaf. Bells play.*) Here comes Kancil now, eating a cucumber and fanning himself with a banana leaf, not seeing the big hole in front of him. (KANCIL *continues walking, crossing downstage. Then he suddenly jumps off stage with a yelp, as if falling into deep pit.* NOTE: KANCIL *may pantomime falling business onstage, if desired. He tries vainly to climb out of pit and onto stage, finally giving up with sigh.*)

KANCIL: Oh dear, dear me. How will I get out of this dark, deep pit? I can't climb out by myself—it's too deep. I'll have to think of a plan.

4TH STORYTELLER: Along jumps Monyet, the monkey. (4TH STORYTELLER *hits sticks in jerky rhythm as* MONYET *enters, jumping about, scratching, making monkey sounds. He crosses to pit and looks in.*)

MONYET (*Chattering*): I say, I say, what's up? I mean, what's down? That is, what's up down there?

KANCIL (*Calling up*): I'm waiting for the end of the world.

MONYET: Is the end coming soon, soon?

KANCIL: Dear me, yes. It's written on this banana leaf, "Those in the pure, sacred pit will be safe."

MONYET: I say, I say, I'm coming into the pit.

KANCIL: No, no, you might sneeze.

MONYET: What's wrong with a sneeze?

KANCIL: It's also written here, "Whoever sneezes shouldn't stay in the pit, for then it wouldn't be pure and sacred."

MONYET: I say, I say, then I won't sneeze. Here I come. (*Jumps into pit with* KANCIL)

5TH STORYTELLER: Along lumbers Kerbau, the water buffalo. (KERBAU *enters, swinging arms and swaying from side to side. He peers into pit.* 5TH STORYTELLER *plays gong/drum.*)

KERBAU (*Bellowing*): Hel-loo. What are you do-o-ing down there?

KANCIL *and* MONYET (*Together*): Waiting for the end of the world.

MONYET: It says on Kancil's banana leaf, "Those in the pure, sacred pit will be safe."

KERBAU: Wo-o-o! I'm coming down too-o.

MONYET: No, no, you might sneeze.

KERBAU: What's wrong with a sneeze?

MONYET: It's also written here, "Whoever sneezes shouldn't stay in the pit, for then it wouldn't be pure and sacred."

KERBAU: Wo-o-o, then I won't sneeze. Here I come. (*Jumps into pit*)

6TH STORYTELLER: Along roots Babi, the pig. (BABI *enters, waddling, sniffing and pawing ground, making snorting sounds.* 6TH STORYTELLER *plays gong.* BABI *peers into pit.*)

BABI (*Snorting*): Sniffle, snorfle, what's happening down there?

KANCIL, MONYET *and* KERBAU (*Together*): We're waiting for the end of the world.

KERBAU: It says on Kancil's banana leaf, "Those in the pure, sacred pit will be safe."

BABI: Snoofle, I'm coming down toofle.

MONYET *and* KERBAU: No, no, you might sneeze.

BABI: What's wrong with a sneeze?

KERBAU: It's also written here, "Whoever sneezes shouldn't stay in the pit, for then it wouldn't be pure and sacred."

BABI: Snoofle, then I won't sneeze. Here I come. (*Jumps into pit*)

2ND STORYTELLER: Suddenly, Kancil holds his nose. (KANCIL *starts to sneeze.*)

4TH, 5TH *and* 6TH STORYTELLERS (*Together*): The other animals gasp with terror. (MONYET, KERBAU *and* BABI *gasp, watching* KANCIL *with alarm.*)

KANCIL: Oh, dear, dear, I'm afraid I'm going to—to—to—(*Sneezes loudly. Others scream.*)

MONYET, KERBAU *and* BABI (*Together*): Throw Kancil out. Keep the pit pure and sacred. (*They push* KANCIL *up out of the pit, then sigh with relief.* KANCIL *dances about, happily, with tiny jumps.*)

1ST STORYTELLER: Orang, the man, is running through the rain forest. (ORANG *enters, breathlessly. Xylophone plays.*)

ORANG: Kancil, why do you look so happy?

KANCIL: I just got out of that frightful pit.

ORANG: Good for you. But you'd better hurry home, as I'm doing, for Harimau is close behind me. And he's hunting for a meal.

KANCIL: Oh, dear me! It's kind of you to give the warning. (KANCIL *and* ORANG *exit, running.*)

3RD STORYTELLER: Along prowls Harimau, the mean tiger. (HARIMAU *enters, slinking, snarling softly, and sniffing air. He slithers to pit and peers into it.* 3RD STORYTELLER *plays drums.*)

HARIMAU: Giant *barongs!* You must be waiting for me to eat you up.

BABI: No! We're waiting for the end of the world. It says on Kancil's banana leaf, "Those in the pure, sacred pit will be safe."

HARIMAU: Let me see that banana leaf. (BABI *hands up leaf.* HARIMAU *examines both sides of leaf.*) There's nothing written on this leaf.

MONYET, KERBAU and BABI (*Together*): Nothing?

MONYET: I say, I say, not even one word?

HARIMAU: Nothing! Kancil fooled you. However, I'm very hungry, so *your* world is going to end right now. (HARI-MAU *leaps into pit, snarling and snapping at animals, who scramble out of pit and, with loud noises, exit, running, pursued by angry* HARIMAU, *who is furiously waving leaf. A minute of music ends the scene.*)

*   *   *   *   *

III.   How Mouse-Deer Saves the Man

SETTING: *Indonesian rain forest.*

AT RISE: STORYTELLERS *are onstage with their instruments. As before, each plays instrument for a particular actor's actions. All properties are pantomimed.*

1ST STORYTELLER: This story tells how Kancil, the mouse-deer, saves Orang, the man. (2ND STORYTELLER *plays bells.*)

3RD STORYTELLER: While Harimau, the mean tiger, is hunting for dinner one day, a large tree falls on top of him. (HARIMAU *enters, slinking, snarling, and sniffing air. Suddenly, he falls backward with a roar, his four paws continue to thrash about, as his body remains still, as if stuck beneath tree.* 3RD STORYTELLER *plays drum.*)

HARIMAU (*Roaring*): Help, help!

1ST STORYTELLER: Orang, the man, is wandering through

the rain forest, looking for a good piece of wood to carve into a figure. (ORANG *enters. He pantomimes seeing fallen tree and crossing to examine it. Meanwhile,* 1ST STORYTELLER *plays xylophone.*)

ORANG: Ah, there's excellent wood in this tree. But what's this wiggling underneath?

HARIMAU: It's me, Harimau. I'm stuck. Please, good Orang, pry this log off me.

ORANG: If I do that, you'll eat me.

HARIMAU: Of course I won't. I wouldn't eat anyone kind enough to save my life.

ORANG: In that case, I'll find a heavy stick and pry up the log. (ORANG *pantomimes finding stick, then prying up log.* HARIMAU *jumps to feet, snarling at* ORANG, *who drops stick in alarm.*)

HARIMAU: Ho, ho! Now I'll eat you. (ORANG *kneels, prayerfully.*)

ORANG: No, no! You promised you wouldn't.

HARIMAU: Tigers don't *keep* promises. They just *make* them. (*Prepares to pounce on* ORANG)

ORANG: Wait, wait! Most tigers are good sports. Give me a sporting chance, please! (HARIMAU *sits down, scratching head thoughtfully.*)

HARIMAU: I suppose you should have a sporting chance. In fact, to show you what a fair tiger I am, I'll give you three sporting chances. The next three animals to pass by will judge whether or not I should eat you.

ORANG (*Rising*): That's fair.

1ST STORYTELLER: Orang is greatly relieved, for he is certain no one will want Harimau to eat him.

4TH STORYTELLER: Along jumps Monyet, the monkey. (MONYET *enters, jumping about as before, chattering.* 4TH STORYTELLER *plays sticks.*)

ORANG: Excuse me, Monyet, we have a question to ask you.

MONYET (*Chattering*): Well, hurry and ask, and make it quick, and be speedy about it.

HARIMAU: Should I, or should I not, eat this man? (MONYET *scratches thoughtfully.*)

MONYET: Man is always teasing and testing me. I say, I say, I'd just as soon you'd eat him up. (*Exits, making screeches.* ORANG *groans with dismay.* HARIMAU *growls with pleasure.*)

1ST STORYTELLER: Although Orang is upset about the monkey's answer, he knows he still has two more chances.

5TH STORYTELLER: Along lumbers Kerbau, the water buffalo. (5TH STORYTELLER *plays gong/drum.* KERBAU *enters as before, swinging and swaying.*)

ORANG: Excuse me, Kerbau. We have a question to ask you.

KERBAU (*Bellowing*): Oo-o-o, all right. Ask me now-ow.

HARIMAU: Should I, or should I not, eat this man? (KERBAU *sits to think a moment, then rises.*)

KERBAU: Man is always working me too-o hard. He whips me, makes me pull a heavy plow-ow, and never gives me any thanks for my labor. I'd just as soo-on you'd eat him up. (*Exits, bellowing.* ORANG *groans.* HARIMAU *growls.*)

1ST STORYTELLER: Orang is even more upset about the water buffalo's answer. But he knows he still has another chance.

6TH STORYTELLER: Along roots Babi, the pig. (BABI *enters as before, waddling, snorting, and hunting for food.* 6TH STORYTELLER *plays gong set.*)

ORANG: Excuse me, Babi, we have a question to ask you.

BABI (*Snorting*): Snoffle, snirfle, ask me anything.

HARIMAU: Should I, or should I not, eat this man? (BABI *roots about.*)

BABI: Man is always hungry to eat *me*. I'd just as soon you'd eat *him*. (*Exits, snorting.* ORANG *groans loudly and sinks to knees in resignation.* HARIMAU *circles him, growling.*)

1ST STORYTELLER: Poor Orang. He has no more chances.

3RD STORYTELLER: And Harimau looks ready for dinner.

2ND STORYTELLER: Just then, Kancil, the mouse-deer, scurries onto the scene. (KANCIL *enters, darting about as before. Bells play.*)

KANCIL: Hello, Orang. How are you?

ORANG: Not long for this world, I fear. The tiger is going to eat me.

KANCIL: How did you end up in this situation?

ORANG: I was foolish enough to save Harimau's life by prying off that log.

KANCIL: Hm-m-m. I don't understand.

HARIMAU: It's simple. Orang pried up this log which was on top of me.

KANCIL: Show me.

HARIMAU (*Pointing*): I was under there.

KANCIL: How far under?

HARIMAU: Very far.

KANCIL: Show me.

HARIMAU: I've never known anyone as stupid as this mouse-deer. Orang, come here and pry up this log. (ORANG *pantomimes prying.*) Now, I was right under there. (*Points*)

KANCIL: Lie down and show me. (HARIMAU *lies on back as before.*) Orang, please drop the log back on Harimau so I can see just how it was. (ORANG *pantomimes dropping log;* HARIMAU *howls.*) Is that how it was, Harimau?

HARIMAU (*Breathlessly, squirming*): Yes, exactly. Are you satisfied?

KANCIL: Completely.

HARIMAU: Then, let me out of here.

KANCIL: Oh, dear me, no. We'll leave that to some other *stupid* creature. (HARIMAU *continues struggling.*) Orang, I hope you learned a lesson. (HARIMAU *howls and snarls.*)

ORANG: Thank you, Kancil. Today I learned many lessons. (KANCIL *exits, jumping and darting.*)

1ST STORYTELLER: And so, Orang, the man, returns home, thinking about his lessons the whole way. (ORANG *exits, thoughtfully.* STORYTELLERS *play music for a minute, then rise, bow, and exit with instruments.* 3RD STORYTELLER *quickly re-enters, pantomimes prying log off* HARIMAU, *and then exits, running and shrieking, pursued by* HARIMAU, *who snarls and snaps angrily.*)

THE END

Production Notes

ANANSI, THE AFRICAN SPIDER

Characters: 11 male or female.

Playing Time: 20 minutes.

Costumes: Animals wear heads made of papier-mâché or paper bag masks. Anansi has two sets of false legs strapped to his body, giving appearance of eight legs in all. Storytellers, Nyame, Forest King, and Tall-Tale Man wear tribal head masks made of papier-mâché. Nyame's mask represents the sun; Forest King wears crown and carries a staff.

Properties: Three African rattles; large "talking" drum.

Setting: Equatorial Africa (Ghana). There is a painted backdrop showing equatorial forest; backdrop curtain may also be used, with vines and shrubbery set in front of it. For Scene 1, cardboard cut-outs of kola nut tree and berry bush are near center. Hornets' nest hangs from bush, and calabash gourd lies on ground. There is a tall stool up center. Paper and cotton clouds are attached to stool, indicating sky.

Lighting: No special effects. Blue flood may be used in night scene of "The First Talking Drum."

Sound: Crocodile chomping on rock and losing teeth; hornets buzzing; drumbeats; chomping, chewing, pounding, etc., as giant drum is built. (Crew of three can make sound effects offstage.)

IJAPA, THE TORTOISE

Characters: 4 male; 2 female; 6 male or female for Priest, Attendant, and Spirits; as many extras as desired for Villagers.

Playing Time: 20 minutes.

Costumes: Nigerian dress. Bush Spirits and Shango Priest wear tribal masks made of papier-mâché. Priest has anklets made of shells strung together and wears raffia costume. Oba wears fringed crown and bib made of cardboard covered with glue and sprinkled with tiny beads in a design. Ijapa and Yanrinbo wear large papier-mâché turtle shells attached to their backs by belts, or, they may wear Nigerian costumes and pantomime the turtle-shell business indicated in text.

Properties: Palm tree (hollow trunk of papier-mâché, with holes for eyes, painted brown, with brown cloth roots to conceal Ijapa when he wears tree, and branches of straightened coat-hanger wire covered with fringed green paper), three yams, nuts, utensils, cloth, and other market-place items (real or pantomimed), gourd rattle, staff (if possible, find a picture of a carved Nigerian "oshe shango" staff and make a copy of it in papier-mâché), large and small bells with striker stick, vine-like rope, water jar, toy or cardboard machete, shoulder bag pouch containing kernels of corn (real or pantomimed), fringed umbrella, palm frond.

Setting: Scene 1, a Nigerian village, and Scene 2, the Nigerian bush. For both scenes, there is a dark backdrop curtain, with cardboard cut-outs of bushes, trees, and huts attached (or free standing). There is a clump of bushes up left in Scene 1, which is moved to up center for Scene 2. There is a throne-stool at center for Scene 1, with the hollow palm tree (see *Properties*) at right. They are removed for Scene 2.

Lighting: Blackouts, as indicated in text.

Sound: Live or recorded African music, as indicated in text.

TWO DILEMMA TALES

Characters: 5 male; 3 female; 2 male or female for Spirits; as many male or female as desired for Villagers; extras if desired for Spirits.

Playing Time: 20 minutes.

Costumes: West African. Chief wears headdress and carries a staff. Spirits wear weird papier-mâché masks with raffia attached to bottom of masks and extending to floor, hiding body.

Properties: Tall African drum, two cloth bundles, pouch, honey pot with shoulder strap (small waste basket or large can), spears for Chief and Villagers of wood or rubber (may be pantomimed), wooden stool.

Setting: A West African village. Backdrop shows rain forest with village huts. In first scene, part of a hut with doorway is at left, angled so rest of hut seems to be offstage. In second scene, hut is moved to center. Hut may be made from a very large cardboard box. To make circular pointed roof for hut, put a tall pole anchored in a can of sand inside box and projecting through top of box. String wires from top of pole to top edge of box, and lay raffia or palm branches over wire structure.

Lighting: Lights dim and brighten, Scene 1, as indicated in text.

Sound: Jungle animal sounds, as indicated in text.

AFRICAN TRIO

Characters: 6 male; 5 female; 9 male or female, including Storytellers. Property Girl is a non-speaking part.

Playing Time: 20 minutes.

Costumes: The Storytellers and human characters wear the costumes of the tribe of their story. The Princess must have sandals, a headdress, cloak, and jewels, worn over a simple dress. The animals can wear large paper bag or papier-mâché masks.

Properties: African drum, mbira or other African harp, yellow pot, red pot, yellow and red cardboard discs, blue crepe paper streamers, cut-outs of palm tree, rainbow, and peacock.

Setting: Slides of East Africa, South Africa and West Africa (Liberia) may be projected on the back wall of stage, or on a screen at rear. The three different houses—veld-style, Masai and Vai—may be cut-outs of painted cardboard. Masai houses are long, low and plastered, and are entered by crawling. Veld houses vary; some are beehive-shaped, and others have circular walls with thatched roofs. The Vai house is round with a tall, pointed, thatched roof. Houses may have working doorways.

Lighting: No special effects.

THE MONKEY WITHOUT A TAIL

Characters: 2 male; 1 female; 3 male or female for Attendant, Storyteller, Monkey, and 1 or 2 male or female for Mej; as many Subjects as desired.

Playing Time: 20 minutes.

Costumes: Draped robes in the style of Amhara people of Ethiopia (use sheets); King and Queen wear crowns. Attendant may carry a fringed umbrella to hold over King's head. Monkey and Mej wear animal costumes (Monkey has no tail), or they may wear tights with matching turtleneck sweaters and papier-mâché heads. Mej wears a rope bridle and a rope sling to hold honey jar.

Properties: Large pottery jars; brilliantly painted jar for Monkey. (Jars may be made of papier-mâché or suggested by cardboard cut-outs.)

Setting: A dark backdrop curtain. In scene 1, forest, cut-outs of palm and acacia trees with ferns are scattered upstage. Left center are two stools covered to look like stones, and a fire, suggested by sticks of wood and crushed red and yellow cellophane. The two thrones in Scene 2, the Palace, may be made by taping cardboard boxes around arms and backs of chairs and painting them gold and other vivid colors in geometric designs.

Lighting: No special effects.

Sound: Drumbeats as indicated in text.

BATA'S LESSONS

Characters: 7 male; 5 female; and 1 male or female voice for Narrator. Palm and Acacia are non-speaking roles.

Playing Time: 20 minutes.

Costumes: Ancient Egyptian dress. For women, long tunics, for men, wraparound skirts (made of old sheets), belted with bright material. Wide, painted, cardboard collars are worn by all but trees and soldiers. Lotus in Scene 2 and Pharaoh have collars made of gold and jewels. Gods wear headdresses, with black yarn attached for hair, and the following symbols: Ra, sun disk; Ament, hawk;

Isis, throne; Khnum, ram's head with wavy horns; and Bata in Scene 2, bull's head. Lotus wears a yellow wig, with a lotus-flower wreath in Scene 1 and at end of play, and a crown in Scene 2. Pharaoh wears traditional "double crown" (see costume book for illustration) and has a beard. Black yarn wigs are worn by Anpu, Soldiers, and Bata in Scene 1 and at end of play. Trees wear brown or black shirts and pants, with branches, made of paper or cloth and wire from clothes hangers, attached to arms, shoulders and head.

Properties: Three sheathed wooden swords, lotus-flower wreath, papyrus reed (made of paper), goblet.

Setting: Ancient Egypt. A painting of the river Nile extends across backdrop and stage, dividing playing area into two sections. There is a yellow backdrop, with river painted on it extending from ceiling height at right to stage level at left, gradually widening. River is painted across stage floor as if continuing downstage into audience. Against backdrop at right and center are small cardboard cut-outs of pyramids as if seen from a distance. For Scene 2, outside Pharaoh's palace, there are two folding screens at center, at an angle to represent corner of palace and placed so they encompass most of river area on stage floor. Left exit leads into palace and right exit leads into city.

Lighting: Blackouts, as indicated in text.

Sound: Egyptian music and bells tinkling for desert crossing. Narrator speaks into a glass for hollow effect and may be backstage or hidden at foot of stage. If voice not loud enough, use microphone.

THE MAHARAJAH IS BORED

Characters: 4 male; 2 female; 4 male or female (Herald, Snake Charmer, Cobra, and Servant); and as many Villagers as desired.

Playing Time: 25 minutes.

Costumes: Indian dress. The Cobra, dressed as a snake, keeps hands at waist. Arms and upper body are covered to give appearance of a hood. He slides about on knees, waving body back and forth. Sitara changes from ragged clothing to a bright, patchwork sari.

Properties: Flute or recorder, sewing supplies, large basket (clothes basket or hamper), scraps of material, wicker chair, water jar, scroll, book, small money box (cigar box painted), fan on long handle, coins, patchwork sari, jacket, and Indian sari.

Setting: Village street in Rajapur, India. Poles, erected in cans of sand, hold up the shop canopy (old sheet). For the well, a large garbage can may be surrounded with paper and painted to give the appearance of stonework. The well must be large enough to hide Cobra. The banyan tree is a cardboard cut-out. A footstool is suggested for the stool. The table is the size of a small coffee table. Upstage, a dark backdrop curtain or a painted street scene may be used.

Lighting: No special effects.

Sound: Drum and flute playing at times indicated in text.

LISTEN TO THE HODJA

Characters: 7 male; 4 female; 1 or 2 male or female for Donkey. More servants may be used.

Playing Time: 20 minutes.

Costumes: Turkish except for the American tourist, who wears an enormous towel over a bathing suit or shorts, and the Donkey, who wears a gray papier-mâché head, matching shirt, pants, tail, and gloves with black cardboard hooves attached and black shoes. There is a saddle blanket across his back, and he has a rope halter around his neck. Servants wear veils, as does Wife for part of play. The Hodja has a gray beard and must have two turbans and two coats. Tamerlane has moustache, beard, a large jeweled pin on his turban, and a curved sword in his sash. Guard wears a bolero-type vest, a curved sword in his sash, and a drum strapped across his shoulders.

Properties: Brass coffeepot, pan with briquettes on red paper; 2 cups, 4 bowls, 4 spoons; a platter of meat, a bowl of pilaf, a bowl of pistachio nuts; drum; 2 bell shakers; broom; bowl of figs; 6 large, uncooked beets with tops, cake of soap, wash cloth, towel, brush, and large pottery water jar.

Setting: The two cutaway houses may be made from cardboard or a large folding screen; coffee table and 7 pillows (one of them should be very large).

Lighting: Spotlight left and right, lighting 2 house areas, and spot in front, lighting Storyteller's area. A blue flood may be used in the street area during Scene 1 to indicate evening.

Sound: Muezzin call may be imitated with an up-and-down-scale nasal singing of "Ah," or a record may be played; drum roll.

THE FLYING HORSE MACHINE

Characters: 5 male; 5 female (including Attendants); 6 or more male or female for Roc, Clouds, and Horse Machine (2 actors); as many extras as desired for Attendants, Clouds.

Playing Time: 20 minutes.

Costumes: Ancient Persian dress, with veils for women, except for Shamour, who wears Indian sari. Attendants wear Persian costumes; in Scene 2, they cover costumes with gypsy shawls with bells on them and wear head scarves, but no veils. They resume Persian dress and veils for Scene 3. King wears tall Persian crown and has black beard. Maroudah wears tousled white wig and beard. Roc has feathery wings made of crepe paper attached to arms, a large papier-mâché beak worn as a mask, and talons on feet. Clouds have cardboard cloud cut-outs painted white, or covered with cotton, which they carry like shields. Cloud cut-outs completely hide actors. Horse has a wooden box on wheels or a wagon as its middle or body section. Box is covered with fringed blanket, hanging to ground to hide wheels, and large enough to be attached to papier-mâché horse's head, worn by first actor, and to cover back actor. Tail is sewn on end of blanket. A large key and a removable knob are on horse's head. A rope is attached to box so front actor may pull it while back actor pushes it.

Properties: Spear; sword; knob.

Setting: Scenes 1 and ₃3 are in a Persian palace courtyard. Backdrop curtains meet at center. A chair up right is draped with material to represent throne. There are plants up center near curtains which may be real or made of paper. In Scene 2, which takes place in a palace in Ceylon, the backdrop curtains are opened and draped, revealing a large Oriental window frame, large enough for Kamar to climb through. Pieces of wood project from either side of window frame to hold back draped curtains. Several large pillows are grouped on floor at right center for couch.

Lighting: No special effects. If desired, when explosion occurs in Scene 1, dry ice may be dropped into pan of water concealed behind plants to create "smoke."

Sound: Explosion (large pan lids banged together); Indian music (from a recording), as indicated in text.

PRINCE RAMA

Characters: 5 male; 2 female; 3 male or female for Storyteller, Ravana's Friend, Hanuman; as many males and females as desired for Monkeys and Demons.

Playing Time: 20 to 30 minutes, depending on amount of dance pantomime used.

Costumes: Indian. Sita wears a sari; Rama and Lakshmana wear knee-length sack-type garments with swords strapped around their waists. Rama, Sita, Ravana, and Monkey King wear crowns. Demons and monkeys wear masks. Monkeys have tails sewn to their pants. Ravana and some demons may have swords and additional arms (made of cardboard) attached to their clothes. In Scene 2, Ravana wears a hermit-style robe (preferably saffron color with one shoulder bare).

Properties: Flowers, wooden cup, earring, gold deer mask with antlers, bows and arrows, cardboard swords, lances, shields, maces, banners.

Setting: Painted backdrop of a tropical forest in northern India with brilliant flowers, birds, and butterflies, done in a stylized fashion. Scene 1: The demon city of

Lanka. A large rock, decorated with a grotesque demon mask, is right center. Scene 2: A clearing in the forest. A tree with a peg on the trunk is at left, next to a stream. Scene 3: The land of the great monkeys. A throne is at center. Scene 4: City of Lanka, same as Scene 1.

Lighting: No special effects.

Sound: Recordings of Indian music —soft, slow, beautiful music for Scene 1; loud, discordant, fast music for Scene 4.

ABU NUWAS

Characters: 3 male; 3 female; and 1 or 2 male or female for donkey.

Playing Time: 20 minutes.

Costumes: Ancient Arabian. Men wear long, loose, wide trousers (old sheets) with wide sashes, outer robes (bathrobes), turbans or scarves with head bands, and beards and moustaches (white for Abu Nuwas and black for Ali and Haji). Ina and Lewa wear full trousers (nylon curtains) over bathing suits, long-sleeved blouses, wide sashes, bolero jackets, head scarves, thin face veils (netting material), and jewelry. Zakia wears long robe and dark shawl covering head and wrapped around under chin then over one shoulder. Shoes are made of cloth material and have long, pointed toes. Donkey wears papier-mâché head, gray costume.

Properties: Mat, shoes, one small and two large cooking pots (large pots of different colors).

Setting: Backdrop painting of ancient Baghdad. Palm trees may be made from long sticks set in flag pole stands with cardboard for trunks and fringed green paper on wire (straightened coat hanger) for branches. A table can be used for the rock, with sides covered with taped together newspapers painted gray.

Lighting: Blackouts, as indicated in text.

PACCA, THE LITTLE BOWMAN

Characters: 5 male; 2 female; 3 male or female for Sakkar, Merchant, and Thief; as many male and female extras as desired for Elephants, Monkeys, and additional Royal Guards (non-speaking roles). The same actors may double as Elephants and Monkeys by changing masks and adding tails.

Playing Time: 20 minutes.

Costumes: Indian dress. Pacca, Katti, Guards, wear white shirts, turbans, bright-colored sashes and capes, and Pacca and Guards have quivers full of arrows (real or pantomimed) slung across shoulders. Merchant, Thief, Sakkar and Prince are similarly dressed. Women wear saris (one length of cloth wrapped around body several times, covering one shoulder and top of head) with blouse underneath. Queen wears a crown. All wear sandals, except Village Girl, who may be barefoot. Elephants and Monkeys wear animal masks and tights or dark slacks; Monkeys have long tails pinned to seat of pants.

Properties: Bows for Pacca and Guards, bag, drum, bells tied on cord, small bag of gold. necklace with red and green stones, and jeweled pin (easily removable from turban).

Setting: A clearing near a river in India. Backdrop, which shows jungle and animals among trees, is painted with bright colors in traditional Indian manner, on sheet or heavy paper. There are several large pillows arranged

down right, with one propped against wall for backrest.
Lighting: No special effects.

THE GREAT SAMURAI SWORD

Characters: 4 male; 4 female; Four Singers and Musicians may be either male or female.
Playing Time: 20 minutes.
Costumes: Japanese kimonos, slippers or sandals, sashes and obis, and flowers or ornaments for the women's hair. Osada and Naoto wear armor in the fencing scene, and fencing masks. All characters have heavy powder on their faces, giving a masklike appearance. The men have heavy eyebrows; Sudo and Kasai have gray beards and hair. Grandmother has white hair.
Properties: Gong, bells, and as many other instruments as desired for Musicians. Two long, curved swords with highly decorated handles. The Great Samurai Sword has a gold sheath.
Setting: A large folding screen or backdrop, painted to give the effect of a Japanese scene: a lake, Mt. Fuji, and houses to right and left of lake. There is a platform for Musicians, and four brightly colored pillows for the Singers.
Lighting: No special effects.
Sound: The Musicians play whenever no character is speaking. The rhythm, tempo, and instruments used vary with the scene and character. Music is used to accompany movements, create moods, and punctuate lines.

WHITE ELEPHANT

Characters: 3 male; 2 female; 2 male or female for messenger and servant; 2 or 4 male or female for Elephants (non-speaking roles).

Playing Time: 25 minutes.
Costumes: Burmese dress. All wear sandals. King wears a pointed golden crown. Elephants (played by either one or two actors) have large papier-mâché heads with stocking-like trunks (so actor can extend arm into trunk to manipulate it) and wear white or gray sheets for bodies.
Properties: Umbrella painted gold with fringe attached to edges; two white shirts; scrub-brush; large cake of soap; scroll; four cardboard cut-outs of pottery tubs— one small, simple, earth-colored washtub, and three fancy, ornately painted tubs for elephant (one too small for elephant; one too thin for elephant—split in center, taped behind with masking tape; and a third, the fanciest and just right for elephant). Other props are pantomimed.
Setting: Painted backdrop showing wall of Burmese palace, with trees and temple tops. Dark curtain may also be used as backdrop. Throne is a low, backless platform or table, painted gold.
Lighting: No special effects.

FIRE DEMON AND SOUTH WIND

Characters: 1 male; 1 female; 11 or more male or female. Well-Digger, Dragon, and Stone Monster are non-speaking roles.
Playing Time: 15 to 20 minutes, depending on amount of dancing and pantomime.
Costumes: Korean women wear long, full white skirts, tied on above waist, and white blouses; Korean men wear full white trousers and white shirts. King, Princess, Wise Won, and Magician wear robe-like coats over their white costumes. Well-Digger wears pointed straw hat, no shirt, and narrow trousers. Dragon-Tamer

wears Chinese pajamas. Dragon has papier-mâché head, claws attached to fingers, and a long dragon's tail attached to tights. Dragon may be played by more than one actor. Fire Demon and South Wind have headdresses to represent their characters. Fire Demon has red and yellow crepe paper streamers attached to arms; Wind has a billowing cape. Monster has papier-mâché head and is scaly, like a salamander, with huge jaws, fangs, and bulging eyes. An alligator-type tail is attached to its trousers, claws are attached to its hands, and a tortoise shell made of cardboard tied on its back. If desired, Monster may attach coffee cans to bottoms of shoes, to make Monster appear tall and to create a clanking as he walks.

Properties: Large scroll, two silk scarves, whip, shovel.

Setting: The Korean countryside. The area at center stage represents a rice paddy. Two large cardboard cut-outs are the only scenery required. One cut-out, placed up right, is cut and painted to represent mountains and a volcano. There may also be a painting of a Korean temple on the mountainside. A ladder for the Fire Demon is behind this cut-out. The second cut-out, up left, is painted to show the Silver Palace. Behind this cut-out are two supports which can be quickly removed to allow the Palace to fall backward, as indicated in text. Exits are right and left.

Lighting: Lights blink several times when Monster roars, as indicated in script.

Sound: Drumbeat and clanging cymbals, as indicated in text.

AH WING FU AND THE GOLDEN DRAGON

Characters: 2 male; 2 female; 10 or more male or female for Poet, Property Man, Chu Yu (tiger), Golden Dragon made up of at least 3 actors—Head, Middle, Tip-of-Tail; Musicians; 2 or more acrobats to emphasize anger of Dragon by tumbling and cartwheeling across stage with great commotion (optional).

Playing Time: 20 to 30 minutes, depending on amount of dancing and singing. Additional songs, dances, and acrobats may be interspersed throughout play.

Costumes: Ancient Chinese dress. Grandfather, long, white hair, long, thin beard, hanging under nose and parted over mouth, attached over ears by string; straw hat; cane. Chin Li, sequinned and beaded cardboard headdress resembling tiara. So San, paper flowers in hair. Chu Yu's face is painted to look like tiger. Head of Dragon, papier-mâché head painted gold, red and green. Middle of Dragon and Tip-of-Tail, long pieces of red and gold cloth attached to sticks which are held by actors. Property Man wears black and no makeup. All wear ballet slippers or socks instead of shoes, and have on hats or headdresses, except in scenes of danger (Ah Wing Fu on mountain and family in boat).

Properties: Cane; fan; Chinese umbrella (Chin Li); two flag-shaped banners, one black and painted with clouds for "wind," the other blue and painted with fish on wild waves for "water"; wooden clappers, gong, bells, cymbals, drums of various sizes, sandblocks, rattle, recorder or flute, Chinese-type stringed instrument (created out of a pan or box with rubber bands stretched around it), for Musicians; chair with sign on it reading WELL; long, low table with sign on it reading MOUNTAIN. All other properties are panto-mimed.

Setting: Up center there is a tapes-try, made of sheet with painting of Chinese garden on it. Sheet is attached to flagpoles in stands.

Lighting: No special effects.

Sound: Musicians make all sound effects, including sound of wind and water. Play gong for begin-ning of scenes and end of play, as indicated in text; sound cym-bals after important sentences; add soft flute or recorder mood music to Poet's lines. Deep drum, clappers and cymbals should ac-company Dragon; sandblocks and little drum, tiger; stringed instru-ment and clappers, Ah Wing Fu; bells, Chin Li and So San; rattle and gong, Grandfather.

JAPANESE TRIO

Characters: 3 male; 1 female; 8 male or female for Traveler, An-nouncer, Yoku, Priest (or Priest-ess), Wolf, Thief, Devil, and Stagehand (non-speaking role).

Playing Time: 20 minutes.

Costumes: Ancient Japanese dress, with papier-mâché masks for Taro, Buso, Fujiko, Wolf, Thief, and Devil. Play may also be per-formed with no special costumes, except a kimono for Announcer, or with all except Announcer and Stagehand wearing masks.

Properties: Drawstring purse con-taining two coins; box, made from four five-foot bamboo poles and four three-foot bamboo poles lashed together to make an open

rectangle; two skewers with pieces of eel (inner tubing may be used); small flat wooden lunch box (use cigar box) containing chopsticks; sack or laundry bag; fans.

Setting: On rear wall there is a painting in Japanese style of a large pine tree. A large pillow for Announcer is down left. There is no front curtain. There is an exit up right.

Lighting: No special effects.

Sound: Musical instruments (wooden clappers, small drum, and gong), as indicated in text—may be played by Stagehand.

FOLLOW THE RIVER LAI

Characters: 6 male; 6 female; as many Bystanders as desired. (There should be a strong resem-blance between Duc and Le Vang, or the same actor may take both parts.)

Playing Time: 25 minutes.

Costumes: Oriental robes over plain shirts and pajama-like pants; mandarin hats for Khiem and Le Vang; headdresses for women. The Soldier is in uniform. The actor playing Le Vang changes to modern clothes, with an orien-tal smoking jacket, if he plays Duc in Scene 4. Khiem's jacket in Scene 2 is heavily embroidered.

Properties: Maps, books, scrolls, small book, backpack with a gourd cup tied on outside; tea tray with cups, cakes, etc.; rake; 2 saucers of burning incense; toy rifle; toy revolver; brush, pen and paper.

Setting: Scene 1: Screen backdrop (a sheet tacked to wooden frame may be used), with a potted plant behind it. Low table, with drawer, covered with books, maps, and scrolls, is at center. There are cushions on floor. Scene 2: The backdrop is painted with a pagoda and red flowers. More flowers, or cardboard cut-outs of them, extend out from backdrop. This scene may be played in front of the curtain. Scene 3: The Land of Bliss. Carved throne is at center, surrounded by real or fake ferns, trees, and flowers. At right is a bridge, with a lotus pool below it. (This may be painted on backdrop.) Clouds may be suspended overhead. Scene 4: The same as Scene 1, except that the plant is moved back, to appear larger in silhouette. Furniture is rearranged, and slightly different from Scene 1.

Sound: Tinkling bell; gong; peddler's voice; appropriate Oriental music and singing, recorded if desired; gunshot and offstage voices, as indicated in text.

Lighting: An upstage flood is used for silhouettes required in Scenes 1 and 4, as indicated in text.

LITTLE MOUSE-DEER

Characters: 1 male; 11 male or female.

Playing Time: 20 minutes.

Costumes: Orang and Storytellers wear Indonesian costumes. Animals wear papier-mâché masks and tights. Kerbau has horns; Harimau has whiskers; Monyet has tail; Kancil has hooves on hands.

Properties: Burlap bag, large banana leaf, instruments (xylophone, bells, large and small drums, sticks, gong, set of small gongs).

Setting: Indonesian rain forest backdrop. There is no front curtain.

Lighting: No special effects.